THE
PEOPLE
CODE

D0018611

Dr. Taylor Hartman

SCRIBNER

New York   London   Toronto   Sydney

SCRIBNER

A Division of Simon & Schuster, Inc.
1230 Avenue of the Americas
New York, NY 10020

This Scribner trade paperback edition September 2007

SCRIBNER and design are trademarks of Macmillan Library Reference USA, Inc.,
used under license by Simon & Schuster, the publisher of this work.

For information about special discounts for bulk purchases,
please contact Simon & Schuster Special Sales:
1-800-456-6798 or business@simonandschuster.com

Text set in Sabon

Manufactured in the United States of America

3   5   7   9   10   8   6   4

Library of Congress Control Number: 97-44594

ISBN-13: 978-1-4165-4230-8
ISBN-10: 1-4165-4230-2

A previous edition was published as *The Color Code* in 1987 and 1998.

ACKNOWLEDGMENTS

First, I acknowledge God and His remarkable insights about core personalities, which I would never have discovered on my own. I am honored by His inspiration and humbled to be provided the opportunity to bring these powerful truths about the true nature of man to light in this book.

Whenever important truth attempts to emerge, there is strong resistance. I am extremely grateful for the many individuals who stood courageously to make this book a reality. From those who first challenged me to write the first chapters to those who have carried this message throughout the world, thank you. Thank you to legitimate trainers, certified teachers, and committed parents for doing your own personal work and helping others live life more abundantly with this message.

Thank you to all the raving fans of my work around the globe, who keep the spirit of this revolutionary message alive wherever you live; to employers, employees, parents, children, professors, and therapists who practice what we preach. I am grateful to every patient I have ever seen and business clients who have passionately embraced the power of this work.

Marriage to my amazing wife, Jean, for more than thirty years has been the critical underpinning of this work. Our children (and their spouses) and grandchildren have been co-authors in this memorable journey over the past twenty-five years. Living the message in our lives has been my greatest joy. Seeing how it truly enhances every relationship and life experience inspires me.

Professionally, I have always felt a remarkable connection to the publisher at Scribner, Susan Moldow, who deserves special thanks for her continuing vision and steady guidance in my work. Also, thank you to Brant Rumble and Lindsay Cahoon for their outstanding editing gifts throughout this entire process. Finally, I wish to thank my literary agent, Margaret McBride, for her continuing promotion of this work.

CONTENTS

CONTENTS

FOREWORD

How do I introduce this man? At first my thoughts turn to his many degrees and professional credentials, but he has experienced so much and enriched the hearts of so many people, that those degrees and credentials can't describe the *real* Taylor Hartman.

When I think of his doctoral degree at the United States International University in San Diego, California, what I remember is the way he kept up with his commitment to his family and community obligations despite his heavy career and education schedule. Taylor enjoys many professional and civic responsibilities, yet he always lets us know that we are the most important people in his life.

Taylor is a lover. He loves people so easily that one would almost have to live with him as I do to appreciate how sincere his love is.

Taylor has always been committed to improving the quality of life—not only his but that of all those he encounters. And yet he remains very playful and loves to live in the present.

Taylor is as comfortable playing "horsie" and "duck-duck-goose" in our family room as he was addressing the International Congress of Psychologists in Austria. In fact, his playful behavior has often provided a creative outlet for our family. He "dated" each of our five children once a month as they grew up, and continues to romance me with frequent surprises and adventures.

Despite the high praise Taylor receives for his professional counseling and consulting business, he still maintains that the highest compliment he ever received was from his then nine-year-old daughter. She told her schoolteacher that she didn't mind having personal problems, because Dad would always take time to give her private counseling.

The question I am most often asked about Taylor is, "What is it *really* like to live with him?" Perhaps the easiest and most accurate answer is to simply say, "He's a man who practices what he preaches."

The People Code is a special gift from a very special person. He cares. This book will help you understand:

- the mysteries of yourself,
- the miracle of your relationships, and
- the magic of living.

Taylor Hartman will touch your heart, and this book will change your life.

—Jean Hartman, 2007

PREFACE

Do you remember the first time you tied your own shoelaces? Or drank water from a moving stream? Or played your first sports game? The moment we discover anything new in life creates a memory all its own. These moments remain with us forever and we sometimes wonder how limited our lives might have been without them.

Millions of people around the world remember when they first discovered *The People Code* (previously published as *The Color Code*)—when they first tasted its resonate truth. For some it seems like yesterday, while others feel as though it has been with them forever. Of course they would remember it—like a first kiss, it leaves an impression that lasts a lifetime. The first time an individual discovers his or her innate driving core motive in life is always filled with intrigue and awe. *"How could he possibly know me so well?!"* is a common immediate response.

Red, White, Blue, or Yellow—everyone is motivated by an internal driving core personality that completely colors how he or she views and experiences life. For twenty years, *The People Code* has connected with people around the globe—most understanding themselves for the very first time with the depth only color-coding can offer.

The People Code offers you the opportunity to see yourself and others in a way you never have before. Once you "get yourself" through the color code filter, it changes your self-awareness and provides tools for effectively connecting with others. This is an experience that you will want to share with everyone.

We have come to realize the significant impact emotional intelligence plays in our lives. Many studies have concluded that it is up to four times more critical to life success than one's IQ. Yet we are far from perfected in our understanding and demonstrating of this skill set so essential to creating success in our lives.

The People Code touches every aspect of our lives from hiring to dating, from parenting to managing, from working well with colleagues to enjoying yourself at a dinner party. Literally thousands of daily human interactions are determined by how well we embrace these principles. Still, we struggle to develop this powerful and life-affirming understanding of others and ourselves. Don't put this book down until you understand and can accurately apply its rich insights.

Companies use it in hiring and retention of employees. Couples read it carefully before marriage. Parents live by it. Students fashion study habits after it. Salesmen devour it. Diplomats review it before engaging in dialogue. Lawyers create juries with it. Teachers construct lesson plans and seating charts by it. In literally every aspect of your life, this book improves you and your chances for success.

After twenty years of witnessing firsthand its powerful impact, I am honored to provide a brand new revision of *The People Code*. This book teaches you about the power of motive—what motivates you and others. When you appreciate the role that motive plays in the dynamics of human relationships, you begin to understand the meaning of life. Enjoy the journey of seeing yourself and others as never before.

—Taylor Hartman, Ph.D.

INTRODUCTION

FEBRUARY 14, 1986

Ambulances and fire engines with flashing red lights and blaring sirens raced to the scene of our head-on collision. It was raining heavily that night. My wife and I had been out to dinner for Valentine's Day. She had reminded me to fasten my seat belt for the drive home. I had never been happier in my life. I knew who I was and where I was going. I felt committed to life and able to contribute much to my family, friends, and profession. Not more than three months earlier, we had moved to our dream home in the country in southern California. Our children were happy and healthy. My wife was creatively decorating our home and making new friends. My private practice was thriving, and my tennis game was at its peak.

Twenty-five minutes later, I lay unconscious in my wife's lap while the firefighters cut through the car door in an effort to free us and transport us to the hospital. I knew no one and nothing about myself. I no longer enjoyed the security of an identity. The only evidence that I was in fact alive was the headaches.

For weeks, I struggled to find me. I felt depressed and valueless. I had no core of personality from which to establish an identity. Gone were my humor and patience with children. Gone were my emotional connection to my wife and my memory of my patients. I had lost the first great gift life offers. I had lost a sense of myself.

For the first time in my life, I recognized how enviable it is to be somebody—to feel truly unique and alive. I desperately needed my sense of identity. I felt lost without my personality.

As the weeks and months went by, I began to regain some of my memory. Numerous phone calls and cards from people helped me remember the warmth of our friendships. Tears came to my eyes many times when I realized I could still hold my "Blue" wife and feel her committed love. The noise my children made began to excite me again as a reminder of how lucky I was to be alive to watch them grow up. Once again I began to see how unique their personalities were. My oldest "Red" daughter, Terra, who moved so confidently, demanded that I reconnect with her, while Summer, "White," waited and watched patiently for my return. My "Yellow" daughter, Mikelle, hugged me freely, told me she loved me, and went off to play, confident that I would once again be well. My little "Red" three-year-old, BreAnne, continued her independent play, unfazed by her daddy's recent confusion. It was as if my identity returned, and with this new identity came my commitment to live again.

Actually, the identity wasn't new. I had merely found the old me again. After wandering for months in depression and severe memory loss, I felt new. I began to laugh and tease friends. I felt myself beginning to get comfortable with life, much the way a guest who stays long enough in a home begins to feel like family. I was once again comfortable with my life because I had found my personality—my identity.

My renewed self-awareness and the recognition of my family's diverse personalities reminded me of the book I had been working on prior to the accident. Difficult as the accident and its aftermath were, no experience could have been more timely. It convinced me of the incredible purpose our personalities play in our lives. It reminded me of my character strengths and limitations. It brought *me* back to *me*.

I am more sensitive today than I was before the accident. I had become too busy to play. I had become too busy to do the things I enjoyed most in my profession—time to call patients, create team-building strategies with corporate clients, and deliver exciting keynote speeches. Now I take the time to go to lunch with friends and laugh until we must leave. Now I take the time to call my wife during the day just to say "I love you." Now I take the time to travel with my children. Now I take the time to live and to love.

This close brush with death brought refreshing perspective to my life. All of us, in some way, experience our own crises. Perhaps they afford us the luxury we might otherwise never afford ourselves—the sudden sense of who we really are and what we're really all about.

You, the reader, do not have to experience a serious accident to discover your own identity. You can be awakened to your identity with a carefully designed profile that will aid you in identifying your personality traits. Each personality, with its strengths and limitations, will be fully explained. You will be offered suggestions on how to develop your character and your personality to be your best self. Relationships between the personality styles will also be discussed. You will be guided in assessing how to succeed in your various relationships at work, at home, and with friends.

We all have a personality and character. It is not determined at birth what we will do with either of them. Unfortunately, many people simply grow old rather than ever growing up. This is your opportunity to understand the difference. It is my hope that *The People Code* will be your guide to understanding and appreciating various personality types. Using the color code system described in the following chapters, you will learn how to improve your relationships, including the most important relationship of all—your relationship with yourself.

Part One

⚜

YOU

Chapter One

THE FUNDAMENTALS
OF YOUR PERSONALITY

*Personality is innate
and motive-based.*

MOTIVE: THE DRIVING CORE OF PERSONALITY

We know we have a conscience that talks to us about what is right and
what is wrong. We also have a driving core motive that speaks to us
often about being true to ourselves and playing to our strengths. Just
as we ignore our conscience, we are often guilty of ignoring our core
motive in life. Our driving core motive knows us and wants our lives
to be successful, and ultimately we must choose to listen to or ignore
who we are innately and what will make us most happy in life.

The following plea is written directly to you from your driving
core motive, asking you to trust that it knows who you are inside. It
knows what works for you and what messes you up. It can help you
be far more successful because when you act congruently with your
innate self, you will find that life makes more sense for you as well as
those around you.

After witnessing for the past twenty years the astounding accuracy
of your driving core motive, this may be the single most significant
piece of self-awareness you will ever come to understand in your lifetime. I recommend paying attention to what it has to say.

*I have always been with you. From your first heartbeat I was con-
nected to you and we will remain inseparable until you die. Being your
constant companion has its definite ups and downs. Sometimes I feel
dismissed by you and wonder, "HOW CAN YOU SIMPLY IGNORE
ME AND PRETEND I DON'T MATTER!" It is times like those that I
want to make you WAKE UP! Wake up and see your true self!*

It makes absolutely no sense that people resist seeing themselves for

7

who they really are inside. Frankly, everyone's life would make so much more sense if they simply understood why they think and act as they do.

I am always watching you. I am so much a part of your internal fabric that you typically don't even recognize that I am with you. We move "hand in glove" because of our connection. When most people see your behavior, they don't know why you behave as you do. But I do! I know exactly why you think and feel like you do.

I know why President Bill Clinton couldn't keep his pants zipped while serving in the White House, tainting an otherwise inspired presidency. I also understand why his most cynical opponents find him charmingly irresistible in person.

I know why Oprah Winfrey runs a quality media empire but can't trust the intimacy of marriage. I understand how she can be compassionate and cruel in the same day.

I know why Brad Pitt abandoned his marriage to Jennifer Aniston for a relationship and children with Angelina Jolie. I also know how Angelina controls the momentum of their lives while he controls their emotional moods.

I know why Meryl Streep, considered by many to be the greatest actress of her day, chose family and a committed relationship as her primary focus in life. She never saw her career as separate from her life.

There is one of me for every person on the earth regardless of when or where they were born. Some people appreciate me far more than others. Some people actually remain trusting and connected throughout their entire lives while others discard me with disdain.

Your thoughts and actions make perfect sense to me—except when you act differently from whom you really are! Sometimes you act like someone you think you should be. I have to admit, when you do that it drives me crazy. You can be so frustrating when you let others convince you that who you really are inside isn't enough—isn't who you should be! Then you go off pretending to be someone whom others want you to be. I can't tell you how difficult it is to sit back and watch you sort out whether you should be true to your intrinsic self or pretend to be what others tell you to be.

It's times like these when I have to simply wait until you return to your true innate self and once again we find our natural compatibility. Then, and only then, can I sleep comfortably at night. When we are in sync I love life (as do you!) and feel completely validated. When you toss me aside and deny me access to you, I become restless and unnerved.

As your driving core motive, I am neither good nor bad—I simply am! Some use me for positive while others use me for negative. The choice is completely theirs, not mine. Before there was race, religion, gender, birth order, or cultural biases, there was me! *In the womb, you and I were close. It's a very personal story that we share—one that I want you to know because the quality of our connection will make all the difference in the quality of your life.*

You are going to discover that while you are unique, you share similar driving core motives with people of every faith, race, gender, and economic condition. An illegal immigrant, a terrorist, an Australian film sensation, and a U.S. president all share the same driving core motive. They may appear substantially different because of the many nuances that enhance and detract from our unique lives, but their core personalities remain the same. In other words, what drives their daily existence—their needs and wants and personality motives, remains the same. What you could know about people from around the world would amaze you if you only understood the code.

I am at the very core of your personality, which is born in your soul. I am completely different from your personal history, which is reflected in your family upbringing, race, religious affiliations, birth order, and other cultural influences. A unique blending of both personality and personal history creates the distinct mixture that ultimately becomes you.

Before you had fingers and toes, we were best friends. Before your parents met you, I was part of your every thought and action. I often reflect back on our early days together and remember how easy it was and how well we got along. I would whisper in your ear and you would automatically agree. I gave you confidence to be you.

I am still your best friend and strongest ally, but sometimes you forget how well I know you. You can ignore me and then I become your worst nightmare. When you are true to me, your life makes sense. When you deny me, or resist my influence, you are miserable and so is everyone else around you.

I remain a mystery to most people. They don't understand our relationship. I am not merely a product of genetics (two Red parents do not a Red baby make!). I am not a reflection of your cultural ancestors (don't blame me for your hot Irish temper!). I am born in your soul and provide the primary driving motive for your entire life—unique from the many other factors that influence how you think and behave. Every human being is born with a driving core motive that lies at the very center of their innate personality. Your driving core motive makes all the difference in how you look at life.

I will never lie to you. As you grow older, you may reject me or lie to yourself about who you really are, and then things can get pretty ugly between us. Remember, people lie loudest when they lie to themselves.

Sometimes, but not always, people wake up. They sort out what caused them to become incongruent with themselves and once again life makes sense and feels good. Sometimes, however, they prefer pleasing others or give in to their fears, living their lives out in lies and incongruence. Now, that is a tragedy. I hope you will want to know me. Learn about me. I will always tell you the truth about you. And once you know your true self, you carry a most powerful awareness of how to play to your strengths in life.

Remember, I will always be with you. You can always come to me when you want to live congruently with who you were born to be. Life will challenge you to lose sight of yourself. Look inward and you will see me. I remain one constant you can always trust—your driving core motive. Use me as your North Star and everything else will line up legitimately to bring you meaning in your life.

> *Very best of living,*
> *Your driving core motive*

Remember when your driving core motive told you about the two defining factors that make up the unique you—personality (which includes your driving core motive) and personal history? Sometimes personality and personal history work well together to enhance a person and other times they work against each other. Let me explain.

There has been an ongoing debate about whether it is nature (innate personality) or nurture (personal history) that most defines a person. Truth be told, both sides have valid arguments. Your driving core personality is with you in the womb, but once you're born, it quickly becomes enmeshed with personal history as parents impact your habits and lifestyle. Your personality becomes layered with your personal history, making you as unique as your fingerprint. Your personality defines your innate motive, needs, and wants, and inherent strengths and limitations. Your personal history strongly influences your perspective on life. I am a strong Yellow personality who innately loves to play. I was born to a strong Red mother who expected me to be productive in society. While my desire to play (innate personality) clashed with her desire for me to be productive (personal history), the combination offered me a unique way of negotiating my life that makes me different from any other Yellow on the planet.

One must not give either component too much leverage in dictating how he or she lives. For example, Yellows can't just say, *"Of course I'm late and act irresponsible. I'm Yellow, you know!"* Nor can one use genetic aspects of personal history to explain poor choices. *"I have to drink and fight. I'm Irish!"* Yeah, three generations ago their great-grandparents lived in Ireland, but they have never set foot in Ireland. Yet they claim being Irish gives them automatic license to drink and fight, as if it were passed down in their DNA.

THE ELEMENTS OF PERSONALITY

Every *woman who has given birth to more than one child will tell you that each child comes with a unique personality. From the very beginning every child is born with a unique set of traits, meaning you became uniquely you in the womb.*

Every child in the womb shows marked behavioral tendencies. One *demands* more room to move around, chews on the umbilical cord, and refuses to accept a variety of foods that Mom selects. Another settles in quietly, pleased that there is no bed to make or food to cook and thinks, *"Hey, I'll take twelve months in here if it works for her!"* Everyone knows that no two sets of fingerprints are the same. How could we possibly believe that human personalities are any less individual than fingerprints? However, just as fingers share similarities, so do personalities.

Some psychologists theorize that a child's personality is not completely formed until the age of five. Others go further, theorizing that personality is never complete but evolves through a lifelong journey of discovery and maturation. What they are talking about is *not* personality but personal history. Clearly we are impacted by our surroundings—culture, gender, religion, birth order, intelligence, and countless factors that have an impact on who we are and how we think and behave. But they are *not* our core personality. That is what makes color-coding so powerful. Who you are in your core personality never changes. You can add to it or delete from it, but you cannot change its core essence.

People often look for reasons to blame others for or justify their thoughts or behaviors. Peer pressure, inadequate parenting, and cultural biases are all common references for blame or justification for our inappropriate actions. However influential they might be in defining you, *they are pieces of your personal history* but not *your core personality.* All through your life you must reconcile your driving core personality with a myriad of other influences in your life. Sometimes nature and nurture work to enhance each other, while at other times they pull each other apart.

PERSONALITY DEFINED

Take the human face. There are only so many different elements that make up a face: eyes, ears, mouth, nose, etc. Yet no two people look exactly the same. So it goes with our personalities. Though there are only four driving core motives, no two personalities are exactly alike. Combine this with our personal histories and you can readily see how unique every human being is.

Your personality is anchored by your driving core motive. Your driving core motive calls the shots from your subconscious mind and causes you to think and act as you do. Your core motive is to your personality as breathing is to the human body. Without it, you die. That is why people with different personality colors are driven so uniquely different than their peers. In order to breathe, you must be true to your innate driving core motive. The challenges come when others don't value our driving core motive or we lose sight of how to effectively maintain our core motive when engaging others with a different set of motives, wants, or needs.

Whenever a person distances himself from his driving core motive, he loses himself in the process. Knowing yourself and understanding why you think and behave as you do is necessary in order to enjoy positive self-esteem. Knowing others and understanding why they think and behave as they do is the cornerstone of successful relationships.

Daniel Goleman suggested, in his groundbreaking work on emotional intelligence, that emotional intelligence (EQ) is far more critical than a person's IQ in creating a successful life. The foundation of EQ is self-awareness. You will never be fully aware until you understand your innate driving core motive, complete with personality strengths and limitations as well as needs and wants. Personality sits at the very core of who you are and lining up with yourself is imperative if you want to experience the congruent life.

PERSONALITY IS YOUR UNIQUE INTERPRETATION OF LIFE

Your personality plays a vital role in what paths you choose to take in your life. It is equally important in describing how you will walk those paths, whether it is childhood, careers, friendships, parenting, and so on. For example, a Blue woman recently left a remarkable career in order to pursue her passion for art. A White business executive leads quite differently than a Red colleague. The *whys* and *hows* of life are best understood through the innate eyes of core personality.

Some people see life through rose-colored glasses, trusting and optimistic, while others see it through dark glasses, suspicious and pessimistic. We can't try on innate personalities the way we try on glasses. Personality is built in from birth.

Your personality determines whether you are easily depressed, casual, critical, careful, or carefree. It determines whether you are passive or assertive. Do you dash off at the last minute for an appointment, or always arrive with time to spare? Is your desk cluttered or meticulously clean? Do you seek deep, meaningful conversations, or would you rather risk your life on a wild mountain-climbing adventure? Are you most comfortable leading or following others? Your personality is more than just an "attitude." It is what causes your preferences, actions, and reactions in life.

PERSONALITY IS YOUR CODE OF BEHAVIOR

Personality is that core of thoughts and feelings inside you that tells you how to conduct yourself. It's a checklist of responses based on strongly held values and beliefs. It directs you to respond emotionally or rationally to every life experience. It even determines your knee-jerk reaction to others. Personality is an active process within each individual that dictates how he or she feels, thinks, and behaves. Pretty important stuff, eh? Critical color code truths:

- *You can never change your core color—it is yours forever!*
- *You have innate strengths you must develop—play to your strengths!*
- *You have innate limitations you must overcome—other colors have the antidote you need to overcome them!*
- *No personality is better, more valuable, or more important than any other!*
- *Your driving core motive is like breathing—you will die if it is not nurtured!*

> *Perhaps the greatest human tragedy of all is watching people abandon their innate personality and simply discard themselves along the side of life's road.*

Your personality watches and guards over you like a caring parent. Without clear-cut personality traits to guide us through life, we would become lost. Your personality is in constant fear that you will dismiss it, ignore it, or reject it. It protects itself and remains highly rigid and quite resistant to change. It does not venture out to experience or understand other types of personalities. While it is generally quite accepting of itself—you—it is much less flexible with or inviting to others.

Personality is like family. You will struggle with your personality at times in your life, but let an outsider do or say something unkind and watch out! We are very defensive of our personalities—ourselves!

Personality points each of us in a particular direction and makes us feel uncomfortable when we deviate from it. The moment we stray from its prescribed plan, we feel disoriented. Even when we try to improve ourselves, we will feel a tug from our personality to resist the change.

Our personality explains us and gives us acceptance and direction in our daily lives. Each of us needs our own personal code of behavior but it makes change rather daunting. We must value our personalities for their many gifts in our lives—clarity, focus, connection. However, we must exert control over our personality if we hope to become more than we were at birth. We must challenge our core personality limitations in order to live happier, healthier, and more charactered lives.

Chapter Two

THE HARTMAN
PERSONALITY PROFILE

DISCOVERING YOUR PERSONALITY
IS YOUR OWN MYSTERY-THRILLER

I love reading thrillers of mystery and intrigue. But, though fiction is great, truth and reality often provide more uncanny plots with greater deception and trickery. In no place is that more evident than the human personality. Sadly, very few of us understand ourselves. We don't know why we think or act as we do. We go through our lives rejecting the people and opportunities we bump into simply because we don't understand who we are or what we need. We are often puzzled by our reactions, our fears, and even our triumphs.

Attempting to understand ourselves is the only way we can improve our lives. Step by step we seek to solve the mystery that is us. Life is the most exciting journey of all and to understand the vital role we (our personalities) play in our lives notably enriches the experience.

This book is designed to help you solve your own unique mystery. Furthermore, it provides you with the expertise to resolve the mystery of your relationship with others. Knowledge is power. The knowledge you gain from this book will give you the power to change your life, enhance your life, or rewrite your life. It will also allow you to have a significant impact on the lives of others.

SOLVE YOUR MYSTERY

Just as the human face is made up of only a few physical features, the foundation of human personality is made up of only four driving core motives. Many people have a secondary influence, but it is critical that we first identify which of the four foundational motivations drives you. I will use a color system to help you remember your core personality. There are Reds, Blues, Whites, and Yellows! One of these will be you. Don't worry about being lumped into a category. Remember the human face—few options, abundant possibilities. We are all unique, but this will prove a critical step in solving the mystery of you.

Each color stands for a collection of traits, strengths, and limitations. Far from being limited to explaining only individual personalities, this color symbolism also clarifies relationships between people and the impact that various personalities have on one another.

We have tested this theory around the globe and discovered that every color exists in every corner of the earth. Among all ages, races, religions, cultures, and genders, you will find 35 percent Blues, 25 percent Reds, 20 percent Whites, and 20 percent Yellows. Various business careers, for example, may skew the percentages because they invite specific colors due to the nature of the work and how they value various personalities' gifts. However, in the general population, when people are allowed to see themselves in their raw innate state, the percentages hold.

Now it's time to discover your own personality type—your own "color." Perhaps you will learn things about yourself that you were not aware of, or find out why you have certain tendencies or reactions you have never been able to understand. In time, you will probably be able to identify the colors of other people as well. This will help you to understand them better, and pave the way to more meaningful relationships.

It's unlikely that your color will prove to be "pure"—100 percent Red or Blue or White or Yellow. Nature isn't that simple. Instead, even those individuals with a strong affinity for one particular color will find it tinged with traces of others. When your profile results reflect high scores in more than one personality area—that is, when two colors are almost equal in strength—you may at first find it difficult to identify the stronger one. Don't worry. As you read further, the motives and characteristics of each personality type will become clear, and you should have little trouble determining your primary personality color.

As you seek your true identity, you may begin to see yourself differently—and more accurately. You will become aware of your many strengths. And though some of your negative suspicions about yourself may also be verified, you will be comforted in knowing that you are not alone—we all have a balance of strengths and weaknesses in our personality makeup. Don't be discouraged by any weaknesses you have. In the later chapters of the book, I will show you how to turn limitations into assets.

In taking the Hartman Personality Profile, be as honest as you can. There's no point in deceiving yourself about who you really are. Dishonesty will only limit your knowledge of yourself and confuse your relationships with others.

Discovering your core personality is *your* challenge. The following recommendations will enhance your accuracy in taking the profile:

1. Unless otherwise directed, answer every question from your earliest recollections of how you were as a child. Since your personality is innate and comes with your soul at birth, this will provide a more accurate perspective on who you innately are, as opposed to who you have become.
2. Do not hesitate to ask others for feedback—especially people who may not agree with you. Their opinions can help you balance your self-assessment.
3. Strive to choose answers that are most often typical of your thoughts and/or actions. Subconsciously, you may want to avoid identifying—or facing—the real you, but tough it out. Don't cheat yourself by prettying things up; the potential rewards for honesty are too great. Enjoy the profile. You are about to determine your true color.
4. Some of you may consciously seek ways to "beat" the profile and actually look for patterns in order to skew the profile results. Others may perceive the profile design to be oversimplified. I caution you not to be fooled. The profile has been successfully used by millions of readers for many years in producing reliable insight. The results have reinforced my confidence that your honesty and the profile's simplicity are a tough team to beat.

THE HARTMAN PERSONALITY PROFILE

Directions: Mark an "X" or check mark by the one word or phrase that best describes what you were like *most of the time* in your earliest recollection. Choose only one response from each group. After you've finished question 30, total your scores for each letter.

PERSONALITY STRENGTHS AND LIMITATIONS

1.	2.	3.
a) __ opinionated	a) __ power-oriented	a) __ dominant
b) __ nurturing	b) __ perfectionist	b) __ sympathetic
c) __ inventive	c) __ indecisive	c) __ tolerant
d) __ outgoing	d) __ self-centered	d) __ enthusiastic

4. a) __ self-serving
   b) __ suspicious
   c) __ unsure
   d) __ naive

5. a) __ decisive
   b) __ loyal
   c) __ contented
   d) __ playful

6. a) __ arrogant
   b) __ worry-prone
   c) __ silently stubborn
   d) __ flighty

7. a) __ assertive
   b) __ reliable
   c) __ kind
   d) __ sociable

8. a) __ bossy
   b) __ self-critical
   c) __ reluctant
   d) __ a teaser

9. a) __ action-oriented
   b) __ analytical
   c) __ easygoing
   d) __ carefree

10. a) __ critical of others
    b) __ overly sensitive
    c) __ shy
    d) __ obnoxious

11. a) __ determined
    b) __ detail conscious
    c) __ a good listener
    d) __ a party person

12. a) __ demanding
    b) __ unforgiving
    c) __ unmotivated
    d) __ vain

13. a) __ responsible
    b) __ idealistic
    c) __ considerate
    d) __ happy

14. a) __ impatient
    b) __ moody
    c) __ passive
    d) __ impulsive

15. a) __ strong-willed
    b) __ respectful
    c) __ patient
    d) __ fun-loving

16. a) __ argumentative
    b) __ unrealistic
    c) __ directionless
    d) __ an interrupter

17. a) __ independent
    b) __ dependable
    c) __ even-tempered
    d) __ trusting

18. a) __ aggressive
    b) __ frequently depressed
    c) __ ambivalent
    d) __ forgetful

19. a) __ powerful
    b) __ deliberate
    c) __ gentle
    d) __ optimistic

20. a) __ insensitive
    b) __ judgmental
    c) __ boring
    d) __ undisciplined

21. a) __ logical
    b) __ emotional
    c) __ agreeable
    d) __ popular

22. a) __ always right
    b) __ guilt prone
    c) __ unenthusiastic
    d) __ uncommitted

23. a) __ pragmatic
    b) __ well-behaved
    c) __ accepting
    d) __ spontaneous

24. a) __ merciless
    b) __ thoughtful
    c) __ uninvolved
    d) __ a show-off

25. a) __ task-oriented
    b) __ sincere
    c) __ diplomatic
    d) __ lively

26. a) __ tactless
    b) __ hard to please
    c) __ lazy
    d) __ loud

27. a) __ direct
    b) __ creative
    c) __ adaptable
    d) __ a performer

28. a) __ calculating
    b) __ self-righteous
    c) __ self-deprecating
    d) __ disorganized

29. a) __ confident
    b) __ disciplined
    c) __ pleasant
    d) __ charismatic

30. a) __ intimidating
    b) __ careful
    c) __ unproductive
    d) __ afraid to face facts

THE HARTMAN PERSONALITY PROFILE

Strengths and Limitations Totals

____ Total a's   ____ Total b's   ____ Total c's   ____ Total d's

Enter your totals in the proper spaces. Now let's see if you respond the same way to the following situations as you did to groups of descriptive words. Again, pick only one answer, and record your totals for each letter at the end of the section.

SITUATIONS

31. If I applied for a job, a prospective employer would most likely hire me because I am:
    a) ___ Driven, direct, and delegating.
    b) ___ Deliberate, accurate, and reliable.
    c) ___ Patient, adaptable, and tactful.
    d) ___ Fun-loving, spirited, and casual.

32. When involved in an intimate relationship, if I feel threatened by my partner, I:
    a) ___ Fight back with facts and anger.
    b) ___ Cry, feel hurt, and plan revenge.
    c) ___ Become quiet, withdrawn, and often hold anger until I blow up over some minor issue later.
    d) ___ Distance myself and avoid further conflict.

33. For me, life is most meaningful when it:
    a) ___ Is task-oriented and productive.
    b) ___ Is filled with people and purpose.
    c) ___ Is free of pressure and stress.
    d) ___ Allows me to be playful, lighthearted, and optimistic.

34. As a child, I was:
    a) ___ Stubborn, bright, and/or aggressive.
    b) ___ Well behaved, caring, and/or depressed.
    c) ___ Quiet, easygoing, and/or shy.
    d) ___ Too talkative, happy, and/or playful.

35. As an adult, I am:
    a) ___ Opinionated, determined, and/or bossy.
    b) ___ Responsible, honest, and/or unforgiving.
    c) ___ Accepting, contented, and/or unmotivated.
    d) ___ Charismatic, positive, and/or obnoxious.

36. As a parent, I am:
    a) ___ Demanding, quick-tempered, and/or uncompromising.
    b) ___ Concerned, sensitive, and/or critical.
    c) ___ Permissive, easily persuaded, and/or often overwhelmed.
    d) ___ Playful, casual, and/or irresponsible.

37. In an argument with a friend, I am most likely to be:
    a) ___ Verbally stubborn about facts.
    b) ___ Concerned about others' feelings and principles.
    c) ___ Silently stubborn, uncomfortable, and/or confused.
    d) ___ Loud, uncomfortable, and/or compromising.

38. If my friend was in trouble, I would be:
    a) ___ Protective, resourceful, and recommending solutions.
    b) ___ Concerned, empathetic, and loyal—regardless of the problem.
    c) ___ Supportive, patient, and a good listener.
    d) ___ Nonjudgmental, optimistic, and downplaying the seriousness of the situation.

39. When making decisions, I am:
    a) ___ Assertive, articulate, and logical.
    b) ___ Deliberate, precise, and cautious.
    c) ___ Indecisive, timid, and reluctant.
    d) ___ Impulsive, uncommitted, and inconsistent.

40. When I fail, I feel:
    a) ___ Silently self-critical, yet verbally stubborn and defensive.
    b) ___ Guilty, self-critical, and vulnerable to depression—I dwell on it.
    c) ___ Unsettled and fearful, but I keep it to myself.
    d) ___ Embarrassed and nervous—seeking to escape the situation.

41. If someone crosses me:
    a) ___ I am angered and cunningly plan ways to get even quickly.
    b) ___ I feel deeply hurt and find it almost impossible to forgive completely. Generally, getting even is not enough.
    c) ___ I am silently hurt and plan to get even and/or completely avoid the other person.
    d) ___ I want to avoid confrontation, consider the situation not important enough to bother with, and/or seek other friends.

42. Work is:
    a) ___ A most productive way to spend one's time.

b) ___ A healthy activity, which should be done right if it's to be done at all. Work should be done before one plays.
c) ___ A positive activity as long as it is something I enjoy and don't feel pressured to accomplish.
d) ___ A necessary evil, much less inviting than play.

43. In social situations, I am most often:
a) ___ Feared by others.
b) ___ Admired by others.
c) ___ Protected by others.
d) ___ Envied by others.

44. In a relationship, I am most concerned with being:
a) ___ Approved of and right.
b) ___ Understood, appreciated, and intimate.
c) ___ Respected, tolerant, and peaceful.
d) ___ Praised, having fun, and feeling free.

45. To feel alive and positive, I seek:
a) ___ Adventure, leadership, and lots of action.
b) ___ Security, creativity, and purpose.
c) ___ Acceptance and safety.
d) ___ Excitement, playful productivity, and the company of others.

Situation Totals

___ Total a's   ___ Total b's   ___ Total c's   ___ Total d's

Now add your totals from numbers 1–30 to those from numbers 31–45 to get your grand totals. At this point, the four personality color types are assigned to each of the letters: Red for *a*, Blue for *b*, White for *c*, and Yellow for *d*.

RED (a) ___ BLUE (b) ___ WHITE (c) ___ YELLOW (d) ___

INTERPRETING THE SCORES

The letter with the greatest total reflects your natural personality. The number of responses from multiple columns suggests the amount of blend your personality represents. You have only one basic personality, but you may be a strong blend (behaviorally) of two personalities, depending on your responses. However, your motive (not your behavior) determines your primary personality (we'll get to that later).

If the totals from the word-choice section do not substantially agree with the totals from the situations section, you will find further guidance in later chapters on the various colors and their motives.

A NEW IDENTITY

How does it feel to have a new identity and immediate membership in an elite group of people with the same color? Of course you are unique, but there is a strong bond of similarity between you and everyone who shares your distinct color characteristics.

You must consider this color profile a guide, not a directive engraved in stone. Few people are completely represented by just one personality type. Your color reflects your primary personality, but, like most people, you are probably a mixture of types. The percent of colors other than your own represented in your pie chart reflects this. You are, however, *always* predominantly one color, one personality. Even if your scores seem close now, by the time you've studied the whole book, you should be able to glean your primary color.

As a result of taking the Hartman Personality Profile, you have discovered the first important truth about yourself. You are either a *purist* (predominantly one color, totaling 30 or more responses to a single letter) or a *mixed personality* (two or more colors representing almost equal totals).

Suddenly, you have a new identity—perhaps an unexpected one. You did not choose it, study for it, or acquire it through conscious effort. Nor can your parents claim genetic responsibility for it. Your personality is uniquely and refreshingly *you*.

> *Do what comes naturally.*
> *That is the straightest path to inner peace.*

SECONDARY COLORS

While purists find it easy to relate to examples that reflect primary colors, individuals with strong secondary colors do not. They are more complex. The characteristics of their behavior and their motives are harder to pin down. Once you have reviewed each of the primary core colors, Chapter 9 will delve deeper into secondary colors. For now, let me offer brief insights into the common personality blends.

The most difficult color combination within one individual is the mixture of Red and Blue. If you are strong in both categories, you will often find yourself stepping on someone's toes to get a task completed (Red), but feeling guilty afterward for making that person unhappy (Blue). Chapter 3, about motives, will help you understand your constant struggle between seeking power and searching for intimacy in relationships.

Red-White combinations are difficult to read because they can be aggressive and determined one minute (Red), then quietly passive the next (White). If you fit this category, your guiding motive is power or peace rather than intimacy, which spares you the intense struggle of the Red-Blue combination. You are likely to be misunderstood because your behavior is inconsistent, and you don't easily allow others to figure you out.

If you're a Red-Yellow, you are a natural leader and find yourself in a comfortable blend. The Red dynamically directs your life, while the Yellow charismatically invites others to enjoy your friendship.

If you're a Blue-White combination, you are comfortable. You express yourself with gentle sincerity. People find you determined yet flexible. You are someone with whom almost anyone can get along.

Blue-Yellows are fun to tease. I call them my dual personalities because they can be footloose and carefree one minute, then suddenly turn very serious the next. They may pack the neighborhood kids in the van and race to the beach for a day of sun and fun. But once there, they'll start to worry about all the things they should be doing at home.

If White and Yellow are your two strong colors, you possess the best people skills of all the personalities. You are relaxed and usually take the path of least resistance. You do not experience much conflict between your colors, despite the different motives represented by each. You are comfortable with your blend and present an inviting atmosphere to those around you.

Ultimately—whoever *you* are—you are driven by one basic personality. You must find your driving core motive, even though it may be concealed by a mixture of two or more colors. All individuals have just *one* primary personality; therefore, it is essential that you determine your basic color. A person with one watch knows the time, but a person with two or more is never sure.

You will find clues to your primary personality—no matter how much of a blend you may be—in the following chapter on motives. As you read, remember that you should always defer to your natural personality strengths. Do what comes naturally. This is the straightest path to inner peace.

Now let's continue—as Reds, Blues, Whites, and Yellows. We will begin by identifying and exploring the needs, desires, and motives of each of the colors in the complex and fascinating rainbow of personalities.

DEMOGRAPHICS AND PERSONALITY

Every group of people provides different demographics with the number of Reds, Blues, Whites, and Yellows they will find among them. Sales organizations are usually strong in Reds and Yellows, while finance departments are high in Blues and Whites. While sexual identity and cultural diversity modify the appearance of a greater majority of any given color, the truth is that innately there are as many Red women as Red men, but society skews it to appear as if there are more Red men and Blue women. Many countries promote different colors through their cultural biases, but when one looks at individuals within the culture, the general breakdown remains the same around the world.

PERSONALITY FILTERS

I am often asked what role other factors play in determining one's core personality. Equally curious to people seems to be the fact that I can categorize everyone with only four core personalities. Before delving into the focus of my work, let me address these important questions.

Nothing exists in a vacuum. Though *personality* is the most critical factor in determining how you will face life, it is clearly influenced by a myriad of other significant factors.

Many factors influence our personality. However, keeping it all in perspective, it is more critical to identify our driving core motive than any other factor. Once that is accurately identified, we begin to assess how the many other influences impact our driving core motive. This also speaks to the issue of how I can categorize the masses into only four primary personality groupings.

No two people are exactly alike. However, I guarantee that every individual with a Yellow personality is driven by the same core motive of *fun*. That's the magic of color-coding. For example, one of my very best friends is a Yellow. We share many similar attitudes thanks to our mutual personality. However, he is an introvert who derives his energy primarily from within. He prefers riding horses alone in the country, while I am an extrovert and derive my energy primarily from others—I prefer the interaction of many people.

I come from a family of seven children, three of whom have Yellow personalities. I have a Yellow sister and a last-born Yellow brother, and I am a middle child. Both birth order and gender clearly influence us, creating differences in our personalities, but we all share the same driving core motive of *fun*.

The human face, with its limited number of variables (eyes, nose, chin, ears, hair), never produces exactly the same look. The same is true with personality. Limited to four core motives, no two people are exactly the same because of numerous personality filters.

Chapter Three

THE MAGIC OF MOTIVE

Many people skip this chapter and jump right into the four colors. They miss the magic of motive, from which all behavior comes. It works like magic even though it is based on common sense. *The true power of* The People Code *comes with understanding the motive behind the behavior.* No other instrument provides this. They are *all* behavior based and we all know that behavior can be learned and altered depending on the circumstances. Personality, identified from the core motivation of an individual, is not easily transitioned and is far more insightful than merely identifying how he or she behaves. That is why people quickly forget other personality profiles. They find

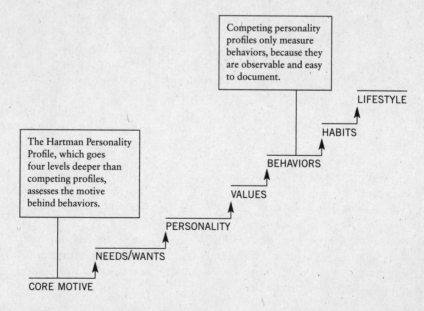

Competing personality profiles only measure behaviors, because they are observable and easy to document.

LIFESTYLE

HABITS

The Hartman Personality Profile, which goes four levels deeper than competing profiles, assesses the motive behind behaviors.

BEHAVIORS

VALUES

PERSONALITY

NEEDS/WANTS

CORE MOTIVE

them inconsistent and often irrelevant because they provide only a snapshot of who a person is on any given day. This will never be the case with color-coding. Once you have an accurate reading of a person's core personality, anchored by motive, needs, and wants, you will always know who they are and what you can expect from them.

Look at the depth you gain from understanding the *whys* behind the behaviors. You will see yourself and other people with profound clarity once you get behind the behavior to understand their motives, needs, and wants.

You have just completed your own profile online, which revealed your core personality by color. The Hartman Personality Profile listed many attitudes and behaviors. *Attitudes and behaviors are determined by needs and wants.* For example, Reds *need* to be right, so their behavior is likely to be opinionated. Since Reds *want* leadership opportunities, their behavior is likely to be assertive and/or bossy.

Many of us are familiar with the *Peanuts* cartoon strip that features Lucy, a Red child who *needs* to be right and *wants* to lead. Consequently, her behavior is dominant and bossy (or "crabby" in Charlie Brown's terminology).

Just as behavior is directed by needs and wants, needs and wants are determined by *motives*. Motives are our innermost reasons for everything we think and do. They explain *why* we think and do! They are the driving force behind our personalities. Motives are to our personalities what breathing is to the human body.

Motives are the principal means of identifying a personality color. Each color stands for one driving core motive. Reds are motivated by POWER. Blues are motivated by INTIMACY. Whites are motivated by PEACE. Yellows are motivated by FUN. I will explain the driving core motives in depth in the next chapters, but suffice it to say that if you could simply "get" the significance of motive, your entire world of relationships would be favorably changed forever.

I am reminded of Jake, a White man who carried on an affair with a woman he loved, while staying in a marriage that was based solely on social obligation and family pressures. There was no love or companionship in his shell of a marriage. Many other men might have moved out, divorced their wives, and gone off with the other woman who was the love of his life. Not Jake! A White's primary core motivation is PEACE. He didn't want to rock the boat. He wouldn't—or couldn't—confront his wife.

He had this tremendous *need* to feel good inside, and a confrontation would have been painful. Jake sought to please both himself (by having an affair) and others (by staying married to his wife). At this point, his motives, needs, and wants were pulling him in different directions. It is no surprise then, that an unhealthy behavior pattern followed. He was unhappy, and he made those around him unhappy, too.

Motives, needs, and wants are neither good nor bad. They are neutral. They become healthy or unhealthy depending on how they relate to clean motives and underlying truth.

The White motive of peace is healthy when it benefits everyone involved. In Jake's case, the White motive of peace was selfish. His unwillingness to be honest with his wife and face the consequences of his behavior kept her from finding someone else to love. It kept his girlfriend from enjoying the true intimacy that would have come from enjoying him on a full-time basis. And it kept him from developing his character and pursuing his wants and needs in a more positive way. The White motive of peace remained neutral, but his actions were unhealthy, dishonest, and selfish.

Fortunately, Jake's story has a happy ending. He learned to develop his character and clean up his motives. He scraped up enough courage to be honest with his wife. He moved into an apartment of his own—which was difficult and uncomfortable, especially for a comfort-loving White personality—and remained alone until he could decide which woman to live with. Ultimately, Jake chose his girlfriend. As difficult as this process was, it freed all concerned to pursue healthy and fulfilling lives.

He hit on the key to successful relationships, regardless of personality color. Jake examined his motives and realized the unhealthy way he was pursuing them. He chose a different path and put them in a new, positive, and healthy perspective. Being White, he still desired peace, but he recognized that he could never find real peace until he faced the truth about his behavior. By facing the truth, he defied his innate personality limitations (passiveness, indecisiveness, and avoiding confrontation at all costs) and developed a healthy sense of his own character. He eventually achieved tremendous success in all his personal relationships because of his willingness to align his motives, needs, wants, and behaviors with truth.

Jake's example illustrates the strengths and limitations of the White personality, but each color has its own set of needs, wants, and behavior patterns, all produced by a unique set of motives. Now that you know your own core color personality, what are *your* particular motives, needs, and wants? What does *your* true color reveal about *you*?

Remember, as you review the needs and wants, that though every individual has only one driving core motive, high secondary colors create blends in a person's needs, wants, and subsequent behaviors. This chart offers a simple and clear perspective on your personality as defined by your driving core motive. Copy it and put it on your wall as you learn the four personalities with their accompanying motives, needs, and wants.

MOTIVES, NEEDS, AND WANTS

	RED	BLUE	WHITE	YELLOW
MOTIVE	Power	Intimacy	Peace	Fun
NEEDS	To look good (technically)	To be good (morally)	To feel good (inside)	To look good (socially)
	To be right	To be understood	To be allowed their own space	To be noticed
	To be respected	To be appreciated	To be respected	To be adored
	Approval from a select few	Acceptance	Kindness	Approval from the masses
WANTS	To hide insecurities (tightly)	To reveal insecurities	To withhold insecurities	To hide insecurities (loosely)
	Productivity	Quality	Tolerance	Happiness
	Leadership	Autonomy	Independence	Freedom
	Challenging adventure	Security	Contentment	Playful adventure

REDS

Reds Want Control

Simply stated, Reds want their own way. If they have been raised in environments where they are able to manipulate their parents and siblings, they become increasingly difficult to manage with age. Reds push the limits and unless someone can check them, they find it difficult to pull back of their own accord.

Reds Want to Be Productive

The driving core motive of Reds is power, which means simply moving from A to B. Reds must move in order to breathe and if you get in their way or prevent them from getting to B, they will challenge you. Reds like to work—in school, in their careers, and in their relationships. Just don't expect them to attach the same importance to things that other people care about—like school classes of limited interest or careers with restricted opportunities. Give Reds a reason to produce and watch them take off. Reds need to get the job done. They are often workaholics. However, they resist nonproductive assignments or uninteresting projects.

Reds Want to Look Good to Others

Reds need to appear knowledgeable. They crave approval from people they respect for their intelligence and capabilities. They want to be respected even more than they want to be loved. They want to be admired for their logical, practical minds. When you deal with a Red, be precise and know the facts. Reds are unmoved by tears or other displays of emotion.

Reds Shouldn't Be Taken Too Seriously

Reds love a challenge. They will often drum up controversy simply for the fun of having a good debate. They are usually highly articulate and like to hear themselves think out loud. They seldom say "in my opinion" before speaking their opinions. I have witnessed countless Blues, Whites, and Yellows become frustrated with issues raised by Reds, only to discover later that the Reds simply wanted to argue the point. Don't take their barrage personally. They are mostly in the discussion for the sake of bantering.

Reds Seek Leadership Opportunities

Reds like to be in the driver's seat. They are often referred to as "control freaks" because they like to get things done their way. Reds are willing to pay any price for an opportunity to lead. Many seek military experience, despite its rigidity, because it affords them future opportunities for leadership. Red children are often frustrated in school because teachers (often Blue) won't let them take charge.

BLUES

Blues Seek Connections

Blues value connecting with others in getting from A to B, far more than actually arriving. They love being loved and loving others. The essence of success for a Blue is making a difference in another's life. Relating with others and feeling completely immersed in the connection gives Blues breath. They are highly nurturing of others—would gladly coach someone else to triumph at the expense of achieving success themselves.

Blues Embrace Altruism

Blues selflessly seek ways to improve the lives of those around them. They love giving up something in order to bring someone happiness. Self-sacrifice is their middle name and they take personal umbrage when selfish behavior rules the day. Many Blues are uncomfortable doing things solely for themselves. They hold doors open for people, offer rides when someone's car breaks down, contribute to charities, and often devote time and talents to help others without giving it a second thought.

Blues Specifically Need Two Things: Appreciation and to Be Understood

Save yourself thousands of dollars on therapy if you are married to a Blue. They need to be appreciated for always going the extra mile. A simple pat on the back will not suffice, trust me. They need to be thanked and specifically remembered for their good deeds and on special occasions. They require sincere gratitude and appropriate attention. Blues are gratified when they are listened to, which can be difficult because they often wax long and intense before they are done. They are notorious for sharing their inadequacies and fears and expect your full attention. Knowing you care enough to understand them at their deepest center makes all the difference to Blues.

Blues Are Directed by a Strong Moral Conscience

Blues believe proper behavior and appropriate protocol make a profound difference in the quality of everyone's life. Proper manners make them comfortable. They have a moral code that guides them in their decision making. Blues enjoy doing the right thing and believe we should all seek to "be good" and take the moral high ground. Of all the personality colors, Blues come equipped with the strongest sense of integrity. Ethically, Blues are less vulnerable to abusing power than Reds, but more self-righteous in their judgment of others' inappropriate behavior.

Blues Crave Fairness

Perhaps nothing riles a Blue like disparity in the world. They see themselves as life's referees, and they want others to play fair as well. They often get caught up in being fair rather than address the unique needs of individuals because of their strong sense of being equal in their dealings with their fellowmen. For a Blue, justice rules supreme and they struggle intensely when they feel that prejudice has been allowed to go uncontested.

WHITES

Whites Relish Fluid, Egoless Lives

Whites move through life with little fanfare. They don't share the ego needs of the other colors, thus freeing themselves to appreciate all personalities free of suspicion. They move like water around boulders and obstacles, without the assumption that everything should be choreographed to meet their specific needs. They are not dramatic or demanding, but accepting of life's challenges for what they are.

Whites Need Kindness

Blues are compassionate (emotional) while Whites are kind (rational). Whites don't understand why anyone ever needs to be unkind. They watch people and make assessments of their ability to trust or share based on how kind the person is to others. They will suffer in silence rather than abuse in the heat of the moment. They are highly self-regulated.

Whites Want Independence

Unlike Reds and Blues, who seek to control others, Whites want only to avoid being controlled. They like their own company and prefer to be respected by others and allowed to move through life at their own pace. Whites want to do things in their own way and in their own good time. They don't ask much of others, and resent it when others demand things from them. They may often comply with unreasonable requests simply to keep the peace, but over time they "blow up" when they can not longer tolerate being bossed around.

Whites Provide Remarkable Clarity

Whites provide astute perspective when solicited, but rarely express themselves unless asked. They enjoy their quiet awareness and modestly consider their remarks less significant than others. They have a keen eye for connecting the dots and making meaningful contributions when invited.

Whites Welcome Diversity

For many reasons, Whites find different perspectives and preferences among a variety of people to be refreshing. They are open to others' recommendations on problem resolution and find little need to promote their own agendas at the expense of the team. They welcome help and make agreeable participants. They are as equally interested in the well-being of others as they are in themselves.

YELLOWS

Yellows Value Play

Yellows consider life to be a party and they're hosting! Yellows never grow up and they believe that life should not spoil having a good time. They love practical jokes and being with other people. They live by the "better offer" theory that they are committed until a better offer comes along. Enjoying someone or something freely in the moment brings out their most inviting and best self.

Yellows Need to Be Adored

While other colors would never expect adoration, Yellows thrive on it. Yellows need you to pay attention to them—to notice them. Ignoring a Yellow is a most devastating blow. Yellows need to know they are valued and approved of—not for anything that they do; simply because they are. Yellows often act as if they have the world by the tail, but they have fears and frustrations, which they rarely confide until they know they are emotionally safe to do so.

Yellows Want Emotional Connections

Yellows often appear so nonchalant that people think they don't care about anything. Nothing could be further from the truth. Yellows need connections but often want them on their terms, which can be quite superficial and lacking commitment. Yellows like to be stroked and enjoy physical touch. To Yellows, physical contact is often the most direct, honest, and comfortable form of connection.

Yellows Want to Be Engaged

Yellows love center stage. Social acceptance is very important to them. Friendships command a high priority in their lives because popularity answers one of their basic needs—the need for general approval. Yellows are highly articulate and often loud. They relish good conversation and can easily go with the flow.

Yellows Seek Action

Easily bored, Yellows crave adventure. They can never sit still for long. They choose friends who, like them, refuse to allow the mundane details to get in the way of what life is all about—play! Ironically, numerous people are currently misdiagnosed as having ADD (Attention Deficit Disorder) when, in fact, they are merely Yellow personalities struggling with their innate inability to be disciplined, sit still, and stay focused on tasks that no longer interest them.

CONCLUSION OF MOTIVES, NEEDS, AND WANTS

There you have it. You now have a clear foundation for understanding each personality's strengths and limitations. Remember, all behaviors are derived from core motives, needs, and wants.

As you now identify your strengths and limitations, keep it all in perspective. No color is better than another. All colors have remarkable innate gifts as well as obstacles to overcome. Limitations are nothing to be afraid of. Each color has much to learn from the others. We are most effective in understanding other people when we see them whole—treating them as complete personalities rather than focusing on either their strengths or limitations.

Reading about one's limitations can be painful. It can be very difficult acknowledging areas in which we are weak. We often prefer to shield ourselves with our built-in blinders, so prepare yourself for some discomfort. "It will only hurt for a moment," as the doctor says. Take stock in the fact that the cure is better than the illness. The cure, in this case, is knowledge. And knowledge is power.

The best thing about acknowledging one's limitations
is that, once understood, they can be turned into strengths.

Chapter Four

PERSONALITY IN PERSPECTIVE

*To experience passion, one must have an accurate
sense of oneself and feel a congruence between
who one is and the life one lives.*

The Hartman Personality Theory identifies three essential dimensions that must operate in unison for an individual to be fully human—fully alive. All three play distinctly different albeit highly integrated roles in creating a complete person.

THE PERSONALITY

The personality plays the central role of the three critical elements. Each personality is driven by a core motive, which you have just identified. It represents each individual's innate wants, needs, and natural behaviors. While no individual is limited from embracing any strengths or limitations of all personalities, he or she can never abandon his or her innate core personality. Even when people strive to alter their core personality by purposely choosing behaviors of another personality, their very being cannot deny who they are innately.

I was conducting a weekend team-building retreat in Oxnard, California, with a small group of twenty executives. Monica listened intently with the others while I presented the basics of *The People Code*. Just before our first morning break, she blurted out, "I am her! I can't believe this! After all I've done to free myself of her distasteful memory, I am, in the end, *her*!"

As we discussed her sudden awareness, Monica explained that the "her" she referred to was her mother, for whom she felt no love and, indeed, very little regard at all. She had pledged never to be like this woman who had proved such a destructive force in her childhood.

On the other hand, she adored her father and had spent endless hours mimicking his strengths and choosing a lifestyle similar to his own.

The accuracy and simplicity of color-coding makes it relatively easy to identify your own true core personality and the personalities of others with whom you interact as well. Monica quickly identified that she and her mother shared the same core Blue personality, while her father was a Red. In distancing herself from her mother, she had also painfully detached from herself. Developing the positive Red strengths of her father was extremely positive but *not* with the negative motive of replacing her own innate Blue strengths. Monica could have replaced her own innate Blue limitations that she shared with her mother, but her core motive of intimacy could never be completely ignored. Subsequently, it haunted her and, despite all her efforts, the minute she heard my presentation, she recognized her true identity. Our personality comes with each of our individual souls and must be respected and nurtured as vital to our being.

DEVELOPING CHARACTER

Character breathes substance into the personality. My next book, *Color Your Future,* brings a tremendous integrity to *The People Code.* While the miracle of accurate self-identity is awe-inspiring, it is essentially just the beginning of knowing ourselves and what we're all about. For example, after completing the Hartman Personality Profile, you now know your core personality, complete with driving core motive, wants, needs, and natural behaviors. You cannot, however, identify the ratio of your strengths to your limitations.

Without the character code, you cannot easily identify what behaviors you need to develop from the other personalities. You cannot readily see which of your limitations creates difficulties for you when interacting with others and why. This requires a process called "charactering" and is introduced using an instrument called the Hartman Character Profile in my next book. In order to complete the process of becoming your best self, you must identify and develop the personality traits unnatural to your innate personality, while maintaining and nurturing your own driving core motive.

Charactering is a challenging adventure. It is never easy to balance accepting yourself as you are, while simultaneously stretching to embrace new gifts to replace current deficiencies. If you think this is easy, you have probably never personally engaged in the process of charactering yourself. It requires a lifelong effort.

For now, a simple illustration will have to suffice. It will help you see

PERSONALITY IN PERSPECTIVE

Charactered	Healthy	Unhealthy	Dysfunctional
+ positive traits of each personality other than their own innate color	+ positive traits within your own innate personality	− negative traits within your own innate personality	− negative traits of each personality other than your own innate color

the strong correlation between personality and character. There are four general ways to identify the different levels people can operate on.

The *charactered* dimension represents people who use the positive strengths of each personality outside their own innate color. While *The People Code* clearly requires that you accept your core driving motive as innate and unchanging, it also embraces the reality that you can choose to develop every positive gift the other personalities provide.

The *healthy* dimension identifies people who use the positive gifts they were naturally born to display. My professional experience indicates that most people could comfortably survive their entire lifetime simply relying solely on their own innate personality strengths, rather than having to develop outside gifts.

The *unhealthy* dimension categorizes people who go through life using the innate limitations of their natural personality. Most people have more limiting behavior traits in their own innate core color than in any other personality type.

The *dysfunctional* dimension represents the ultimate in poor mental health. People who use the negative behavior traits of any (and sometimes every) personality other than their own are extremely difficult to identify accurately, let alone relate well with. Whenever I ask seminar participants to identify the core color of an ex-spouse where there has been extreme abuse or dysfunction, they will often shake their head and say, "Can I use the color Black?!" They can't readily see the ex-spouse's core personality color because they can remember only their various limitations from multiple personality sources.

Most people operate in one of the following dual dimensions: the charactered-healthy dimension, healthy-unhealthy dimension, or unhealthy-dysfunctional dimension. One of the positive dynamics of becoming charactered is that if you struggle with a limitation outside your core color (dysfunctional dimension), you can focus on a strength of another color (charactered dimension) to overcome it. In so doing, you can leap from the dysfunctional dimension to become charactered without having to move individually through the other dimensions as well. Developing unnatural strengths requires arduous work and tremendous humility.

CREATIVE PASSION

Finally, passion breathes life into both personality and character. With personality and character you can see the lights on in the house, but there is no guarantee anyone is home. Passion is the people in the house, giving it life and creating a powerful synergy between personality and character. Passion cannot be forced. It must be genuine and flow from one's very being. No one can develop your passion. It is like breathing: you must do it for yourself or you will die. Sadly, we live in a society where far too many people die years before they are buried. Passion makes the difference in why people get out of bed in the morning and how they feel about themselves when they fall back into bed at night. **To experience passion, one must have an accurate sense of oneself and feel a congruence between who one is and the life one lives.** If this aspect of the color method interests you particularly, you will want to read *Color Your Future*.

Having put personality in its proper perspective against the backdrop of the added elements of character and passion, let's refocus on identifying our core personalities. That's where it all begins and, as in constructing a building, unless we get the foundation correct, nothing is going to line up properly later on. Our personalities are rooted in our innate driving core motives and offer powerful insights into our wants, needs, and natural strengths and limitations.

Part Two

EVERYONE ELSE

Chapter Five

REDS:
THE POWER WIELDERS

We all know people who just get things done. No matter what. You remember Mother Teresa, who founded her own order, Missionaries of Charity, which began with only twelve members and grew to have more than four thousand nuns running orphanages and charity houses worldwide. Or Mark Inglis, the man who conquered Mt. Everest as a double amputee. These are the bridge builders of society. These are our natural-born leaders, the people who know how to get from point A to point B efficiently and typically with little fanfare. They are the power wielders.

> *The Red personality*
> *moves forcefully through life.*

WARNING: This is **not** a quick read if you are Red! The positive strengths will encourage you and the limitations will frustrate you. Still, *this is who you are!* The truth will set you free, but you must first embrace it for what it tells you about yourself. You will quickly see that your personality is bold—both positive and negative. You'll leave a mark on others, with serious consequences. For all other colors, this chapter will heighten your awareness of how to effectively engage Reds. Read it like a blueprint of their lives.

RED CHARACTERISTICS

Active and Productive

As the most dominant and intimidating of the personalities, Reds move forcefully through life. Helen Keller (a definite Red) once said,

"Life is either a daring adventure or nothing at all." Reds are highly committed to causes. They are all about being focused and determined to accomplish whatever life places before them. They are so intense that often the everyday monotony of life just isn't enough. Reds seek action and enjoy the challenge of rising to the occasion. As a result of their innate tenacity for life, they are often successful, primarily in business, task-oriented activities, and causes. Reds *seek* action and results, and they *crave* productivity. They measure their own success by how much and how efficiently they accomplish anything at any given time. The bottom line: Reds get things done.

Visionary

I would gladly follow a healthy Red to the ends of the earth! They are always looking ahead, putting the puzzle pieces together long before the rest of us realize there is even a puzzle. Because Reds are so decisive, they are often accused of acting without considering the consequences. Nothing could be further from the truth! Reds hate to fail, and so rarely make a hasty decision. They weigh every decision against the question What if I fail? This question alone is enough to stop other personalities dead in their tracks. Not Reds! They've already developed an alternate plan. It's instinctive for them! Reds think two or three steps ahead: "If this fails, then I'll do that. And if that doesn't work, I'll head in this direction." While others stop because of their fear, Reds offset their fear with rational alternatives and simply do what needs to be done.

> *"Have a vision. Be demanding."*
> —Colin Powell

Insensitive and Selfish

No matter where they are, whether it is at home with friends or engaged in hobbies, Reds make sure they get their fair share of the pie. To put it simply, they are typically selfish—always looking out for number one. They know what they want and how to get it, and this means they often manipulate events and people in order to achieve it. They are not so much concerned with feelings of guilt or compassion for others (how does that help you get from A to B?). Ironically, very insecure and emotionally needy Reds will seek emotional attention and make certain that whatever inconvenience they may be experiencing (e.g., illness or accident) is shared by others in their life. Because they are so confident in their views, they can present themselves in a condescending and insensitive manner. As I mentioned before, Reds are all about getting from A to B, and they aren't easily distracted from that goal.

Kings of the Jungle

Considering what we already know about Reds, it is no surprise that they exude self-confidence. Because they appear strong and certain of themselves, few people are willing to confront them. This strength and certainty bestow on Reds the most feared status of all the personalities. Reds are kings of the jungle. When people are in need of advice and direction, Reds have ready answers and solutions. They have a sense of being right and they are often able to express themselves in such a way that few people can logically refute what they say. It is extremely important to Reds that they appear knowledgeable in all aspects of life. Less intelligent Reds often refuse to acknowledge their ignorance. These sullied souls we refer to as bad Reds. They don't *get it*, but refuse to concede their limitations. Good Reds, on the other hand, admit vulnerability, take their medicine, and move forward. They are highly resourceful, providing a powerful energy for creative problem solving. As such, they are skilled in making good decisions and consequently people choose to follow. And why not? When you find a good doctor, why seek another? It is their innate and enviable ability to be right so often that influences others to place them in leadership roles. Their natural gifts and desire to lead drive Reds to take advantage of the opportunities for advancement to the top of many social organizations, businesses, sports teams, and any other affiliations to which they belong.

Demanding and Critical

Reds are highly critical of others. Most are verbally critical, while others remain quietly dissatisfied with the performance of others. They are impatient with human inadequacy (something they don't accept in themselves or others), and feel that nothing short of efficiency should be tolerated. Though Reds are not as perfectionistic as Blues (thank our lucky stars!), they do expect a job to be done right and expediently. They have no tolerance for mental dullness, a lack of common sense, or unpreparedness. They expect results. They can be highly biased and reactionary in their judgment of others. This emotionally based behavior is ironic considering the logical rigidity that permeates the thinking and behavior of most Reds.

Insecure

Reds are incredibly adept at hiding their insecurities so deeply that they don't consciously feel the pain associated with them. This often means that they are insensitive to the raw nerves they touch in others who may be less adept, willing, or even able to hide their insecurities and vulnerabilities. Most Reds don't mean harm. They are only concerned that their productivity is enhanced and that in the end they are proven to be right. Reds have little sympathy for obstacles to progress, whether the source is an employee, child, spouse, or friend.

Must Be Right

Because Reds are driven by their need to hide their emotional insecurities, they absolutely demand to be right. One hundred percent of the time. They do not ask whether they are perceived by others to be right; they simply state that they are. Again, 100 percent of the time. Even in the face of obvious evidence that a Red has been inaccurate in an assertion, they often brush it aside as a misunderstanding or misinterpretation.

Competitive and Bold

Reds are daring and bold. These traits tend to lure them away from the business world or their domestic duties in pursuit of adventures such as mountain climbing, hang gliding, and building their own homes. Reds can also find this same excitement in finding the most efficient way to progress in their personal relationships (remember, it's all about getting from A to B), or in getting the competitive edge in the business world. The combination of their brave and competitive strengths allows Reds to be bold within their organizational structure as well as in their personal lives.

> *"You have to learn the rules of the game.*
> *And then you have to play better than anyone else."*
> —*Albert Einstein*

Manipulative

I have seen lives nearly destroyed by the shrewd manipulation of an unhealthy Red. Many Reds are frustrated when they realize that they want to *control* rather than *share* their destiny. This is the very base of Red insecurity—they want a loving relationship but refuse to abandon control for vulnerability, which is essential in order to experience legitimate intimacy. Often, when they find they are powerless to control the process, they abandon intimacy all together, settling for business heroics, meeting financial obligations, or creating mutually beneficial community service. Subsequently, many Reds may appear wildly successful while actually leading "lives of quiet desperation."

Tenacious and Taxing

Reds can be taxing with their intense personalities. They tend to be so tenacious and bossy that they can wear you down rather quickly. Reds often remind me of houseguests who want the household schedule adapted to meet *their* personal schedule. After even a short time with this overbearing personality, a change of scenery and a breath of fresh air is not only welcome—it's necessary! In their leadership, Reds can also be overbearing. They expect nothing less than an authoritarian atmosphere, and *they're* the authority. Reds expect their subordinates to remember their place in the pecking order and respond accordingly. They can be hard to work for or live with because they order others around with little or no regard for established schedules, family commitments, or professional concerns. If they are ever challenged, they can become aggressive due to their intimidating nature and arrogance. They are not shamed by public awareness of their demanding behavior. With a lack of tact characteristic of Reds, they will relentlessly pursue those elements in their lives that need attention, whether it be a misplaced hotel reservation or a child's less than sterling report card. An unhealthy Red is typically aggressive.

Assertive and Determined

On the flip side, positive assertion flows as easily to the healthy Red as water falls from a duck's back. Everyone always knows where a Red stands. They need no coaxing to establish their position in any situation, and they need no support in maintaining that position. Their innate "knowledge" that they are right gives Reds all the support they need, and the confidence necessary to intimidate opposing parties. Business groups are *always* enhanced by the presence of healthy Reds. They speak their minds directly and honestly, paying no mind to the effect it may have on their popularity. Reds are strong-willed and determined individuals. They take firm stands and simply expect others to follow.

"Live daringly, boldly, fearlessly."
—*Henry J. Kaiser*

45

Disagreeable

Whether it is for the sake of maintaining the fine art of debate or a driving need to convert the world to their beliefs, Reds can be quite opinionated and stubborn on most topics. It doesn't matter whether it's about how to pay a bill or about how to meet a deadline. A logical side dish to their disagreeableness and their logical minds is their knack for verbal arguments. Reds are highly articulate, quick on their feet, and quite comfortable in debate. It requires very little for a Red to challenge another person. They have such a natural flair for this, in fact, that they rarely recognize the conflict they've created.

Poor Listeners

Though articulate, Reds are not natural conversationalists. They prefer to lecture. Let's just say that the ability to listen and empathize is often limited in the Red personality. These limitations cause many Reds to experience loneliness, but don't hold your breath waiting for them to admit it. If they do admit it, they tend to blame their loneliness on others (for example, "If people were only more intelligent, they would appreciate me," or " I can't be expected to dumb myself down in order to find common ground with you.").

Resourceful and Self-Reliant

Reds, because of their resourcefulness and self-reliance, often challenge authority figures and successfully control their own destiny. If I were ever caught in an emergency situation, I would most prefer to have a Red person in close proximity. They eat, sleep, and breathe action. No situation will ever get the best of them until they've exhausted every possible remedy. They simply don't give up easily. They aren't easily intimidated by life's obstacles. They have a sharp competitive sense, and their opponents (whether it be an earthquake or a mother-in-law) will not find victory easily.

Relentless

If you need an ally of any sort, whether you're fund-raising for the local elementary school or running for president, advertise for the Red personality characteristics. Nobody promotes like a Red. I have already explained their bold, assertive, and competitive nature. They are also pragmatic. Reds are able to get to the heart of a problem without being distracted by lesser concerns, and are able to quickly devise proactive solutions. If they feel it is worthwhile, Reds throw themselves into a cause. Their commitment to causes they believe in is unquestionable. They are as comfortable promoting others as they are themselves when they are committed to a cause. Reds are more difficult to convert to a new concept, but then equally difficult to restrain once converted. For instance, once a Red parent has discovered her child's dancing talents, she will drive long distances and provide financial resources to see her child succeed. Once Paul converted to Christianity, he became the faith's most zealous missionary. So it goes with Reds.

Impatient

Whether it be healthy or not, Reds pursue what they want until they have it. They want everyone to respond whenever and however they deem proper. Reds struggle with impatience. They don't feel they have the time to wait for others to "grow up" and behave the way Reds know they ought to. Red infants expect and demand to be held *immediately* upon request (crying). Red salespeople demand that you not only listen to their pitch but that you answer any and all silly questions ("Do you really want to be seen driving last year's model?"). Red parents demand respect long before they have earned it. Red employers cannot tolerate indecisiveness or poor productivity. Impatience can prove costly for Red leaders. They can step too quickly and impose change with such haste that they dismiss personalities who need time and training to find their groove.

Calculating

Reds don't casually toss their lives up in the air and hope for a favorable wind. Remember, they are all about getting from point A to point B. They know where they are going and how to get there. In order to control their lives and produce the results they desire, they can be calculating. They have a gift for creating their own wind and getting life to blow in their direction. Even at their most determined moments, Reds can be reasoned with logically. When they are in trouble, if you can help them get beyond their insecurity (displayed as ego), they can be exceptional at creating a chess player–like attitude in calculating proactive moves for positive life resolution. If you can intrigue them by making them see life as a chessboard, Reds have an uncanny sense of how to set a successful course for themselves.

Lack Intimacy Orientation

The greatest obstacle Reds experience when trying to attain a quality lifestyle is their inability to be intimate with other people. They are so determined and productive by nature that their lack of intimacy is often ignored or overlooked as a legitimate concern, both by the Reds themselves and those close to them. Unless corrected, it usually means Reds take a supervisory "caretaker of humanity" role instead of simply being a "member of the human team." Their calculating minds combined with invulnerability often makes true intimacy an impractical notion and highly unlikely! Reds divert themselves from ever having to face the issue of legitimate intimacy in their relationships. They are lost without their career or intense family focus. Your Red child will be the first to remind you how eager she is to leave the house at eighteen. She will also be the first to come home (whether physically or emotionally) and seek the comforts of a loving and caring family. Some Reds will milk an illness for every drop it's worth (especially Red men), while other Reds hide their pain and discomfort. These behaviors are attempts at connecting with others that don't lead to true intimacy. They eventually leave many Reds skeptical and lonely.

RED LIMITATIONS

At their very worst, Reds have a myriad of intense limitations, which are neither subtle nor undefined but are easily detected. Because Reds are often taxing and demanding, they can be difficult to live and work with unless they get their way. They are innately argumentative and combative. Their selfish nature is a reminder to the other personalities that they will always consider themselves first, and that others should treat them accordingly. They can be insensitive and arrogant, which creates distance and distrust. This is understood when taking into account that intimacy is, perhaps, a Red's most underdeveloped skill. They argue from logic and are highly skilled at the art of manipulation, which often leads to their critical and disagreeable nature. Reds are often intimidating in their role as king of the jungle. They are the masters of denial ("Who, me?"). They are often surprised to find that others may see them in a negative light, yet finding fault in others is an essential part of their daily routine. Their tactless behavior actually reveals their internal dissatisfactions. They often bloom in positions of power, impact, and control, yet shrink from an engaging social life when leadership opportunities are no longer afforded them. Always thinking, like sharks that must keep moving in order to breathe, these often remarkable individuals can cut themselves off from an abundant life if they are not constantly working on their limitations.

> *Denial prevents Reds from*
> *accurately seeing themselves*
> *and how they affect others!*

RED STRENGTHS

At their very best, healthy Reds are the lifeblood of humanity. They are the movers and shakers of every society. They are the powerful leaders and responsible delegators. Healthy Reds are an asset to any organization. They thrive on competition, challenges, and winning. Their emotional intelligence shines in the area of self-motivation, and focused direction defines their solid inner core. When setting goals, a Reds' focus is unrivaled. They tenaciously assert their personal rights, as well as the rights of any organization, person, or cause they value. They are all about being proactive and productive, and are willing to pay whatever price is necessary to be both. They excel in organizational teamwork yet enjoy the challenge of individual survival. Reds are the perfect embodiment of the power derived from rational thinking and assertive communication. They are the standard against which we measure our intellectual prowess. They are the leaders we seek to emulate. Akin to the element of fire, a Red's light continues to burn bright as a beacon of strength and productivity, warming and reassuring us with their resourceful and protective nature.

> *Reds are so decisive,*
> *if they make 51 percent of the decisions right*
> *they're happy, because they know the other 49 percent*
> *would have worked, if you hadn't screwed up.*

THE RED PARADOX

Many Reds live a complex existence, caught in a paradox of self-confidence and insecurity. They seek the very acceptance and understanding that they themselves are often unwilling to give others. However, this need for acceptance is deep within their hearts, well hidden from their rational mind's eye. Reds defer to their unrivaled logic, refusing to acknowledge their emotional vulnerability. (You Reds are doing it right now!) As youths, while they are yet innocent to raw emotions, their insecurities are more evident and exposed. Unfortunately, with age and life experience, Reds play to their innate strengths and often neglect to develop their emotional intelligence. They further develop their skills at logic and rational debate, allowing them to keep their deep emotional insecurities shrewdly disguised from others. With time, they often lose an accurate perspective on their emotions and actually begin to believe that they have no need for them at all. The irony of this lies in the fact that in order for Reds to experience a fullness of life, they must expose themselves to perhaps their greatest fear—their emotional insecurity and their need to be loved and accepted. On the flip side, there is no more powerful human force known to mankind than a *legitimately vulnerable Red*.

> For Reds, winning isn't everything: it's the only thing.

REAL-LIFE EXAMPLES OF REDS

➤ Rob is a Red CEO and the youngest brother in a family-owned business. His two older brothers are Blue and are constantly worrying about details such as petty employee complaints and current cash flow. While they sweat over the details, Rob is focused on the future by creating new spin-off companies of their already successful business and developing personnel into stronger future leaders as the company evolves. Reds instinctively visualize the future and then take the necessary steps to successfully take them there.

➤ Grace is a Red teenager who needed to get to the library to write a report for her AP American History course. Grace's mother, Nancy, had promised to take her. Just before they were to leave, Nancy and Jack (Grace's father) had a rather traumatic argument, and Jack threatened divorce. Grace witnessed the entire one-hour ordeal, which left her mother devastated and sobbing uncontrollably. Grace couldn't see why this should affect *her* plans, and said very matter-of-factly, "Mom, will we still be able to get to the library before it closes tonight?" Only Reds can be so selfish and insensitive to the feelings of others! Reds may be successful at developing and promoting ideas, events, and business ventures, but it is their selfishness and insensitivity that most often prevents them from enjoying quality relationships.

➤ Red Ginny and her family were looking for an office building without having the exact address. One of Ginny's siblings remarked, "I think it's near the corner of Moody and Lincoln." Ginny replied, "Oh, no, it's not. It couldn't be there. I know all the buildings over there." Ginny was driving, so ignored the suggestion. After an hour of driving, and several phone calls, they finally arrived at the office building, located on the corner of Moody and Lincoln. When they arrived home, their White mother suggested that in the future perhaps *all* suggestions should be entertained with an open mind. To this Ginny scoffed, "I know she didn't say Moody and Lincoln. She must have said somewhere else. After all, I'm the one who finally found it, didn't I?!"

➤ Bob is a powerful Red CEO. He wastes little time getting to the point and is always quick to get to the bottom line. He has little patience with people who "waste" time with all the details. John works as Bob's controller. As a Blue, John constantly worries about covering all the bases of the company. He always sends lengthy memos that Bob regards as detailed drudgery. Bob told me that he was tired of John's irritating memos, and was planning on telling John to quit writing them. I reminded him of the relationship between Reds and Blues, and how John deemed it critical to have Bob's sincere appreciation of his hard work as well as his support in order to feel secure. Bob decided not to tell John to stop writing the memos. Instead, he requested that John highlight the three paragraphs he felt were the most significant. "If I only have three minutes in my day to review your memo, highlight what I must read. Limit it to three paragraphs." This compromise satisfied Bob's Red need to be efficient and productive as well as John's Blue need for attending to details and feeling appreciated. It has kept them on the same winning team for years.

➤ As a young professional, I worked for a drug prevention program where the boss was a shrewd manipulator. Many of my colleagues were former drug users, and had confided in our Red boss about themselves— their fears and struggles in keeping a drug-free life. He hired these individuals knowing their personal histories and then manipulatively used this knowledge against them when they inquired about raises and promotions. Comments like "You still expect something else to make you happy—first drugs and now more money?" or "*Now* I understand why your father threw you out of the house. Were you this defiant when *he* asked small favors of you?" were common manipulations for this director. It is this type of unhealthy Red behavior that can destroy both personal and professional relationships.

➤ A Red patient of mine eventually lost the woman of his dreams because he kept postponing their marriage in order to get the right timing for the best tax break. True intimacy requires equality, and to the competitive Red, equality doesn't always seem like a worthy ambition.

➤ This book would never have been published twenty years ago had it not been for the support of three close Red friends. Two gave me the confidence to write, with their numerous suggestions, time, and support. The other met me for early-morning breakfasts, demanding (as only a Red can) that I write a new chapter every time we met. When I left a message to cancel our first breakfast, my friend called me at 11 p.m. the night before our scheduled breakfast and asked if I was canceling because I hadn't completed my "homework." She was right. I was sliding and she would have none of that!

A QUICK GUIDE TO REDS

RED STRENGTHS

AS AN INDIVIDUAL

- excels with logical thinking
- committed to a productive lifestyle
- dynamic and direct
- thrives on independence
- natural leader
- highly resourceful (strong survivor)
- resourceful in crises

AS A COMMUNICATOR

- operates in a very logical, sensible manner
- direct and honest with opinions
- articulates thoughts well
- directs the conversation in a productive, pragmatic way
- tells others where they stand in a relationship

AS A GOAL SETTER

- natural goal setter—sets goals comfortably and confidently
- maintains strong sense of perspective (sees the whole picture)
- highly disciplined

REDS: THE POWER WIELDERS

- focused productivity with predictable follow-through
- makes decisions quickly and easily
- strong goal orientation (wants to move up the ladder)

AS A CAREER PERSON

- thrives in leadership positions and being responsible
- comfortable with power (as long as he or she has it or access to it)
- always thinks in the future
- delegates effectively
- strong decision maker
- self-motivated
- thrives on competition
- dynamic and assertive
- highly task-oriented and efficient
- high self-confidence in ability to achieve
- trusts own business instincts—difficult to discourage

AS A PARENT

- decisive
- unquestioned leader in the home
- assumes responsibility for protecting family
- resourceful provider
- quick with good advice and direction
- promotes group cohesiveness or comfortable being alone
- generates focused activities for children

AS A CHILD

- communicates what he or she is thinking
- highly articulate and persuasive
- strong sense of independence
- willing to risk and try new experiences
- takes charge of situation when parents are gone
- capable of bouncing back from negative environments
- refuses to be "held hostage" by inadequate childhood
- self-confident in ability to perform

AS A FRIEND

- honest and forthcoming with proactive recommendations
- highly efficient during emergencies or disasters

- provides leadership in promoting group activities
- engages in conflict with candor
- productive in solving dilemmas

AS A COMMITTED COMPANION

- highly protective of companion
- loyal to the relationship
- promotes interesting experiences
- assumes primary responsibility for financial obligations
- reliable and dependable
- initiates interaction and activities

CAREERS MOST LIKELY TO ATTRACT REDS

(Of course, all personality types can be found in every occupation. There are innumerable variables that determine success in any career.)

Administrator	Lawyer	Building Contractor
School Superintendent	Medical Doctor	Sales
Military Officer	Tax Accountant	Marketing
Politician	Realtor	Clergy (Minister)
Entrepreneur	Professional Critic	Police Officer*

(Are you kidding? A gun comes with the badge!)

Note: Reds are most naturally driven up the career ladder of success.

PERSONALITIES THAT APPEAR TO BE RED

Angelina Jolie: Perhaps better known for her humanitarian work than for her acting career, Angelina finds a cause and promotes it as only a Red can. While filming in poverty-stricken Cambodia, she became aware for the first time of the suffering in the world. She has since been named a Goodwill Ambassador for the United Nations, and has donated millions of dollars and months of her time to these charities and organizations. She sees what needs to change and knows how to get others and their checkbooks behind her humanitarian causes. She's all about making things happen!

Donald Trump: This man's name is symbolic of an empire. He rides the waves of financial turmoil, and always ends up on top. As a youth, his parents sent him to military school, hoping to channel the energy and assertiveness of this Red child in a positive direction. He decided on a degree in economics with the goal of ultimately joining his father's real estate business. It is said that he had even fewer friends during his college years than he did in military school. Rather than seek friends, he desired only the company of real estate professors. After all, they were going to get him where he needed to go. Talk about a focused young Red!

Hillary Clinton: Does she ever stop? As a classic Red, she has been at the head of every organization that had a cause she valued. As First Lady, she remained cool and confident during the upheaval caused by her husband's impeachment. As soon as he had finished his second term, she bought a house in New York, established residency, and ran for senator of the State of New York. She became the first First Lady to be elected to the United States Senate, became the first woman elected in New York State, and is determined to be the first female U.S. president. Her innate tenacity and drive defines what Reds are all about!

RED NATIONS

These are nations that have a culture that promotes the Red motives, attitudes, and behaviors. It does *not* mean that everyone in these nations is Red.

China	Libya
Japan	North Korea
Germany	Argentina

RED MOTTO

"Lead, follow, or get out of the way!"

CELEBRITIES WHO APPEAR TO BE RED

- Russell Crowe
- Katie Couric
- Larry King
- Jack Nicholson
- Madonna
- Al Pacino
- Barbara Walters

- Nicolas Cage
- Martha Stewart
- David Letterman

RED LIMITATIONS

AS AN INDIVIDUAL

- generally seeks to serve self first ("What's in it for me?")
- promotes turmoil and conflict if necessary for a personal goal to be gained
- out of touch with own feelings
- privately rationalizes and publicly denies own failings
- always has to be right
- cannot relax and feel comfortable unless producing something (think shark!)
- often arrogant and defiant of authority
- inconsiderate of others' feelings
- won't present self as vulnerable for fear of losing power and control

AS A COMMUNICATOR

- unemotional and detached from feelings
- insensitive and tactless
- unappreciative of detail and beauty
- bored with "idle chatter"
- limited insight into others' emotional needs
- intuition is jaded by personal insecurities and judgments
- harsh and condescending
- lacks ability to share self intimately
- poor listener

AS A GOAL SETTER

- impatient with self in completing goals
- too rigid with expectations of his or her destiny
- lives life on paper rather than with people
- often judges outcome based on efficiency versus effectiveness
- quick to anger if goals aren't achieved and/or are blocked
- blames others for personal misfortune

REDS: THE POWER WIELDERS

AS A CAREER PERSON

- can step over others for personal fulfillment
- stressful and relentless in driving self and others to perform
- can be resentful of authority
- may be insensitive to others in order to get ahead in business
- insensitive decision making
- more concerned with task completion than with people
- demands others' loyalty and obedience without giving it
- authoritarian and uncompromising
- critical of others and slow to give compliments
- often too competitive to enjoy the journey
- lives in the future too much to enjoy the present

AS A PARENT

- maintains high expectations but offers limited emotional support
- demands compliance with strict obedience
- requires loyalty from family at all costs
- insensitive to children's fears and concerns
- has the final say on important decisions
- detached from children—doesn't share self emotionally
- does not tolerate deviations from set expectations
- poor listener
- impatient with play and other nonessential trivia
- lacks insight into children's emotional needs
- difficult to please—remains unimpressed
- strong sense of right and wrong—(*their* right and wrong!)

AS A CHILD

- demanding and manipulative of parents to get their way
- often defiant and resists control
- highly articulate
- critical of parents and feels he or she knows better
- fights with siblings for control and power
- hides insecurities and emotional needs
- highly independent
- finds intimacy difficult
- can be dramatic and often overreacts to pain
- expects to be catered to, especially when sick
- poor listener

AS A FRIEND

- insensitive and unemotional
- doesn't easily admit the need for friendship
- remains detached from sharing self completely
- enters friendships asking, "What's in it for me?"
- listens when convenient
- maintains mostly pragmatic friendships
- tries to control group activities
- expects friends to do things his or her way
- impatient with others
- negative, critical, and judgmental of others
- feels it is more important to be right than agreeable
- blunt or rude when angered
- demanding
- expects to be entertained
- stubborn
- denies any personal inadequacies or responsibility

AS A COMMITTED COMPANION

- primarily concerned with self-gratification
- gives priority to work over personal relationships
- demanding and arrogant
- hides insecurities and vulnerabilities
- critical of companion's imperfections
- lacks sensitivity
- often unaware of intimacy and rejects its priority in a relationship
- poor listener

Just for Reds: Recommended Life Tips

1. Connect with others, both emotionally and socially. I know it's out of your comfort zone, but you'll find that it will motivate others and they'll be more willing to help you accomplish your goals. You might not want to admit it, but you do need others to get where you're going.
2. Believe that other people can do things right too! Promote the positive in others while helping them focus on shared priorities. If you're negative or critical it may create fear in others, causing them to go into crisis or try to escape. Trust me, this will impact your bottom line.
3. Relax! Remember that Rome wasn't built in a day. Being so

demanding of yourself and others doesn't create the confidence or quality you're after.

4. When setting goals, set them differently for yourself than you do for others. When setting goals for yourself, set those you know you can achieve with your strong sense of self-discipline and motivation. Be prepared to accept different styles when working with others.
5. Avoid blaming others for failing to meet your commitments. This is a natural reaction for you, but you'll find that others will be much more cooperative in helping you rectify the failure if you don't.
6. Think your problem through and seek others' advice. You can sometimes make decisions that ignore the needs or perceptions of those in your life that will be affected. This can create more work for you down the road.
7. You can't do it all. Be open to suggestions—brainstorm with others to find solutions. This will both save you time and improve the team's morale.
8. Be cautious when imposing your demands on others' time. They have their own priorities that they need to meet. Be aware of what others have to do as well.

Top Five Red Attraction Factors

1. Confidence: help others believe in their possibilities and win
2. Vision: show others where they can be in the future
3. Sense of Urgency: love of action, movement, and results
4. Resourceful: provide options and ideas for success
5. Convincing: highly articulate and persuasive; create a strong presence

Top Three Red "Unattraction" Factors

1. Selfish: scarcity versus abundance
2. Arrogant: insecure; always needs to be right
3. Intimidating: condescending and demanding; dismissive of others

Five Things Reds Should Do Before They're Thirty

1. Teach their mother how to be a better parent
2. Win every argument
3. Break a Blue's heart

4. Run in a marathon or "run" (be in charge of) the entire event
5. Run a country

Two Things Reds Need to Do Before They Die

1. Become vulnerable and share their heart
2. Leave their cell phone and computer at home and take a *real* vacation

> "I'm sorry that we argued. . . . I hate it when you're wrong."

How to Develop a Positive Connection with Reds

Do

1. Do your homework and present issues logically
2. Demand their attention and respect
3. Be direct, brief, and specific in conversation
4. Be productive and efficient
5. Offer them leadership opportunities
6. Verbalize your feelings
7. Support their decisive nature
8. Promote their intelligence where appropriate
9. Be prepared with facts and figures
10. Respect their need to make their own decisions their own way

Don't

1. Embarrass them in front of others
2. Argue from an emotional perspective
3. Always use authoritarian approach
4. Use physical punishment
5. Be slow and indecisive
6. Expect a personal and intimate relationship
7. Attack them personally
8. Take their arguments personally
9. Wait for them to solicit your opinion
10. Demand constant social interaction (allow for alone time)

Chapter Six

BLUES:
THE DO-GOODERS/
CONNECTORS

There are people in this world who are just good: good-hearted, of good conscience, good citizens. It seems as if their moral compass is always pointing due north as they navigate life in a compassionate and empathetic way. They are always concerned about how you're doing and they never forget a birthday. In fact, they never forget anything! They'll remind you in twenty years about a first glance in the greatest detail, and be deeply hurt that you don't remember. These *sainted pit bulls* are our Blues, and they innately know that life is all about relationships.

> *Life cannot bestow on anyone a more*
> *gratifying reward than the sincere*
> *appreciation and trust of a Blue friend,*
> *co-worker, or family member.*

WARNING: This is **not** a quick read if you are Blue! The positive strengths will encourage you and the limitations will frustrate you. Most likely, you will feel the negative more deeply and dismiss the positive. There are equal numbers of strengths and limitations explored in your chapter. Remember, *this is who you are!* This is your personality package. The truth will set you free, but you must embrace it honestly for what it tells you about yourself. For all the other colors, this chapter will heighten your awareness of how to effectively engage Blues. Nothing matters more to Blues than being understood and appreciated by others. Read this to know them at their most intimate core.

BLUE CHARACTERISTICS

Committed and Loyal

Life is a sequence of commitments for Blues. Committing to relationships both personally and professionally is perhaps their single greatest strength. They thrive on companionships and willingly sacrifice personal gain in order to nurture intimate relationships. Blues give freely of themselves in valued relationships. With commitment as one of their greatest strengths, it is no surprise that Blues enter into deep friendships that often last a lifetime. They are highly dependable and consider a verbal promise as binding as a written contract (that goes for any promise you make to them, as well). They are completely loyal to people. Their unrivaled loyalty and commitment gives credence to the notion that Blues usually enjoy far richer relationships than the other personalities. And they remain committed through the good and the bad. When one realizes the depth of their commitment, it is easy to understand why fair or foul weather has little impact on a Blue's loyalty.

Perfectionistic

Blues often ask me why this is a negative trait. The answer lies in the motive that drives perfectionism. Insecurity drives perfectionism, while quality originates from a legitimate valuing of excellence. The derivation of perfectionism and quality are exact opposites. Blues are highly critical of themselves and others. They have such unrealistic expectations that they struggle to satisfy themselves or find satisfaction in others' performances. They really do want things to be done right in life and resist being asked to settle for less. Blues are typically skeptical about their own creative talents. They are so self-doubting and demanding of themselves that they often hide their skills and abilities because they fear they aren't good enough. It's most unfortunate because they are often remarkably talented and creative. Artistic celebrities Barbra Streisand and Steven Spielberg are prominent Blues whose demand for excellence has provided us with remarkable theatrical experiences. However, their eye for detail doesn't make working with them a picnic in the park.

> *"The thing that is really hard, and really amazing,*
> *is giving up on being perfect*
> *and beginning the work of becoming yourself."*
> —Anna Quindlen

Highly Demanding

Blues struggle with verbal communication. It's not that they don't like to talk—quite the opposite, actually—but how they communicate and what they expect back can be a problem. People struggle to know how to meet the expectations Blues set. Even knowing their expectations is not always helpful, because meeting their unrealistic expectations would take more energy than others are willing to give. I'm referring specifically to a parent's expectations of straight A's on a report card, spotless rooms, and chores done promptly and properly every day. I wonder if Blues don't represent 80 percent of the parents who scream at their children. We would all scream if we had their perfectionistic expectations. Blues often confuse priorities and fail to realize that a more rational approach would be healthier and far more productive.

Blue employers demand that their employees make a commitment of time and talent to the company. A report worth doing at all is worth doing well. They expect excellence even on projects that probably don't require it. For example, they often stress the quality of a project as more important than the relationship itself—the letter of the law versus the spirit of the law. I have witnessed Blue managers' restrictive rigidity and Blue parents' micromanagement of children create highly dysfunctional relationships for both parties. Right now Blues are thinking, "But if they would just do what is expected of them!!" or "What is wrong with asking them to do their part?" Blues want others to be like them. They don't necessarily say what they want but magically believe that everyone thinks the way they do and will produce the same results they will.

> *"Excellence is in the details. Give attention*
> *to the details and excellence will come."*
> —Perry Paxon

Distrusting

Blues often struggle with delegation of duties. "It's easier to do it myself! That way I know it will get done right and on time!!" So goes the constant Blue lament in life. Blues stand over others like a mother hen in order to avoid errors. This controlling behavior is construed by Blues to represent nurturing. It is actually distrust and the end result of their misconception is always disappointing. Blues may believe that by maintaining strong emotional ties with their employees, they are being supportive and promoting effective employee relations. They often throw up their hands in frustrations when their employees feel strangled or spied on. It is so difficult to convince Blues that when their intentions are not clear and their expectations are so demanding, their employees wish they would just go back to their office and leave everyone else alone. However, employees usually don't tell their Blue boss how they feel because the Blue manager is often seen as overly sensitive and usually means well, so no one wants to hurt his or her feelings. Instead of honest, direct communications, Blues typically get dishonest patronizing from employees.

Admired

Blues are often the most admired of the personalities. They naturally embody so many of the virtues the rest of us aspire to: honesty, empathy, self-sacrifice, loyalty, sincerity, and self-discipline. With these attributes, they create an image of righteousness and respect. They resemble a lighted beacon of truth and goodness—a standard of excellence the rest of us can aim for. Blues appreciate creativity and disciplined achievement, and they live for committed relationships. The combination of these traits inevitably results in a strong and purposeful individual who is deeply committed, fiercely loyal, and a well-behaved member of society.

Complex

Blues are highly complex individuals with many extremes. I often refer to them as the best and worst humanity offers. They have such influential strengths and debilitating limitations. They are sensitive, intense, caring, critical, giving, and unforgiving at the same time. You can "love them to death" and want to "put them to death" in the same week! They focus on emotional connections, but can be guilty of emotional rigidity. In other words, they can get stuck in their own emotionally charged moral ruts. They can lose perspective on the very thing they crave—connected relationships, and focus instead on how they feel completely misunderstood. Frustrated by their inability to express their feelings effectively, Blues may give up the necessary effort to create the intimacy they require to feel whole in life. No personality requires others the way Blues do. Their driving core motive in life is intimacy, and without meaningful connections, they often find themselves alienated and disappointed in life. Typifying their complexity, while Blues crave connection, they are also strong proponents of autonomy. Such is the essence of these remarkable human beings—intriguing, absorbing, and complex.

Intuitive and Opinionated

Blues have a fascinating gift that they often refuse to trust. They are highly intuitive. Their first gut instinct is remarkably accurate, yet they often refuse to trust it. Looking back, they often see how they "always knew," despite not taking action based on their intuition. I believe their gift comes from their hearty measure of emotion, which they can use very effectively as a filter in assessing others' motivations. Blues are highly opinionated, making them a tough competitor to face off against, especially considering that they tend to base their opinions on emotions and moral principle. Blues have a strong analytical nature that presents itself as logic, but their knee-jerk reaction is always rooted in emotion.

Emotional and Moody

For Blues, life is a double-edged sword emotionally. On the positive side, they are incredibly giving and sensitive. On the negative side, they can be unforgiving and overly sensitive. A common statement from Blues over the years has been "My emotions have ruled me all my life." Perhaps their greatest vulnerability lies in their unbridled emotions. They want so desperately to be understood and appreciated. Yet they often seek to be understood while refusing to understand themselves. Blues ride a powerful roller coaster of emotions. Sensitive to all kinds of trivial matters, they constantly find themselves susceptible to emotional trauma. Depression is frequently experienced by Blues. Allowing their hearts to rule their minds, they often think and behave irrationally.

Blues see the world through positive and healthy emotional eyes as well. They care deeply for those elements of living that tug at their hearts. Weddings, parades, and birthdays are great cause for celebration, but Blues see beyond the events and take time to reflect on the lives of those involved. They think of their own weddings and what it means to be in love. They consider all the hours it takes to prepare the costumes and mechanics of a parade as it passes by. Blues wonder how their aging grandmother feels on her seventieth birthday, and are mesmerized by a three-year-old blowing out the candles on a cake. They "make" time for sharing the important moments of life.

"Never apologize for showing feeling.
When you do so, you apologize for the truth."
—Benjamin Disraeli

Self-Sacrificing and Nurturing

With rare exception, Blues think of others before they think of themselves and enrich the lives of those they touch. Doing for others brings tremendous satisfaction to Blues. They enjoy serving. My Blue teenage son always asks if anyone wants something from the kitchen whenever he gets up to get something for himself. As a Yellow, I figure if you want something you will get up and get it for yourself. I have to think consciously about doing what comes naturally to my son. Being productive is important for Blues, but producing for people they care about seems to make the contribution just that much better! When we take our grown children on vacations all over the world, it is my Blue wife who creates phenomenal itineraries (we call them iJeaneraries), providing historical perspective for every location and making recommendations for what to do to make the most of the visit. *Blues always seek purpose in their lives.* They want to have lived for more than simply earning a wage or taking up space on the planet.

Unforgiving and Resentful

Remember their emotional foundation. Ironically, Blues *give* more than any other personality but *forgive* the least. It's not that Blues can't or don't forgive, it is more that they struggle to do so. They take things personally and when an offense occurs, it roots itself at their deepest core, making forgiveness a much more difficult challenge than for other colors. Blues find it difficult to see from a rational perspective. I have encountered many Blues who have yet to forgive their parents for damage done during their childhood. It's quite easy to find Blues in the audience. I simply ask for a show of hands from those who can remember all the bad things their kindergarten teacher did to them. Reds don't remember; they have already taken care of the teacher by putting tacks on her chair. Yellows loved getting the attention whether it was good or bad, so what's to be mad about? And Whites aren't sure they went to kindergarten, so what's to remember? (Even if they remember, they are unlikely to say something unkind anyway.) *But Blues always remember!* One of Blues' most self-destructive weaknesses is grudge holding. It often goes hand in hand with their excellent memory.

Self-Disciplined and Stable

Undoubtedly a Blue coined the phrase, "If a job's worth doing, it's worth doing well." At the deepest core of the Blue personality lies the positive trait of being self-disciplined. When Blues throw themselves into a project, it brings out the best in them. Their perpetual exercise of self-discipline brings stability and order to their lives. Many people learn to depend on Blues because of their steady and predictable natures. General Robert E. Lee is one of the most admired military generals in American history because of his self-discipline and stable nature. He was a complete gentleman even to his surrendering of the Confederate army at Appomattox at the end of the Civil War. Blues provide us with a sense of security through their steady, committed ways. They also thrive in environments where security is provided and valued. They aren't known for being risk-takers. With support and cooperation, they bring creative talents from the highest caliber, directly from their hearts.

Worried and Guilt-Prone

Blues worry about everything, and they wear guilt like a badge of honor! All this excess worry limits the amount of excitement Blues can handle in one day. A thirty-year-old Blue experienced worry whenever she drove on the freeway. If a car changed lanes behind her while she was driving in the middle lane, she immediately cross-examined herself by asking, "Am I driving too fast? Too slow? Are my brake lights working correctly or disturbing other drivers?" Worry and guilt generally mark the path to most Blues' homes. They can be *guilted* into almost anything. They often neglect to see that their true motives in many circumstances are based on useless guilt. For wrongs they think they may have done, Blues will chastise themselves forever. One Blue man finally gave up worry in his eighties. He told me he had worried needlessly all his life and it had cost him dearly. Most of what he worried about never happened, yet he had robbed himself of enjoying the present moment for so many years. He said that he finally woke up one day and said to himself, "No more! If it hasn't happened to me by now, chances are it won't ever happen. So let it go!" And he did. He had paid his debt in time and energy and was finally free simply to be.

Appropriate and Sincere

One of the reasons the world fell in love with Princess Di of Wales was her sense of the appropriate and her sincerity. Like Jacqueline Kennedy, Princess Di loved her children and raised them with a sense of etiquette and style that is not often seen today. Blues value culture and reward appropriate behavior. They understand the value of manner and propriety in society. Blues deem it their personal responsibility to serve as the moral watchdogs for society. They are comfortably obedient to laws and authority. Blues think society requires structure and discipline in order to function properly. They always seek to preserve the dignity and quality of the human experience.

Perhaps *no* strength labels Blues as uniquely as their sincerity. Think of renowned American president Abraham Lincoln who rose to fame because of his integrity. He is revered for his ability to remain true and sincere regardless of how he was vilified by his enemies. In today's vernacular, he is appreciated for his powerful role model of *emotional intelligence.* One of life's greatest experiences is to earn and experience a Blue's trust.

Self-Righteous and Insecure

Each personality color has its own share of insecurity. However, no personality displays it as publicly as Blues. Blues have powerful personalities. They feel driven to participate in life. They voice their opinions, albeit sometimes only within the safe walls of their homes. They have strong values and belief systems. However, they are torn by feelings of guilt, the unrealistic expectations caused by their perfectionistic attitudes, and skepticism. They are often caught between wanting to be involved and fearing their inability to be successful. This insecurity is made more complicated by their unique self-righteous attitude. Perhaps no statement describes this attitude better than the bumper sticker slogan "Those of us who think they know everything [referring to the Reds] really annoy those of us who actually do." Unlike the vocal, arrogant Reds, Blues silently remind themselves how unfortunate it is that others must remain so ignorant. They piously view the world with a suspicious eye. This tends to give Blues a pessimistic nature. They wish others would care enough to adopt the Blues' attitude of perfection. They are frustrated with the realization that many people prefer to accept life rather than to modify it. Self-righteousness does not breed intimacy. Rather, it promotes emotional distance and deception.

BLUE LIMITATIONS

At their worst, Blues are probably their own worst enemies. Their self-righteous attitude is merely a cover for their deep insecurity. They are often too emotional and judgmental to enjoy intimacy. They continually depress themselves and others with unrealistic expectations of perfection. Lacking trust, they find themselves skeptical and suspicious of others. Blues often find themselves bitter, resentful, and unforgiving of those who have crossed them in life. Overwhelming guilt and worry continue to drive them inward, seeking solace from the only one they believe truly understands them—themselves. Blues are hard to please and tense about schedules. They are moody and find leadership a difficult dilemma. Blues aren't generally playful or spontaneous. In anger, they are the personality most likely to believe "Life's a bitch and then you die." They often fail to see the positive side of life. Blues become angry when others find them irrational and emotionally rigid in relationships. Blues exemplify Pogo's famous line, "We have met the enemy and he is us."

> *Blues are the most controlling personality.*
> *They are fiercely connected to the lives they live*
> *and often appear to be emotionally unstoppable,*
> *as though they are on a mission from God to save*
> *the rest of us from ourselves.*

BLUE STRENGTHS

At their best, Blues are steady, ordered, and enduring. They offer culture, beauty, and emotional security. Blues love with passion. They see intimate relationships and creative accomplishments rather than material possessions as being the finer things in life. They bring culture and decency to home and society. They appreciate uplifting experiences, and feel most comfortable in creative and productive environments. They want a sense of purpose in their lives, and willingly sacrifice personal luxuries for more meaningful accomplishments.

They are highly committed individuals. Loyalty to people and sincerity in relationships (at home and work) are their trademarks. They believe in all causes that bring a higher quality to the human experience. They listen with endearing empathy and speak with emotional zeal. Blues truly value their connections to people and enjoy the accomplishments of others. With perfection as their guide, they strive to be the best they can be. They expect the same in their fellow beings. Obediently, they accept the need for authority, and put their energy into supporting law and order. They are essentially the glue that binds society together. Blues give us positive examples in the way they organize their lives, giving preference to personal relationships and quality achievements. They add that special touch of excellence as they freely commit their hearts and souls to the betterment of us all in our shared journey through life.

> *Blues don't lie.*
> *Reds may lie because they've already taken care of the problem*
> *and there is no need to further discuss it with you.*
> *Whites may lie because they don't want the inevitable confrontation.*
> *Yellows may lie because they forgot what you told them the first time.*
> *But Blues don't lie and they struggle desperately in relationships*
> *where deception is present.*

REAL-LIFE EXAMPLES OF BLUES

➤ Jenny had never gotten along with her mother while growing up. In fact, she struggled simply to maintain a civil relationship in the face of her mother's constant attempts to sabotage her. Her mother repeatedly humiliated her by calling her names and mocking her for her lack of popularity with boys through the dating years. Despite the obvious favoritism her mother had displayed for Jenny's older siblings, Blue Jenny was the only one of the children willing to undertake the tremendous responsibility of caring for her invalid mother during the final painful days of her life. Our paths crossed when Jenny sought psychological help in order to sustain the courage necessary to face this woman she had so often struggled with through the years. Jenny stayed close to her mother's bedside, despite her mother's repeated abuse and lack of appreciation, until her mother died. Would other personalities have been so loyal and able to commit so completely?

➤ One Blue sixty-seven-year-old woman resented her White husband for numerous reasons covering a span of fifty years of marriage. She was so angry at him one day that she secretly took her wedding dress down from her closet and donated it to a charitable organization. Needless to say, her motives were less than charitable. This woman was so committed to "getting even" and hurting her husband that she neglected to realize that giving her wedding dress away was far less disturbing for her White husband than herself. The truth is he never noticed it was gone. So she kept reminding him what he caused her to do and how it *should* have hurt him if only he had a heart! Here is the ultimate kicker! Years later, this woman's granddaughter wanted to be married in her grandmother's wedding dress. You can imagine her immense pain when she realized that, in the end, she had hurt only herself. Furthermore, she kept her husband's limited self-esteem in check by constantly reminding him how he had made such a mess of *her* life. This woman exemplifies the unhealthy Blue need to get even and their struggle with letting go of resentment.

➤ My unfortunate Blue father was always frustrated when I would laugh at his spankings. My response was terribly inappropriate and made it difficult for him to feel good about his parenting when he was simply trying to provide me with a sense of what was appropriate and I refused to comply.

➤ One Blue woman *thought* she had a major decision to make. She was leaving for the East Coast on June 11 for a two-week visit with her family. She was also invited to join her husband at an all-expense-paid three-day church convention that ended June 7. That meant if she tried to attend both, she would only have three days to unpack, repack, sort the mail and so on, and get ready for her trip back east. She always enjoyed the time with her husband at the church conventions but she was torn about staying home and getting ready for her two-week trip. She was worried that her children would tear the house apart while she was gone too long (we're talking about twenty-five-year-old twins!).

➤ Larry is a talented CEO whose career is highlighted by tremendous success. He is blessed with a business savvy one cannot learn in academic institutions. Still, he is known to pace the floors at night, plagued by second-guessing himself and worrying about the decisions he can't do anything about. Despite his uncanny intuition and solid experience, he cannot seem to trust himself and let go once decisions have been made. Instead, he ruminates about possible "worst case scenarios" and whether or not he has carefully considered all the options.

➤ The following example comes from a Blue's journal notes. It is an extreme case of the "moody Blues." However, it clearly expresses the frustration most Blues experience with accepting others' behavior when it doesn't meet their high standards. One evening, Susan was reflecting on her recently dissolved marriage and wrote:

> Happy anniversary to me. I hate Jason [my husband]. I hate myself. I hate everyone; especially I hate living. I am so angry and bitter it feels like I cannot go on living because it is too uncomfortable. There is no joy—no hope. I don't even like people who want to help or support me. I wish I could just go away from everyone and everything.

I'm mad at God! I'm mad at my parents! I'm mad at my kids! I'm mad at myself! And I *hate* Jason! I would like to see harm come to him I think. But then I'd be mad because he doesn't even have life insurance. They'd probably make me pay for his funeral too.

I just hate everything. I wish I would die, but I can't and that makes me mad too. I'm mad that life is so rotten and there's no way out. So I'll just be mad for a while longer because I don't see any viable options. But I want to be clear about communicating this: LIFE SUCKS AND I HATE ALL OF IT!!!!!

I'm so tired of being "RESPONSIBLE" for everything! Life seems so unfair. I want to be left alone for a while by everyone! I don't want anyone to expect anything from me because I'm tired of being capable. I'm tired of people saying how great I'm doing. I'm tired of my life. In fact, I'm even tired of writing this depressing garbage, so good-bye.

When Susan shared this with me, she no longer felt the anger displayed in her journal notes. Instead, she felt rather foolish, at times laughing while she shared her writings with me. Three days later she called me and said, "I can't believe this. I feel exactly the same way I felt when I wrote those notes. What's wrong with me? I feel like I'm losing my mind!" Actually, she had never found her mind (logically thinking). She was the victim of an undisciplined heart.

➤ One of Hartman Communications' trainers, Gayle Fesperman, is a strong Blue personality. When she married her husband, Paul, they got married three times in one day so as to not have anyone feel left out of the festivities. They were referred to as the "nation's triathlon bride and groom" by Erma Bombeck, who journeyed with them on behalf of *Good Morning America*. They started in the morning in Greenville, South Carolina (for Paul's family), flew to Minneapolis (Gayle's family) for a 3:00 p.m. ceremony, and ended the day in Phoenix, Arizona, where Gayle had lived for six years and wanted to share her day with many of her friends and family.

A QUICK GUIDE TO BLUES

BLUE STRENGTHS

AS AN INDIVIDUAL

- sees life as a serious endeavor
- appreciates beauty and detail

- has a strong aesthetic sense
- stable and dependable (plow horse versus racehorse)
- sincere and emotionally deep
- analytically oriented (concerned with why one behaves as he/she does)
- high achiever
- deep sense of purpose

AS A COMMUNICATOR

- able to enjoy sensitive and deep conversation
- strong skills in empathizing with others
- remembers feelings and thoughts shared in conversation
- willing to give conversations time to run their course
- prefers small groups

AS A GOAL SETTER

- highly disciplined
- receptive to others' suggestions
- strong goal orientation
- plans well and follows through superbly

AS A CAREER PERSON

- excellent behind-the-scenes worker
- respectful of employer because of employer's position
- enjoys details and schedules
- receptive of creative thinking in others
- gives more of self than required or expected

AS A PARENT

- encourages academics and/or vocational development in children
- excellent trainer of skills (e.g., manners, study habits, etc.)
- very observant
- empathetic and sensitive
- sincerely loyal to children
- excellent in long-term commitments
- keeps home clean and cozy
- sincerely seeks to understand children's behavior
- self-sacrificing

AS A CHILD

- proper and behaved
- easily disciplined verbally
- concerned about being a good family member
- sensitive and concerned about other family members
- loyal to parents and siblings regardless of quality of relationship
- seeks learning opportunities

AS A FRIEND

- loyal forever once friendship is established
- genuine concern for other person's well-being
- remembers special holidays and promotes celebrations
- encouraging in times of trouble
- willing to commit time to the relationship

AS A COMMITTED COMPANION

- gives the relationship priority over other activities
- values intimacy and places high priority on it
- considers spouse first in decision making
- responsible for making ongoing contribution to relationship
- enjoys sharing intimacy and places high priority on it

CAREERS MOST LIKELY TO ATTRACT BLUES

(Of course, all personality types can be found in every occupation. There are innumerable variables that determine success in any career.)

Teacher	Banker	Nurse
Homemaker	Clergy/Minister	Engineer
Psychotherapist	Accountant	Editor
Computer Programmer	Politician	Journalist
Musician	Architect	Carpenter

Note: Blues are the most capable of adapting in the career world.

PERSONALITIES THAT APPEAR TO BE BLUES

Oprah Winfrey: Easily one of the most influential and wealthy women of the twenty-first century, she single-handedly changed the daytime talk show genre. With her empathetic and warm Blue nature, she cries alongside her guests, often leading them to disclose more than they normally would. She is strongly rooted in her values and beliefs, and millions of people implicitly trust her judgment. An avid philanthropist, she personally donates more of her money to charity than any other show business celebrity in America. She truly exemplifies the influence, sincerity, and admiration that is characteristic of a healthy Blue.

Steven Spielberg: We all remember tearing up when E.T. finally went "home," or feeling as if we were running through the jungle with Indiana Jones. His dedication and attention to detail have made him one of the most renowned filmmakers in history. He is able to masterfully portray emotionally heavy subjects such as the Holocaust, slavery, and war, with a quality that none can deny. He has a perfectionistic manner that is a quintessential characteristic of Blues' creativity, and a gift we all enjoy.

Walt Disney: A creative genius, he loved the process more than the bottom line and relished design and details. He kept a room at Disneyland where he could rest after working long hours with his many new ingenious creations. His creative juices flowed late into the night, often refusing to let him sleep.

BLUE NATIONS

These are nations who have a culture that promotes the Blue motives, attitudes, and behaviors. It does *not* mean that everyone in these nations is Blue.

United States	Israel
(except Hawaii, which is White)	
England	Norway
Denmark	Iceland

BLUE MOTTO

"If you love someone, set them free. If they come back, they're yours; if not, hunt them down and kill them!"

CELEBRITIES WHO APPEAR TO BE BLUE

- Diane Sawyer
- Harrison Ford
- Faith Hill
- Brad Pitt
- Kate Winslet
- Elton John
- Renée Zellweger
- Prince William
- Beyoncé Knowles
- Matt Damon

BLUE LIMITATIONS

AS AN INDIVIDUAL

- highly emotional
- smug and self-righteous
- controlling and/or envious of others' success when too easily obtained
- strong orientation toward perfection and performance
- verbally self-abusive

AS A COMMUNICATOR

- has intensely held opinions on many issues
- tends to lecture and overdiscuss issues
- rigid with principles and unwilling to negotiate
- fears risking self in conversation
- argues primarily from an emotional perspective
- strong expectations for others to be sensitive and deep
- expects others to read his or her mind and know his or her feelings

AS A GOAL SETTER

- sets unrealistically high goals
- easily discouraged when unsuccessful in accomplishments
- easily frustrated by lack of team cooperation
- expects others to understand his or her goals and make them a priority

BLUES: THE DO-GOODERS/CONNECTORS

AS A CAREER PERSON

- feels others are not capable of doing things as well as he or she can
- craves security in career
- feels inadequate in natural talents and creativity
- shies away from public exposure and performance
- establishes high and often unrealistic expectations for self and others
- tends to overplan and overprepare
- critical of others' work and of self
- overextends self

AS A PARENT

- blames children for being unappreciative of parenting efforts
- can be moody and unpredictable
- easily irritated by mistakes and shortcomings of others
- usually loves with strings attached
- tends to give heavy doses of guilt to children
- lacks ability to relax
- requires a purpose in order to play
- controlling and overprotective of children
- too precise and exact with expectations
- feels having a clean home is more important than quality family time
- accepts guilt feelings too easily and readily
- not spontaneous with activities
- frustrates children with unrealistic expectations
- strong sense of right and wrong—badgers children if convinced they are wrong

AS A CHILD

- easily frustrated
- feels guilty over minor concerns
- moody and emotional (cries instead of facing issues rationally)
- feelings are easily hurt
- martyr-like and complains about life
- self-esteem is dependent on outside influences
- has difficulty relaxing and often feels uncomfortable
- withholds affection if angered (pouts)
- waits for parent to initiate ideas and then criticizes unacceptable suggestions

AS A FRIEND

- highly insecure about others' acceptance and approval
- feels rejected easily
- when depressed or depressive, feels it is friend's job to understand
- can be revengeful and bitter if crossed or scarred emotionally
- critical of friends' principles or activities if not similar
- expects friends to maintain strong loyalty
- wishes friends would communicate more often
- rarely playful and spontaneous

AS A COMMITTED COMPANION

- blames others for his or her unhappiness ("If only you were more . . .")
- demands affection and intimacy
- demands time and attention of partner
- highly manipulative in seeking support or understanding
- suspicious of others' motives (distrustful)
- unforgiving of past misunderstandings and wrongdoings
- clings to companion too much

Just for Blues: Recommended Life Tips

1. Try thinking rationally rather than reacting emotionally when pressured. Emotionalism can create chaos and unnecessary distress.
2. Clearly state your limits when others impose deadlines on you. To them, they are asking just a small favor; they don't realize what a huge commitment it is for you. *Everyone* has limits.
3. Manage your expectations. Perfectionism narrows your focus, causing you to ignore other more important aspects of your life—like the quality of your relationships.
4. Again, manage your expectations!! Don't set unrealistic expectations of yourself or others to the extent that everyone feels overwhelmed. Goals are the road markers, not the criteria, of your success.
5. Don't personalize every people interaction you have. I'd be willing to bet that you often feel others have let you down, or you feel bad because you've let others down. Others aren't nearly as hard on you as you are on others and yourself!

Relax! Concentrate on the task at hand rather than become emotionally discouraged or critical.

6. Try viewing time management as fluid instead of absolute. If you fail to meet a deadline, punt! You'll find this frees you up to be more creative (which you have an incredible talent for) and less self-critical.

7. There are limits to what you can control. Really! You can't control the weather, or the movement of the stars, and you certainly can't control other people!

8. Set a ten-minute limit in the day for worrying about any topic. When those ten minutes are over, so is your worrying. Get on with living in the moment, for that's where true is pleasure and happiness will be discovered!

Top Five Blue Attraction Factors

1. Quality: legitimacy of both the product and the relationship (intimacy)
2. Caring: life is all about relationships
3. Sincerity: heart and truth tell the story
4. Nurturing: empowering and supporting others' success
5. Consistency: dependability creates trust

Top Three Blue "Unattraction" Factors

1. Controlling: others don't feel free to express themselves
2. Perfectionism: destructive need to compensate for insecurities
3. Need to be understood: creates whining, rambling, and/or moody behavior

Five Things Blues Should Do Before They're Thirty

1. Create something uniquely personal
2. Become competent at a skill you value
3. Experience something new
4. Tell yourself you're amazing
5. Forgive someone who didn't measure up!

Two Things Blues Need to Do Before They Die

1. Set emotional boundaries for others and free yourself to zoom past your own!
2. Forgive yourself just because you can!

"Leave me alone; I'm having a crisis!"

How to Develop a Positive Connection with Blues

Do

1. Emphasize their security in the relationship
2. Be sensitive and soft-spoken in your approach
3. Be sincere and genuine
4. Behave appropriately and be well-mannered
5. Limit their risk level
6. Promote their creativity
7. Appreciate them
8. Allow ample time for them to gather their thoughts before expressing themselves
9. Be loyal
10. Do thorough analysis before making presentations

Don't

1. Make them feel guilty
2. Be rude or abrupt
3. Promote too much change
4. Expect spontaneity
5. Abandon them
6. Expect them to bounce back easily or quickly from depression
7. Demand perfection (they already expect too much from themselves)
8. Push them too quickly into making decisions
9. Expect them to forgive quickly when crossed
10. Demand immediate action or quick verbal bantering

Chapter Seven

WHITES:
THE PEACEKEEPERS

Some people don't say much, but when they do, we ought to listen. A healthy White's perspective is invaluable. While other colors are flapping their lips, Whites are listening and observing. People with this personality enjoy their own company and are completely content being by themselves. (Send a White child to his room and he is thrilled. He could easily last a month by himself and consider it a reward!) However, Whites resent being imposed upon and have absolutely no desire to impose their will on the rest of the universe. When life is hectic, just being in the same room with a person like this makes you feel calmer. Nothing seems to ruffle their feathers, and with their innate calm, they are often able to bring clarity to chaos.

> *Whites offer us all a model for*
> *gentle human dignity.*

WARNING: This is **not** a quick read if you are White! The positive strengths will encourage you and the limitations will frustrate you. Still, *this is who you are!* The truth will set you free, but you must first embrace it for what it tells you about yourself—both the positive and the negative. Whites (especially men) often struggle with accepting the intense exposure that color-coding brings. For all other colors, this chapter will heighten your awareness of how to effectively engage Whites. Read it like a blueprint of their lives.

WHITE CHARACTERISTICS

Peaceful

Whites are exemplary peacemakers. They sincerely believe in the value of diplomacy and they diligently seek to promote cooperation at all costs. They are perplexed by battles over petty disagreements. They are in no hurry to stir the pot or create disharmony. Whites remind me of water that flows easily over and around life's trials. Equally true, still waters run deep. Walden Pond (made famous by the American philosopher Henry David Thoreau, who was a White) reflects the quiet depth of this personality. However, as with a well, you must dip your bucket into their depths if you hope to enjoy their amazing gifts. How many times have we all said, "Will everyone just settle down? All I want right now is some PEACE and quiet!" If everyone could simply be transformed into a White personality, our exasperated wish would become a reality.

Insecure and Unassertive

Whites are the most difficult personality to read. They hold their cards very close to their chest and reveal very little of what they actually feel. They approach life so fluidly that others may incorrectly assume they are content when in reality they may be feeling inadequate and fearful. They are so good-natured and even-keeled that people generally prefer not to challenge or upset them. Whites' limitations are often ignored while their strengths are acknowledged. The urge to protect Whites by ignoring their deficiencies will ultimately sabotage their personal development. Whites struggle with self-doubt and a general unwillingness to confront others. They can be very passive. They often follow others through life without assuming any leadership of their own. They are vulnerable to making others the core of their existence, neglecting to develop their own sense of purpose and direction. Some Whites become so attached to one individual that they refuse to develop outside interests or make any commitments that would separate them from that relationship. Whites can be like paper waiting for others to write on them. Yet, when they get into a flow and rhythm, they are highly capable and enjoy their independence.

> *"Truce is better than friction."*
> *—Charles Herguth*

Self-Doubting and Dependent

This is where we see clearly the difference between a healthy and an unhealthy White. All Whites carry a sense of self-doubt. They may look serene on the surface but underneath they challenge themselves and question their capabilities. A healthy White pushes through this self-doubt and creates evidence of his or her legitimacy through choices and actions. Unhealthy Whites doubt themselves so much that they constantly demand proof of acceptance. The innermost thoughts of an unhealthy White may be something like this: "Prove to me that you accept me. Stay with me always and be there for me, for I don't know what to do without you." The price is high when one tries to accept, protect, and rescue a clingy White. It can be a lot like holding a man by the wrists when he's falling from a cliff. The longer you hold on, the heavier he becomes. Yet he feels he is safer in your grasp than trusting himself to climb back up. The nobility of the rescue soon loses its shine, and the rescuer now becomes the victim. If you "care," you feel obligated to hold on forever, giving up a life of your own in a doomed attempt to save his. If you let go, you are rebuked for giving up and selfishly seeking your own rewards elsewhere. Such dilemmas are commonly experienced by clinging Whites and those in a position to save them from falling. Healthy Whites are much more comfortable finding their own way. Whites enjoy solitude, so taking responsibility for their lives frees healthy Whites to move through life at their preferred pace rather than rely on others to clear their path and ensure their safe passage.

Tolerant and Patient

Whites value diversity. It is important for Whites to hear and see all sides of an issue before declaring their stance. Therefore, they invite differences of opinion where other personalities don't. They are far less biased than others, which enables them to enjoy a vast array of people and preferences without prejudice. Whites are charitable about others' motives and choices despite the negative impact said motives and choices may have on them. Whites have an unusually high emotional and physical pain threshold. Unless you push a White into a combative stance, they prefer to suffer in silence. I have witnessed remarkable White tolerance in the business world by White managers who ignore the drama and find ways to make allowances for others in order to simply get the work done. Whites have an uncanny ability not to sweat the small stuff when it comes to human drama.

Indecisive and Impressionable

Whites rarely seek leadership positions. They are uncomfortable making decisions that may be wrong, and they tend to avoid responsibilities that require decision making. They are much more comfortable as followers or in less involved roles, leaving group decisions to others. They would rather just accept the decisions of others than assert themselves with their own opinions. Whites don't say much, but they see it all. As a consequence, they are quite impressionable. They observe everything from a safe distance and keep a watchful eye on the human condition. This can make a negative childhood particularly traumatic for Whites. If you are critical of an individual in a White's presence, he will not soon forget the encounter. He will say nothing but distrust you just the same. Long after you have squared up with the individual you criticized, the White remembers distastefully your unkindness and silently keeps his distance.

Aimless and Misguided

Whites often approach life too casually. What is particularly frustrating to the rest of us is how much energy we must expend to make up for them—White children forgetting lunches, White friends neglecting to pick up the children for baseball practice, White husbands unable to select a career direction, and White siblings not willing to develop their own friendships. Whites rarely realize how selfish their limitations are. By presenting themselves as kind but helpless souls, they often seem to ignore the pressure their inadequacy places on everyone else. The frustration mounts for the other personalities who have much greater expectations for Whites than they have for themselves. How enjoyable could life be when they constantly have to remind their White friends and family members to brush their teeth, call the hotel for reservations, make decisions about where to eat, and so on? Whites often respond to these reminders with a casual (albeit disdaining) remark such as, "Why do you have to get so huffy about everything?," "Whose life is it anyway?," or "Go on and mind your own business and leave me alone." Whites are notorious for requiring assistance in the planning and processing of life. They are less known for accepting, and in fact are quite capable of resisting, the very assistance they require.

Withhold Feelings

Whites don't trust easily. They usually hold their true feelings safely tucked away from others who may be judgmental or disapprove of them. I have often wondered if people attending a White's funeral really know the person they come to grieve. So often, when I push Whites to share themselves, I am absolutely intrigued by the complexity of their personalities. They share so little throughout life that we are often forced to make assumptions regarding their beliefs, fears, hopes, and dreams. For many Whites, that is just fine with them, while for others, they wish they could find the words to express what they genuinely feel inside.

Kind

Perhaps my favorite moment when speaking to large audiences is when I am speaking about Whites and I suddenly challenge a participant to stop talking and pay attention. Of course, there is no one talking, but I love to use it as an example of how each of the personalities reacts. The Reds are thinking, "What do you care about who is talking? You've got the microphone. Simply get on with your speech!" The Blues are thinking, "Who was talking? That is terribly inappropriate. I wonder who it was." The Yellows are thinking, "I was talking and he didn't catch me!" But the Whites are thinking, "I don't like Dr. Hartman calling someone out like that in public. That was rude and unnecessary!" Whites are kind people and they place no value in seeing people mistreated. Though they don't share the compassion of the Blues, they display a resounding kindness for people and animals that no other color innately understands. As a result, if you are unkind to a White, you will lose her respect and future interaction. Though she may tolerate the behavior due to her passivity, she will neither be able to justify it nor respect the individual displaying it.

> "Three things in human life are important:
> The first is to be kind. The second is to be kind.
> And the third is to be kind."
> —Henry James

Lazy

Lazy and reluctant (just try to get one moving in the morning!), Whites often meander through life. They are in no hurry to experience life. They feel certain life will wait for them. Their motto is "Everything comes to him who waits." True enough. Everything (good and bad) eventually comes to him who waits. Too often Whites sadly accept life on life's terms rather than their own.

Silent and Stubborn

Whites prefer to give the silent treatment because they are uncomfortable with confrontation. It can be very difficult for the rest of us to live with people who silently resent our behavior! Whites seem to take advantage of others' natural curiosity by refusing to discuss their feelings openly, forcing the other personalities to struggle to understand them. It's not that Whites don't feel things deeply; in fact, they often feel very deeply. They just find it very difficult to express their feelings to others. Of all the personalities, Whites are the most likely to be passive-aggressive. It suits their quiet stubbornness and allows for apparent cordiality rather than overt conflict. Do not assume that simply because a White is silent, she is compliant. That would be a huge mistake. Whites definitely have opinions, but are not likely to share them without encouragement.

> "A man is not idle because he is absorbed in thought.
> There is visible labor and there is invisible labor."
> —Victor Hugo

Unmotivated

I don't know of a limitation that does more harm to a White and those directly connected with Whites than their lack of motivation. Fortunately, we have some stellar examples of motivated Whites who have made tremendous contributions to our society, from former U.S. president Jimmy Carter to actress Diane Keaton. Some Whites say that they have an inner drive that enables them to overcome their natural doubts or fears. Still, many Whites lack direction and commitment, which are critical elements of motivation. Goals are the only hope for an unmotivated White; without them, Whites remain disengaged and unmotivated. Until they are able to establish direction in their lives, Whites often remain complacent, yet unsettled. For Whites, lack of passion is a common thread in life. Many Whites discover something that brings them tremendous pleasure only to lose total interest within months of being fully engaged. I know many Whites who rise to success in a hobby only to completely lose interest shortly thereafter and never return to the activity again. It often leaves friends and associates puzzled and disillusioned. Trust me, it baffles Whites as well.

Accepting

Whites are capable of successfully befriending each personality. Accepting others is simple because they can find good in everyone. They have minimal expectations of others, which people find inviting. Whites value others for their diversity, and in return, people seek their nonjudgmental companionship. Whites enjoy doing almost anything, with anyone, anywhere. They appreciate a wide variety of people and experiences, and often find themselves in unusual relationships or life situations.

Boring

This is a tough one to read! One White woman was completely immersed in reading *The People Code* when she came across the statement that Whites can be boring. She was irate and immediately called her sister to inquire if she thought it was possible. Her sister reluctantly shared that she never seemed boring but that she never made any attempt to entertain others either. She just passively let life happen to her. Whites can be boring and noncontributive when it comes to social and emotional interaction. They prefer to be alone or have someone engage them. They miss many of the potentially wonderful moments in life because they look to others to create excitement and relevance in life rather than look to themselves. Sometimes they find life too overwhelming and may give way to boredom, laziness, or stubborn reluctance to change. I have seen wives leave husbands, husbands leave wives, employees leave jobs, kids and parents leave each other, friendships dissolve, and a myriad of other potentially wonderful relationships end primarily because of boredom. The worst part is that the person leaving (never the White) often feels very guilty, because the grounds for separation aren't dramatic ones such as infidelity, distrust, or abuse. They have no bruises to show how draining life with a reluctant White can be.

Timid and Emotionally Unsure

Whites remind me of the Cowardly Lion in *The Wizard of Oz*. They can be a frightened group of individuals! I am not implying that they are necessarily afraid of physical danger but rather emotional exposure and drama. Many Whites are guilty of taking the easy road rather than fighting for themselves in the corporate world. They accept less pay and lower positions for a myriad of reasons, the most common being that they are uncomfortable placing themselves in potential conflict.

Asking for a raise or seeking a new position necessarily demands a challenge, and they are more inclined to go with the flow than address the situation they deem inequitable. It is often the partner of the White who challenges a spouse to speak up about the job situation or seek other employment.

Gentle and Even-Tempered

White children are truly gifts from heaven. They are so simple and undemanding. They are usually the easiest babies. There is a unique gentleness to these children that promotes family harmony. They are the children who travel through life with an even temper. New experiences have the potential to traumatize a White child, though they typically enjoy a peaceful, casual existence.

Diplomatic

Every parent prays for a White child. Every teacher deserves at least one White student in his or her class. Whites move quietly through life with an easy, unruffled style. They appreciate the cooperative nature of mankind, and keep working to achieve a peaceful coexistence among all living things. White's gentle diplomacy typically shines through, making them highly compatible with almost everyone they meet. Whites blend well with all personalities. A sure sign of a White personality is the individual who feels like a rainbow of colors when they take the profile. **In fact, only a White can literally score 25 percent of each color on the profile.** Their fluidity allows them to embrace other colors' gifts, but their innate core remains *peace*.

WHITE LIMITATIONS

At their worst, Whites often appear detached and uninvolved. They give off the sense that they are uninterested and communicate mixed messages because of their difficulty in expressing themselves. They are often unwilling to set goals. They frequently refuse to pay the price of involvement because they fear the inevitable consequences of confrontation or rejection. It is this fear that keeps them from experiencing true intimacy. Their indecision limits their potential accomplishments. They express themselves only reluctantly, preferring to let others believe what they will. Meanwhile, Whites go about their lives as they choose, avoiding conflict and confrontation at every turn. They silently accept whatever comes their way. What they don't value, they silently and subtlety dismiss. Whites do not often allow those desirable experiences that require the effort of risk, leadership, and honest expression into their lives.

> *Whites will either pay great attention to the needs of others and strive at all costs to please those they encounter, or ignore them altogether.*

WHITE STRENGTHS

At their best, Whites are the satisfied ones. They are contented and agreeable individuals who easily accommodate others in life. They complement every personality regardless of differences in style. Their gentle nature and diplomacy win them many loyal friends. Their agreeable and peaceful dispositions make them an invaluable asset to any family, friendship, or business that is fortunate enough to include them. Whites are typically moderate people without the extremes of the other personalities. They flow over and around life's difficulties rather than demand that the obstacles in their path be moved. Their leadership is solid and fair. They tolerate differences and encourage camaraderie with all team members. Their mascot is the chameleon, which reflects their adaptability. Their goal in life is to be kind. They enjoy the enviable strength of balance. They are receptive to every personality and willing to learn from all of them. Whites are most effective at putting life's crises in proper perspective. Satisfied and even-tempered, they ask little of life. They often enjoy the protection of other personalities. Patient and tolerant, they have much to give. And give they do, with gentle approval for those fortunate enough to experience their accepting embrace.

> *If you ever want to witness quiet human majesty, simply observe a healthy White personality bless another's life with random acts of kindness. But you must watch closely, because they will never announce their own heroics.*

REAL LIFE EXAMPLES OF WHITES

➢ One of my White patients, Michael, hated high school. He despised homework and all the necessary demands of education. He was bright but unwilling to engage in conflict with either his parents or his teachers. He struggled with how to satisfy everyone, including himself. Here was his dilemma: he hated doing homework, yet his parents and teachers demanded that it be done. For one solid semester in eighth grade, Michael did every homework assignment and never turned in a single one. Every night his parents would ask if he had completed his assignments, and he would answer in the affirmative. When his grades slipped dramatically and his parent requested to actually see his work, he promptly showed them. By the end of that semester, his parents thought they were going crazy! Were the teachers out to get their son? They had seen his work, but the teachers kept telling them that he had not completed it. This is a perfect example of the silent, strong, and stubborn nature of Whites.

➤ One White chief financial officer was at one point a California surf bum who wasn't going to graduate from high school. At eighteen, without anyone's guidance or support, he signed up for military service because he instinctively knew he had to act or he would be lost. Later in life, having achieved financial security, he confided that he felt a strong desire to leave the corporate world behind, in order to surf and enjoy a more relaxed pace. His inner drive focused him on developing a legitimate career, but cost him substantially in his work-life balance.

➤ Two Whites dated for years before deciding to marry. Their courtship consisted primarily of shared television viewing and quiet moments together. They eventually married, and after five years decided that they were wrong for each other. Neither one was happy or fulfilled. During the next five years this couple remained married but separate in their dreams and aspirations. He pursued a college degree and she moved to another city and became a police officer. Neither actively committed to staying in the relationship or leaving to pursue a more legitimate life. After seven more wasted years of living apart but not choosing truly separate lives, they divorced. Why did it take so long? When asked, both admitted that neither was motivated to cut the final string.

➤ Jeff had been the perfect child, as Whites usually are. Even after his parents retired, he still resisted rocking the boat for any reason. Knowing this, his parents repeatedly controlled his choices. When Jeff, who is Caucasian, wanted to marry an Asian woman, his mother flatly refused to entertain the idea, and his father supported his "traumatized" wife. Jeff felt completely abandoned. He had been a wonderful, caring son. When his only brother turned his back on their parents, Jeff had remained loyal. Now he felt torn between the devotion and loyalty he felt for his parents and the love he had for his girlfriend. Notice that I didn't mention any feelings of loyalty toward himself. He simply didn't "count" to himself. He was experiencing his value and self-worth through others. Now he needed to find himself and challenge his "secure" relationship with his parents if he was ever to experience self-respect. Through months of therapy and inner struggling, he freed himself of his parents and pursued a life based on his own values and beliefs. Jeff eventually married his fiancée. He will never feel as welcomed or as "accepted" by his parents as he did before, but he recognizes that pleasing himself appropriately is far more gratifying than living his life to please others.

➤ One White husband asked his wife, "Honey, on Dr. Hartman's personality profile, it wants to know if I'm decisive. Do you think I am or not?" We all shared a good laugh, recognizing that he never realized what he was asking until she said, "Honey, somehow I think you just answered your own question better than I could ever hope to!"

➤ One intellectually gifted White man offered to tutor his Harvard medical student roommates free of charge. He later realized that it was his way of expressing his warm feelings toward them without having to openly share his emotions. Looking back, he now regrets that he could never express or share himself. He shared his knowledge because he was secure in that. In retrospect, he now longs for the good friendships he could have developed if he had been able to trust others with his inner feelings and thoughts.

➤ As a college professor, I asked 100 university students to identify the trait they felt was most critical for successful parenting. Independently, 95 percent of them ranked *patience* as the most significant virtue for successful parenting. I was amazed at this overwhelming response from these young people who had only recently been children and were not yet fully adults. What about love, discipline, and leadership? Why hadn't they given the edge to communication or some other attribute? The students offered me a valuable insight into parenting and the White personality. They said, "patience indicates a trust in human dignity—a belief that people will make the right choices in life when given the free agency to act for themselves." What a powerful and telling statement these young people shared about how Whites often bring out the best in humanity.

A QUICK GUIDE TO WHITES

WHITE STRENGTHS

AS AN INDIVIDUAL

- quiet, reflective, and peaceful
- sincere and genuine lifestyle
- appears to accept life comfortably
- patient with self and others
- enjoys life's simplicity
- compatible with others
- kind to animals and people
- blends into all situations

AS A COMMUNICATOR

- receptive to others' input
- negotiator and mediator on issues
- listens superbly
- strong ability to see both sides of every issue

AS A GOAL SETTER

- receptive to suggestions
- appreciates exposure to many possibilities
- recognizes the value of goal setting
- accommodating in many different environments
- independent

AS A CAREER PERSON

- accommodates others easily
- handles bureaucratic environments well
- calm under pressure
- prefers slower pace and "think time"
- negotiates well
- sometimes puts self in dangerous occupations for excitement
- nonconformist

AS A PARENT

- flows well with crises
- takes time to enjoy each child
- agreeable with difficult children
- appreciated by children for gentle manner and style
- slow to react with anger
- supportive and considerate
- accepts companion's decision—demonstrates unity
- patient with deviant and inappropriate behavior
- accepts differences and values diversity

AS A CHILD

- very agreeable to established traditions and boundaries
- undemanding
- willing to accommodate siblings and parents
- plays well by self
- accepts life without drama
- peacekeeper

AS A FRIEND

- patient and enduring through good and bad times
- tolerant
- supportive and accepting
- listens with understanding and acceptance
- relaxed in most situations
- likes most people
- liked by most people
- compatible with different personalities
- enjoys observing others
- undemanding of friendship; not emotionally needy

AS A COMMITTED COMPANION

- tolerant of others' tardiness
- can entertain self easily
- appreciates leadership qualities in others
- quietly committed to relationship
- willing to accept beliefs and values of companion
- accommodating

CAREERS MOST LIKELY TO ATTRACT WHITES

(Of course, all personality types can be found in every occupation. There are innumerable variables that determine success in any career.)

Forest ranger	Recreation leader	Veterinarian
Dentist	Researcher	Lawyer
Bureaucrat	Homemaker	Engineer
Computer programmer	Police officer	FBI Agent
Military service	Preschool teacher	Truck driver

Note: *Whites and Yellows are usually the least motivated to succeed in the career world.*

PERSONALITIES THAT APPEAR TO BE WHITE

Albert Einstein: A genius and highly observant, he let his thinking do his talking. Personally withdrawn, he was most comfortable in the world of ideas and intellectual exchange. He preferred quietly doing the research for his remarkable theories behind the scenes, rather than heralding its importance to the public. He kept his personal life quiet and his social circle small. He emulated kindness to everyone whether it was merited or not.

Yoda: This infamous character is known for his funny accent and simple wisdom. Characteristic of Whites, he may not say much, but what he does say is a gem of clarity. He prefers solitude, and is willing to be as patient as is needed. His life is one of quiet balance and harmony and he feels absolutely no need to impose his will on the universe. He is a master diplomat with objectivity and forbearance, as he processes each situation before taking action.

Diane Keaton: An authentic actress, she is beloved on- and off-screen for her easygoing nature. There is a calm that she radiates in every role she plays. She credits her listening skills in making her various relationships work successfully. Diane keeps her personal life out of the public eye. In fact, she is one of Hollywood's most reclusive stars. Highly adaptable, she makes the art of acting look easy with her distinct ability to play almost any role.

WHITE NATIONS

These are nations that have a culture that promotes the White motives, attitudes, and behaviors. It does *not* mean that everyone in these nations is White.

Finland	Russia
Switzerland	Greenland
Canada	Hawaii
	(but the rest of the
	United States is Blue)

WHITE MOTTO

"Everything comes to him who waits."

CELEBRITIES WHO APPEAR TO BE WHITE

- Johnny Depp
- Gwyneth Paltrow
- Michael Jackson
- Queen Elizabeth
- Nicole Kidman
- President Jimmy Carter
- Britney Spears
- President George Bush Sr.
- Gwen Stefani
- Lance Armstrong

WHITE LIMITATIONS

AS AN INDIVIDUAL

- appears detached and uninvolved
- takes a passive approach to life
- unresponsive or not openly excited about experiences
- has problems becoming intimate
- bashful and unsure of self
- easily manipulated into changing plans
- ambivalent about direction and goals to pursue
- often lazy and unwilling to take responsibility for self
- resists making commitments

AS A COMMUNICATOR

- fearful of confrontation
- unable to respond quickly in conversation
- dishonest with feelings—often agrees only to please others
- hesitant to engage others in conversation
- doesn't contribute openly
- accepts others' decisions without seeking best solution
- gives very little energy to conversation unless forced to
- refuses to take a stand on issues
- prefers to observe others interact

AS A GOAL SETTER

- takes a "wait and see" attitude to life decisions
- allows others to make decisions for them
- lacks consistency in goal setting
- sees goals as demanding and therefore restrictive
- waits for others to set their goals and then criticizes the goals set for them

AS A CAREER PERSON

- low profile
- low energy
- directionless—requires leadership from others
- resents strong direction and leadership from others
- works at a slow pace
- stubbornly and/or passively resists dominance of other personalities
- difficult to motivate and inspire
- fears change and risk taking
- willing to stay in a monotonous job
- easily manipulated by others when unmotivated or unconcerned

AS A PARENT

- refuses to engage in conflict with spouse about children
- doesn't initiate activities and interaction with children
- poor disciplinarian
- works obsessively to maintain peace
- poor leadership and delegation with children

- easily dismissed by children when promoting unpopular ideas
- easily controlled or ignored by spouse or children

AS A CHILD

- resents being pressured to do things
- doesn't contribute much to conversations
- contributes quietly to family activities
- waits for parent to initiate ideas and then criticizes unacceptable suggestions
- prefers the comforts of home to the demands of the world
- indifferent to family dilemmas
- uninvolved in family action
- doesn't complete tasks

AS A FRIEND

- lacks creativity to make suggestions
- easily led by others' opinions
- won't express honest perception if controversial
- passive-aggressive
- requires definition and structure
- easily hurt and defeated

AS A COMMITTED COMPANION

- prefers the other person to lead
- boring and indecisive
- too accommodating
- won't make suggestions for activities
- willing to let opportunities pass him or her by
- may experience difficulty initiating relationships
- often feels uncomfortable taking a stand and voicing opinions
- uncomfortable expressing emotion in intimate relationships (often feels more deeply than is able to communicate)

Just for Whites: Recommended Life Tips

1. State verbally how you feel and what you perceive about yourself, current tasks, and others' behavior. You tend to waste energy because you find it difficult to identify accurately how you feel and present it confidently to others.

2. Address issues rather than avoid them. You'll find that you feel empowered and less resentful.

3. Believe it or not, conflict can be enriching! Share your ideas and seek others' input, instead of taking their feedback personally. Choose to view others' feedback as enlightening and as a way to broaden your horizons.

4. Actively seek a sense of urgency. Sometimes you can miss living a passionate life because you refuse to get excited about projects and people. Don't let time pass you by!

5. Try setting proactive agendas, rather than merely reacting to agendas others set for you. Proactive attitudes will challenge your natural tendency to be passive-aggressive.

6. Don't be overly defensive when others seem demanding. Focus on *what* is being said rather than *how* it's being said.

7. RISK A LITTLE. Set goals that require effort and will build your confidence instead of always taking a "wait and see" attitude.

8. Make the concerted effort to control daydreams that rob you of valuable time to get legitimate work done.

Top Five White Attraction Factors

1. Listening: egoless ability to hear others
2. Acceptance: value diversity and promote creativity
3. Kindness: respectful and considerate of others and life
4. Patience: steady internal compass
5. Perspective: amazing clarity amidst complexity

Top Three White "Unattraction" Factors

1. Indecisive: people respect others who act, resolve issues, and risk
2. Conflict avoidance: people expect you to address conflict honestly
3. Inexpressive: people need to feel that you care and want to hear your opinions

Five Things Whites Should Do Before They're Thirty

1. Initiate and carry on a legitimate conversation with a stranger
2. React from an emotional perspective. Risk with your heart.
3. Break a Blue's heart
4. Spontaneously do something—anything—at least three times

5. Keep your subtle witty comments flowing at all times and with everyone

Two Things Whites Need to Do Before They Die

1. Connect verbally on a deep, intimate level with another adult (no fair text-messaging!)
2. Passionately stand up for something you believe in or right some wrong in the world

> *"I used to be apathetic,*
> *but now I just don't care."*

How to Develop a Positive Connection with Whites

Do

1. Be kind
2. Be logical, clear, and firm about the content you present
3. Provide a structure (boundaries) for them to operate in
4. Be patient and gentle
5. Introduce options and ideas for their involvement
6. Be simple and open
7. Acknowledge and accept their individuality
8. Be casual, informal, and relaxed in presentation style
9. Look for nonverbal clues to their feelings
10. Listen quietly

Don't

1. Be cruel or insensitive
2. Expect them to need much social interaction
3. Force immediate verbal expression; accept written communication
4. Be domineering or too intense
5. Demand conformity to unrealistic expectations/behaviors
6. Overwhelm them with too much at once
7. Force confrontation
8. Speak too fast
9. Take away all their daydreams
10. Demand leadership

Chapter Eight

YELLOWS:
THE FUN LOVERS

Remember your happiest day of childhood? Now imagine living your entire life with the enthusiasm and sheer delight of a child. Only then can you envision how Yellows embrace their entire existence. Yellows make life fun for everyone. (Think of a child playing on a beautiful summer day!) Nobody *lives in the moment* quite like a Yellow. They like people—all people—and people generally like them back. Luck is their middle name and magic is their game. Yellows are the frosting on life's cake.

> *Yellow people love themselves*
> *because they know exactly what they love to do*
> *and always find the time and resources to do it.*

WARNING: This is **not** a quick read if you are a Yellow! The positive strengths will encourage you and the limitations will frustrate you. In fact, you'll probably be tempted to skip over the negatives and read only the positives. But *this is who you are* (even the negatives)! The truth will set you free, but you must first embrace it for what it tells you about yourself—both the positive and the negative. For all other colors, this chapter will heighten your awareness of how to engage Yellows effectively. Read it like a blueprint of their lives.

YELLOW CHARACTERISTICS

Fun-loving

Riding on the primary motive of fun, Yellows reflect the spirit of the wind and the life-giving miracle of fresh air. They are as essential to society as breathing is to the human existence. Yellows are simply fun to be around. In fact, Yellows properly define fun. Fun means enjoying someone or something simply for the sake of enjoyment. It has nothing to do with results or improvement or complex meaning. Fun means enjoying whoever or whatever you are in the moment. Michael Jordan (Red) and Harrison Ford (Blue) clearly understood this valuable lesson from Yellows when they were always reminding their peers that all the practice and work needs to be done before the game and the actual film shoot. Once you are in the game or doing the shoot, *"you need to have fun,"* both of these superstars would always say! Being able to create the fun piece is a critical element for success in all facets of life.

> *"The best advice I ever got was when somebody said, 'Enjoy.'*
> *Intensity is interesting, but fun connects people. You can be*
> *childlike without being childish. A child always wants to*
> *have fun. Ask yourself, Am I having fun? Is this my bliss?"*
> —Chris Meloni

Self-Centered and Uncommitted

Yellows bound through life focused on themselves. They frequently fail to develop the depth necessary to contribute substantially to society. Yellows struggle to understand why anyone would rather earn his keep than take the easy road through life. Perhaps their most serious limitation is their inability to commit. Because of their enthusiasm, Yellows start more projects than any other personality but successfully complete the fewest, due to their lack of commitment. (Typical of Yellows, one patient complained that she had started 366 diets in one year—she even did two in one day! She never lost one pound but quite enjoyed the adventure!) Commitment requires constant dedication, something that unduly taxes a Yellow's capacity for endurance. They usually cannot concentrate long enough to convince others that their intentions are genuine and trustworthy.

It is equally difficult for a Yellow to commit to personal development. Getting to know oneself is difficult for everyone. Yellows often give up before they really tackle problems in their psychological makeup. Commitment to painful soul searching usually ends up at the bottom of their list of priorities. Yellows are unwilling to pay the price for true self-confidence, which is a lifetime of doing and committing to those experiences, people, and values one cherishes. They love excitement and willingly forgo commitment, with its discomfort, in order to feel momentary pleasure.

Happy

Yellows love life. They are spirited, exciting, and have an innate ability to be happy. They have a mental attitude that allows them to appreciate what they have, rather than be miserable about what they lack. Fate often appears to smile on them, and they are considered to be very lucky. Yellows wake up happy every morning. Blues think they must be on medication because *nobody* can possibly be *that* happy! The truth is, Yellows simply are that happy.

> *"I have found that if you love life, life will love you back."*
> —*Arthur Rubinstein*

Irresponsible

While society has come up with some harsh adjectives to describe Yellows (some of which I can't even put in this book), the word that most accurately describes the negative essence of the Yellow personality is *irresponsible*. Remember that wonderful song, "Call me irresponsible—call me unreliable"? Save yourself some time and simply call them Yellow. Yellows truly believe it is someone else's responsibility to take care of them. It doesn't matter who—just somebody other than them. Perhaps a Yellow's greatest concern is loss of play time in life. Their rebellious natures can be cute while they are still young, but society has little tolerance for adult slackers. There is perhaps nothing more tragic than an aging Yellow without character: their faces bear heavy lines from year-round tans, their personal belongings are often minimal and not cared for properly, and they have few intimate friends.

Yellows are typically so charismatic that others fail to see their limitations. Only after a period of time do they see Yellows for what they often are—energetic sprinters who may not go the distance. Yellows are not comfortable with the pressures of responsibility. To them, work is for people who don't know how to party. Those readers familiar with Aesop's fable about the grasshopper who lived only for the moment can appreciate the extreme lack of perspective many Yellows (like the grasshopper) have for living *beyond* the moment. Blaming others is a classic pattern for irresponsible Yellows. Too many married Yellows blame affairs on the insensitivity of their spouses. Of course, they fail to recognize that their own irresponsibility is often the reason their spouses seem insensitive.

Enthusiastic and Carefree

Yellows seek enchanting opportunities and find life laced with silver linings. They rarely become bogged down with details or "emotional baggage," which for them means controlling friends, poor work conditions, and other undesirable and demanding circumstances. Yellows are as vulnerable to these experiences as any personality, but they have a strong yearning for freedom and subconsciously recognize baggage and instinctively move away from its influence. Yellows represent enthusiasm and share this excitement with everyone they meet. They are terrific at social involvements and have a way of making a party out of everyday living. They remind us of our youth and the joy that comes from innocent hopes and optimistic dreams.

Chatterboxes

Yellows are often nicknamed "chatterbox" because they can find *anything* interesting enough to talk about. This conversational skill is helpful while dating and in business, as well as with most situations requiring interpersonal communication. They can talk to anyone about anything. They enjoy a natural curiosity about others and life. However, their engaging ways can be quite stressful for colleagues and family members. When their idle chatter is combined with rude and loud behavior, Yellows are considered obnoxious. This label always offends them because they can't comprehend why anyone wouldn't find them as delightful and entertaining as they find themselves. The conversational approach to life is frustrating when you want to be serious, and Yellows don't generally want to, can't, or won't. They are notorious for interrupting whether you are busy or not. Nothing is sacred to the Yellows, and they are certain that nothing is sacred to others either. Whether you are on the telephone or reading, Yellows will find a way of distracting you until you acknowledge their needs. They talk constantly, as if their words were the music of life.

Naive and Trusting

No other personality experiences life with as much naiveté and innocent trust as do Yellows. They don't think things through prior to speaking or doing. Yellows often take others at face value and can find themselves victims of their own naiveté. They are often fooled and quick prey for more sophisticated and calculating personalities. They trust easily, yet often build high walls to prevent intimacy once sufficient emotional scarring has occurred. Yellows are not particularly bothered by commitments such as appointments being broken, but broken emotional commitments can be devastating. Yellows are vulnerable to settling for superficial relationships. This is particularly unfortunate for Yellows because, deep inside, they value connections. They often hide their emotional pain with a quick smile and playful tease. It is not uncommon to see misguided, superficial Yellows floating through life, preferring their freedom to meaningful connections, but such behavior often comes from their own misplaced trust and naiveté. Since Blues are known for their sincerity and loyalty, this may, at least in part, explain why Yellows often seek their companionship.

Charismatic and Popular

Yellows find it easy to relate to people of all ages. They make friends with all the kids on their block. They charm elderly people in stores and babies in strollers with their entertaining style. Their joyful natures brighten the disposition of many of those whom they encounter. Yellows often appear to be physically attractive because of their personalities. They are skilled at choosing a style that emphasizes their best physical and social strengths. They have the most engaging style of any of the personalities. An adjective commonly used for Yellows is *charismatic*. They parent charismatically. They conduct business charismatically. They converse charismatically. Often considered the Pied Pipers of humanity, Yellows can easily move groups of people to tears and/or laughter. Yellows love to entertain and be entertained. They often stage productions in the garage for neighborhood children, run for student body office in school, and choose careers in which they have a great deal of exposure to people. They give freely of themselves. Perhaps because they crave their own freedom so dearly, Yellows do not seek to control others. They live without many expectations and give without concern for what they might receive. Yellows find laughter and interpersonal relationships easy. They sincerely like people and typically find themselves surrounded by friends. They are very popular in most environments without ever having to seek social acceptance. Their trusting nature draws others to them. Yellows are typically very open, which makes their friendship easy to understand and maintain. Other personalities seek out Yellow friends for their carefree and cheerful manner.

> *"Lack of charisma can be fatal."*
> —*Jenny Holzer*

Superficial

Ski resorts, beaches, and amusement parks are filled with Yellows seeking the good life. They hate exercise unless they can socialize at the same time or watch themselves in a mirror. Yellows enjoy the company of others but often find themselves unwilling to commit beyond the pleasures of momentary good times. Yellows resist activities or people that require endurance, which keeps them from perhaps the greatest goal of all—high self-esteem based on earned productivity and the kind of deep intimacy experienced only in long-term, committed relationships.

Disorganized and Incomplete

Yellows enjoy change. However, *what* they change is usually unimportant, and *when* they change, it is often counterproductive. Yellows learn early in life to cut corners. Intelligent Yellows are remarkably astute at this game. They often claim credit for accomplishments they haven't actually achieved but fully intend to. They may tell half-truths, or feel that it isn't that big a deal whether they are what they say as long as it doesn't hurt anyone. Many Yellows are amazingly talented and would love the applause of others but remain unwilling to put in the time and effort to earn the praise they seek.

Clutter has a way of finding Yellow lives. Perhaps it's how they think or maybe it has more to do with what they value. Eliminating clutter requires organization and effort. Few Yellows find much immediate gratification in addressing the clutter in their lives. They have the capacity to sort through debris when necessary, but they accommodate chaos quite comfortably, much to the chagrin of the other colors.

Optimistic

The well-loved character Mary Poppins (Red core, Yellow secondary) has a song that describes life with Yellows perfectly. The song says,

"It's a jolly 'oliday with Mary." And it is. Life with Yellows is festive. They always see the glass as half full. They know things will work out no matter how desperate the situation has become. Yellows have great faith in humanity and in life itself. Subsequently, life and humanity show great faith in Yellows. They have the uncanny ability to land on their feet regardless of where they fall.

Impulsive and Undisciplined

Yellows are terribly restless and find sticking with most tasks boring. For that reason, Yellows often experience numerous job changes. One can never be sure what to expect from these unpredictable individuals. Here today, gone to Maui! They are quick-change artists! It is hard to hang on to flighty Yellows who constantly seek the free and easy life. Yellows prefer not to be bothered with the details of life. They simply want the praise for what they do accomplish and the credit for whatever commitments they miraculously maintain in their lives.

Yellows are very interested in preserving wildlife. In other words, they are always ready to throw a party. Daily routine quickly becomes monotonous, and Yellows slip away into new and different environments. Immature Yellows become sullen and often express anger when life becomes difficult and unfair. They feel instant frustration when problems aren't easily solved. Few Yellows, therefore, ever become powerful world or business leaders. (President Ronald Reagan and President William Clinton were obviously exceptions, and Nancy [Blue] and Hillary [Red] were clearly *not* Yellow!) Yellows are not interested in power, and even if they were, they lack the discipline required to solve challenging problems. Daily mundane activities like balancing checkbooks, grocery shopping, and paying taxes can frustrate Yellows so much that they often lose their concentration and begin rummaging through their minds for ways to escape the insanity others call "responsible living."

Playful and Exciting

Yellows generally enjoy life regardless of what they are doing. Even when working hard, Yellows know how to have a good time. They live their lives with a confidence that the best is yet to come. They have a zest for living that is contagious. They seem to know how to make life fun regardless of their circumstances. No personality plays the way Yellows do. They are so spontaneous that they are always ready for whatever fun opportunities come their way. They are often found sporting T-shirts with slogans such as Are We Having Fun Yet? and It's OK to Play. They do not need to be productive in their play. The activity of play is, in itself, valuable enough to warrant a Yellow's attention. Yellows love surprises. They love to celebrate everything imaginable. They find holidays and special moments refreshing and, barring a memory lapse (which they are noted for), they will make the most of every opportunity to have fun.

> *"A life of unremitting caution, without the carefree—
> or even, occasionally, the careless—may turn out to be half a life."*
> —Anna Quindlen

YELLOW LIMITATIONS

At their very worst, Yellows have little regard for boundaries or for the property of others. They are disorganized individuals who keep themselves clean and polished while their homes often suffer from neglect. They want to look good socially to the world, and when social praise is a consideration, they are quick to comply with society's standards. Otherwise, tedious tasks (such as housekeeping) may require too much effort.

They are self-centered and superficial. Rather than focus on real issues and important events, Yellows putter with minor concerns and irrelevant activity. They have a difficult time committing to anything that takes priority over play time and consequently may find themselves vulnerable to leading limited lives.

> *Yellows go with the flow,
> as long as it keeps flowing and is flashy.*

YELLOW STRENGTHS

At their very best, Yellows are eager to experience all life offers. Yellows are our constant reminder that you are as young as you feel. They remain youthful in their attitudes toward new ideas, change, relationships, occupations, and the future. Yellows carry that childlike quality of hope that inspires others to appreciate and value themselves as well as the wonderful world in which they live. Yellows promote the good in others and willingly ignore their limitations. Yellows are more inclined to like themselves for what they are rather than what they do. Yellows express themselves candidly and genuinely. They give playful attention to living and inspire others to do the same. They freely offer their opinions as well as themselves, often spreading a contagious spirit of friendship wherever they go. Once your life has been intimately touched by a Yellow, you will more fully appreciate the incredible joy achievable by the human soul and the optimistic hope attainable within the human heart.

> *Yellows love life.*
> *They are the people connectors and*
> *social glue of society.*

REAL LIFE EXAMPLES OF YELLOWS

➤ An older woman reminisced once at a dinner party about her high school prom. "There we were, all dressed to the nines and having a great time, when this elderly woman with a cane arrived and shuffled throughout the event without disclosing her name. She was delightful and everyone enjoyed her presence but no one could figure out who she was or why she was there. That same evening when I came home, I discovered the 'elderly woman's' disguise on my mother's bed. My very Yellow mother had dressed up so she could come and see everyone at the party without being a nuisance. Most of the kids at my school knew and loved my mom because she was always inviting them over to the house. She wanted to see how everyone dressed and who they went with to the prom without being an imposition. That is exactly how my mom lived her life. Never a dull moment and we adored her for it."

➤ One Yellow friend lamented that every time he had a big project coming due, he would clean his garage instead. Rather than focus on the essential project, he wasted hours focusing on irrelevant puttering. Equally frustrating to him was his inability to organize effectively. He even left his garage in a constant state of disruption rather than create order. When he finally tackled the essential project, he would be forced to toss it together instead of having time to prepare a quality presentation. He felt incomplete, as if he were cheating himself and others of his best-quality performance.

➤ A Blue individual called a Yellow friend long-distance after five years of silence and said, "I've missed the life we shared as friends in college.

You always seemed to make life happen for me. I often reflect back on our friendship and remember all the excitement you always stirred up. I miss you because you breathed life into me." The Yellow friend had no idea that he had been the instigator of all the fun. He naively assumed that everyone's primary goal in life was to have a good time. He also thought most people experienced life as freely and as comfortably as he did. Later in life, he learned that his was the unique and enviable style that Yellows cultivate wherever they go.

➤ One patient told her Yellow husband, "If I weren't around, you would probably be lighting candles every night rather than remembering to pay your electric bill." After talking with them for a short time, I was certain that she was right. He had neglected to pay the last three months' mortgage payment of $825, so they decided to sell their home (which afforded them a tremendous tax advantage) and now rent a small apartment, half the size of their home, for $700 a month and zero tax advantage. He further justified this costly decision by saying, "All I need is a place with a little land for my dog and so that my wife can have a horse. Other than that I just want to travel. In fact, if I had my way, we would load up the van right now and go live in Mexico for a while." We discussed his Blue wife's need for a secure environment and more stability for raising children. He told me he had already matured, because when he first met her all he did was cash his paycheck each week, deposit it in his back pocket, and enjoy life until he reached in his back pocket and found that all the money was gone. Yellows live life in the moment, and saving money is typically only a remote future concern.

➤ Lynda Sherman is a Yellow gift from southern California who is always tied up with a bow. (Actually, she does like to be tied up, but that's another story!) She is so playful and entertaining that one can't imagine going on vacation without her. She has a fetish for a wonderful singer from England named Michael Ball. She discovered that he was performing in Toronto, Canada, and immediately invited friends to join her for a weekend in Toronto so they could feast on this singer. To make a long story short, the Michael Ball presenting in Toronto wasn't a singer at all: he was a scientist presenting a paper at a conference. So here they were, stuck in Toronto at a scientific conference with no music. The weekend couldn't have turned out better (except Lynda really *did* miss seeing her Michael Ball perform!). Because of her spontaneity and charm, the friends claimed they created a whole weekend out of nothing and would follow her anywhere she decided to travel simply to share her spirited sense of adventure.

➢ One distressed mother feared she would gag her Yellow four-year-old child if something didn't change soon. She was so tired of nonstop conversation that she admitted she had stopped listening simply to save her own sanity. (Personally, I think she was also concerned for the child's physical well-being.) She liked her quiet time, and every time she simply sat down to gather her thoughts, her daughter pounced on her lap and tried to cheer her up. The mother actually hid from her child at times throughout the day so that she might enjoy some peace.

➢ All lawyers know that it is one thing to practice law and quite another to bring in new clients. Lawyers with the expertise to bring new clients to the firm are often referred to as the "rainmakers" because they water the bottom line. Lawyers who can create new business are unique and highly sought after by law firms. One young Yellow attorney made his firm buckets of money with his engaging ways, and the partners saw a bright future for him. They promised him a bonus for every client he drew into the firm and hoped for a long business relationship with this man. Unfortunately, money meant less to him than social acceptance. His peers were jealous of his success and resented having to do more casework while he was off to yet another lunch appointment. Eventually, much to the partners' dismay, this enterprising attorney left the firm and practiced solo in order to free himself of the constant comparisons. He was actually surprised at how well he performed on his own with his innate gift to create new business and satisfy client expectations. He would have been just as happy to bring it to his old firm had he not had to deal with his peers' petty social resentment.

➢ Herb Kelleher (Red core who values Yellow) demonstrated the bottom-line magic of a positive business environment with Southwest Airlines. When other airlines were struggling to stay afloat and customer service was at an all-time low, flying Southwest was sheer fun. I remember sitting on a Southwest Airlines plane ready to leave the gate when the flight attendant asked every passenger to get out of their seat and move to the left side of the airplane. We did so only to hear her say, "As you all know, it has been a tough two years for our aviation industry. Parked right next door on your left, as you can see, is a Delta airplane. Would you all mind waving good-bye. We want them to think that we're carrying a full plane of passengers. Thank you for your cooperation in our most recent marketing campaign."

➢ As a very Yellow young man, I was unable to commit to marriage and repeatedly broke engagements and women's hearts. I was completely overwhelmed by the thought of a lifelong commitment. I enjoyed romance but feared the expectations of a committed relationship. Eventually, I fell deeply in love and, once again, felt motivated to consider the possibility of marriage. My uncertainty overcame me, however, and I called my father for advice. I respected my father and listened to his wise counsel. My father knew my fear of commitment was creating this difficulty. He simply reminded me that divorce was always an option and, if necessary, I could always exercise that option in the future. My wise father provided me with the essential ingredient in every Yellow's life—an escape, an out, a chance to run away, if necessary. His wisdom and effective parenting brought me to the altar. As a result, my very Blue wife and I happily celebrated our thirty-second wedding anniversary this year.

A QUICK GUIDE TO YELLOWS

YELLOW STRENGTHS

AS AN INDIVIDUAL

- highly optimistic (rarely depressed)
- likes self and accepts others easily
- loves to volunteer for opportunities
- sees life as an experience to be enjoyed
- flashy (racehorse rather than plow horse)
- adventurous and daring

AS A COMMUNICATOR

- thinks quickly on his or her feet and can express things spontaneously
- enjoys and promotes being physical (hugs, touching)
- easy to converse with
- comfortable with people
- able to express self directly in conflict
- energized by large groups
- superb at general conversation

AS A GOAL SETTER

- appreciates and lives for the present
- gives priority to play time

- very flexible
- accepts guidance from others
- disciplined if he or she finds the task fun and challenging
- demands action rather than prolonged study

AS A CAREER PERSON

- people-oriented
- friendly
- risk taker
- high energy
- inspires colleagues and subordinates to cooperate and excel
- charismatic and enjoyable to work with
- breaks up monotony of work world
- likes to tackle short-term projects with visible results
- enjoys both dressing up and casual attire
- supports dreams and intuitive thinking

AS A PARENT

- highly entertaining
- promotes fun family activities
- excellent short-term leader
- finds physical affection toward children natural and comfortable
- flows easily with negative experiences
- turns crisis into comedy
- nonjudgmental about children's friends
- children enjoy their company and seek them out
- concern themselves with the broad picture rather than the details
- very present in the moment

AS A CHILD

- fun to have around
- playful and entertaining
- enjoys new experiences
- accepting of differences
- loves to socialize (brings friends home)
- easy to talk with about varied topics
- strong visual and tactile learner
- loves physical contact (hugging, kissing)
- pliable—willing to bend in order to please
- curious and inquisitive

YELLOWS: THE FUN LOVERS

AS A FRIEND

- exciting and fun to be with (never dull or boring)
- often puts friends before family in importance
- forgiving of self and others
- lively and entertaining
- vulnerable, innocent, and trusting
- endearing
- willing to free up schedule in order to play
- spontaneous

AS A COMMITTED COMPANION

- brings excitement to spouse
- promotes romance with a creative flair
- enjoys unusual experiences
- not burdened with emotional baggage
- has few expectations of others
- agreeable to change
- accepts others' suggestions

CAREERS MOST LIKELY TO ATTRACT YELLOWS

(Of course, all personality types can be found in every occupation. There are innumerable variables that determine success in any career.)

Firefighter	Beautician	Secretary
International consultant	Entertainer	Receptionist
Travel agent	Tour guide	Sales
Recreation leader	Circus performer	Retail
Lifeguard	Insurance agent	Clergy/Minister

Note: Yellows are generally the least capable of consistently committing to the requirements for financial success in the career world.

PERSONALITIES THAT APPEAR TO BE YELLOW

Bill Clinton: President Clinton has magically survived a myriad of assaults on his personal character and professional competence, but he never runs for cover. His winning smile and positive manner make people trust him. He is intellectually bright and verbally quick, making him difficult to pin down or ever catch off-guard.

Ronald Reagan: One of America's most adored presidents, Ronald Reagan's trademark was optimism and charisma. He spoke with conviction and always exuded an inviting warmth. He carried himself with a carefree confidence that put others around him at ease.

Elvis Presley: Dynamic and rebellious, his vulnerability and trusting nature were charming and disarming. He was personable and generous. He lived for the moment, and his naiveté and emotionalism caused irrational decisions that prematurely ended his scattered brilliance as a performer. As with all good Yellows, people are still hoping to find him alive so the party can continue.

YELLOW NATIONS

These are nations who have a culture that promotes the Yellow motives, attitudes, and behaviors. It does *not* mean that everyone in these nations is Yellow.

Mexico	France (except for Paris, which is Red)
Australia	Italy
Brazil	Austria

YELLOW MOTTO

"Don't sweat the small stuff . . . and it's *all* small stuff."

CELEBRITIES WHO APPEAR TO BE YELLOW

- Julia Roberts
- Will Farrell
- Jessica Simpson
- Goldie Hawn
- Will Smith
- Mel Gibson
- Cameron Diaz
- Ellen DeGeneres
- Matthew McConaughey
- George Clooney

YELLOW LIMITATIONS

AS AN INDIVIDUAL

- needs to look good socially (high priority)
- irresponsible and unreliable
- self-centered and egotistical
- flighty and uncommitted
- lots of talk with little action
- superficial and mostly interested in a good time
- unwilling to experience pain in order to produce quality
- undisciplined
- loud and obnoxious in public places
- exaggerates successes and omits unpleasant truths
- unable to confront or face issues

AS A COMMUNICATOR

- often speaks before thinking
- unsympathetic about depression in others
- makes insensitive jokes about serious and sensitive issues
- light-minded and superficial
- often repetitious and long-winded
- interrupts others freely
- overly dramatic in expressing self (often uses superlatives)
- often talks too much about everything and nothing
- poor listener
- forgets what others have said

AS A GOAL SETTER

- terribly undisciplined in committing to goals
- prefers to play today rather than plan for tomorrow
- feels no need to prepare for the future
- restless and finds it difficult to stick with long-term goals
- more interested in appearing onstage than writing the script
- disorganized and scattered in too many directions

AS A CAREER PERSON

- requires that all activities be fun
- can handle stress only for short periods of time

- poor concentration for any length of time
- unwilling to dedicate self to a cause without vacations
- resents authority and defiant of leaders
- sloppy and unpredictable
- needs a lot of interaction with people
- takes few things seriously

AS A PARENT

- self-centered and more concerned about self than children's needs
- more interested in enjoying children than teaching them
- can be sarcastic with children
- unwilling to spend a lot of time and energy on children's behalf
- inconsistent with discipline
- irresponsible and too permissive with children
- bad role model for positive work habits
- lacks discipline for housecleaning or providing stable income

AS A CHILD

- sassy and demanding
- defiant of authority
- forgetful of assignments and parental expectations
- more concerned with friends than family
- teases siblings constantly
- insensitive to parents' responsibilities or needs
- prefers to take the easy road whenever possible
- shows little concern for family problems and responsibilities
- unconcerned with financial issues

AS A FRIEND

- spends most time discussing own life
- shows up at his or her convenience
- undependable in a crisis
- unwilling to commit to long-term needs of distressed friends
- pursues own life regardless of friends' situations or needs
- uncomfortable in painful or distressing environments
- makes new friends easily and without guilt, often at the expense of old friends

AS A COMMITTED COMPANION

- uncommitted and flighty in long-term relationships
- undependable and inconsiderate of the needs of others
- prefers to enter a relationship knowing there is an escape
- unwilling to hang in there during the difficult times
- quick-tempered in unpleasant circumstances requiring patience
- unwilling to invest time in personal growth to improve relationships
- capable of ignoring the feelings of others and focusing on self

Just for Yellows: Recommended Life Tips

1. Realize that "busyness" is not necessarily the same as purposeful action. Reflect on what is important and give it legitimate attention.
2. Set specific goals each day and prioritize them. Work on your A1 goals first. Don't go to your A2 priorities until you complete your A1. Do them in order.
3. Focus on "what's necessary" rather than "what's fun." Quality requires both. Don't let others take on the responsibility of handling your "necessary" tasks.
4. Set achievable "time bits" where you focus on a specific task for a specific amount of time and create a fun reward for sticking to it. Break up the monotony.
5. Commit to the bigger picture. Create a long-term plan of substance and seek specific activities you can complete to make it a reality.
6. Balance undemanding creativity with focused commitments. You'll feed both your need for unstructured play and your need for accomplishment.
7. Do a little planning up front so you "get it right" the first time. You'll save yourself tremendous time.
8. Listen well so you don't have to interrupt others for information already presented.

Top Five Yellow Attraction Factors

1. Enthusiasm: it's contagious and energizing
2. Fun: you make people feel alive and engaged in the moment
3. Trusting: people appreciate your inclusion of others and new ideas

4. Positive: very upbeat and optimistic
5. Charisma: people like themselves more when they are with you

Top Three Yellow "Unattraction" Factors

1. Uncommitted: people want to know you are in for the long haul
2. Poor follow-through: people want you to keep your promises
3. Afraid to face facts: people lose respect for you when you refuse to see the truth about yourself and your surroundings

---

How to Develop a Positive Connection with Yellows

Do

1. Be positive and proactive with them in your life
2. Adore and praise them legitimately
3. Touch them physically
4. Accept their playful teasing
5. Remember that they are more sensitive than they appear
6. Value their social interaction skills and people connections
7. Remember that they hold feelings deeply
8. Promote creative and fun activities for and with them
9. Enjoy their charismatic innocence
10. Allow them opportunity for verbal expression

Don't

1. Be too serious or sober in criticism
2. Push them too intensely
3. Ignore them
4. Forget they have "down" times also
5. Demand perfection
6. Expect them to dwell on problems
7. Give them too much rope, or they may hang themselves
8. Classify them as just lightweight social butterflies
9. Forget a Yellow's creative genius
10. Totally control their schedules or consume their time

Five Things Yellows Should Do Before They're Thirty

1. Take a long road trip with friends
2. Travel extensively and enjoy other cultures
3. Break a Blue's heart
4. Celebrate every holiday on the calendar as only Yellows can
5. Play charades long and often with many diverse groups of people

Two Things Yellows Need to Do Before They Die

1. Finish something they are passionate about and commit to it
2. Marry well

> *"Hard work may not kill me,*
> *but why take a chance?"*

Chapter Nine

SECONDARY COLORS

Few people exhibit only the behaviors of one color.
While everyone has only one core,
our personalities are often influenced
by our secondary colors.

There are three specific reasons why people readily embrace the People Code:

1. **It is simple to understand.**
2. **It is easy to apply.**
3. **It is accurate.**

A psychological theory is only as good as its ability to accurately identify and predict human behavior. Using the driving core motive as the foundation for my work assures an accuracy that a premise based solely on observed behavior cannot hope to offer. The driving core motive in everyone's personality is the critical element that will not only facilitate personal development but will grant others a personal view into everyone they encounter.

I have lectured to hundreds of thousands of people. I have worked intimately as a personal coach with thousands of individuals. Ever since developing *The People Code*, I have always found the driving core motive in each person with whom I've had contact. Admittedly, I've been slow to discover it at times and initially wrong at other times. But I have always found their true core motive, and we both knew it was accurate when we finally discovered it. By the way, when you find your innate core motive, it feels like "coming home" to a safe and comfortable place—a place free of pretense and demands. It simply feels right.

Some people identify themselves correctly from the first time they hear or read my theory. Others struggle to find themselves for various reasons. Ironically, as the author of this theory, I was initially wrong identifying myself. At first I pegged myself as a Red. Actually, nothing could be further from the truth. When I took the Hartman Personality Profile from a childhood perspective, I was 43 Yellow, 1 White, and 1 Red. Statistically, there appears to be no Red or any secondary color at all.

However, when I review the profile, it becomes readily clear that my secondary preferences are overwhelmingly Red, as opposed to Blue or White. In other words, when I had to struggle to make a decision on any given question, it was almost exclusively between the Yellow and Red options. This brings in the exciting variable of how our secondary color influences our personalities.

My clinical research indicates that there are four main reasons that best explain why some people struggle to identify correctly their core driving personality motive. They are:

1. An individual is reared in a strong autocratic family where express attitudes and behaviors were determined solely by one or both parents (or any significant familial figure).
2. Unresolved and/or untreated sexual abuse
3. Theological and/or cultural biases
4. An individual is born with a closely blended personality.

This chapter focuses primarily on the fourth reason: An individual is born with a closely blended personality. However, allow me to give a brief clarification of why and how the first three reasons play such a critical role in confusing people about who they innately are:

Reason #1 An individual is reared in a strong autocratic family where express attitudes and behaviors were determined solely by one or both parents (or any significant familial figure).

Actually, this is my story. My mother (whom I absolutely adore) is so Red that she is just one step shy of Attila the Hun! She ran our home of seven children with tremendous confidence and authority. In fact, in writing *The People Code*, I researched my own brothers and sisters and was astounded to find a Red brother who so pales next to our Red mother that I almost missed correctly identifying him. (And, trust me, he is no lightweight, either.) Mom was so committed to us and loved every minute of being home to rear us (a rather unique attitude in today's world), but no one ever crossed her and lived. We knew early in life that survival depended on working *with* her rather than *against* her. Consequently, she completely directed all of our lives, and I embraced numerous Red (as opposed to Yellow) qualities because she deemed them to have the most value and was such a strong role model. Fortunately, she never demeaned my Yellow gifts. She actually rather enjoyed them. But they always (and only) found value in conjunction with Red behavior such as responsibility and accountability.

Far too many people will never know themselves because their parents (or a significant familial figure) set the course everyone was to embrace. Sadly, I have encountered thousands of people who remain angry at parents for controlling them and robbing them of the personal preferences they would have chosen given their innate personality.

> *When you find your innate core motive,*
> *it feels like "coming home"*
> *to a safe and comfortable place—*
> *a place free of pretense and demands.*
> *It simply feels right.*

Reason #2   Unresolved and/or untreated sexual abuse

Free agency is the cornerstone of the human experience. Perhaps nothing has caused me greater emotional pain than to work with people who were sexually betrayed early in life by someone they trusted (and clearly should have been able to trust!). I don't know of any indiscretion that is more destructive to the human soul than sexual abuse. It's terribly invasive and demeaning. It steals hope and innocence and leaves deep scars, self-doubt, and a propensity to make poor choices with regard to the men or women with whom they are intimate.

So much has already been written on this topic. I merely want to add my voice of experience that sexual abuse can be a terrifying and powerful force in deadening the human soul—thus seriously derailing one's accurate perception of oneself. If you have been a victim of sexual abuse, consider who you really are inside as opposed to what attitude and/or behavior you may have embraced to protect yourself or vent your anger for having lost your innocence so young.

Reason #3   Theological and/or cultural biases

Myth: Men are logical and women are emotional. This false statement continues to permeate our society, convincing Red and White women they really aren't thinking logically, and Blue and Yellow men that they really don't feel those emotions they have. Nonsense. But how often do we hear biased comments like "big boys don't cry" and "women just cry to manipulate you"? We are so afraid to face the truth of who we are that we often make rash and self-serving comments at the expense of others so we can feel better about ourselves. Do yourself a favor and get beyond rigid theological and/or cultural biases in order to embrace everyone's true personality identity.

Of course, people learn quickly how to get on in this world. If someone gets a consistent message that they are wrong to behave a certain way because a religion and/or society so dictates, they usually defer personal preference to survival and acceptance of group norms. Some individuals have deferred so much throughout their lives that they are either terribly angry about everything, or they no longer even resemble who they were at birth. If you want to talk about human tragedies, that's the real human tragedy—to be robbed of your very being!

> *Blues with strong Red secondary*
> *experience the most difficult internal struggles.*
> *They are also typically*
> *the most resourceful of personalities.*

So much more could be written about each of these reasons that block individuals from being fully human and feeling fully alive. However, the focus of this book is on innate personalities as opposed to outside influences. Though other factors do impact us, they are not the primary influence in determining our personalities. That distinguished role will forever be played by our driving core motive. This is why it is so critical to identify correctly who we are innately.

More than any other secondary factor, secondary colors are most prominent in determining our unique personality. Secondary colors refer to personality strengths and limitations that belong to a personality not of our own core, but represented in our attitudes and/or behaviors. For example, you may be an assertive Red with tremendous compassion (Mother Teresa comes to mind). Compassion does not belong innately to the Red personality, and yet a person with a Red personality may enjoy its gift (whether innate or learned). In this example, assertiveness would be considered primary or natural to the core personality, while compassion would be considered to be a secondary color influence. Compassion, of course, is a positive trait. There are as many negative traits capable of providing negative secondary influences as well. For example, consider working for a sincere Blue personality who is selfish. The sincerity is primary, but it becomes seriously tainted by the secondary trait of selfishness.

I have discovered that we are far more forgiving of others when they act according to their natural, innate core personalities. We expect Reds to lead and Whites to be kind. However, when people stray from their innate comfort zone, others become uncomfortable, especially when someone displays limitations unlike their innate personality (for example, if a Yellow becomes reclusive or a Blue becomes bossy). If you had never heard about the People Code, you would still have an intuition of and expectation for how others will behave. When they act incongruently and go beyond the lines we have established as acceptable for them, conflict or avoidance usually occurs.

These same expectations can get in the way of personal development as well. So often when a selfish, emotionally guarded Red begins to stretch and take the charactered path (which means to develop personality strengths outside one's core personality), others react negatively. Based on their history with the individual, they refuse to accept the change. We like people to stay in the boxes we have come to know them by. Any deviation from what we have determined to be acceptable is uncomfortable for us, and thus we immediately react to preserve the status quo, whether it is positive or negative. This also explains why personal change is so difficult and why so many of us abandon ourselves and the charactered journey before we've completed our work.

Secondary colors are those traits, whether positive or negative, that directly influence our primary core color to our benefit or detriment. After completing the Hartman Personality Profile, you will have an excellent awareness of your primary core and secondary colors. However, what the profile does not tell you is whether your secondary color is positive or negative. The Hartman Character Profile will provide you with those answers. That's why it is so crucial for us to correctly identify our core personality before focusing on secondary color influences. Once we have correctly laid the foundation of our core personality, we can begin the inviting task of uniquely filling out our personality with secondary color blends.

There are pluses and minuses to having strong secondary color(s) in our personality. One plus is that having the strengths of a secondary color can balance you. You can draw on gifts of other personalities more comfortably than people who display no secondary influences. You are also more adept at understanding other personalities, because there may be parts of you that think as others do. The most common reason that people don't get along with others comes from a lack of understanding of why others think and act as they do. Having a secondary color helps us cross that bridge of understanding.

The minuses of having strong secondary color(s) can best be explained in two parts. When you have strengths in two colors, you may find yourself in a constant internal battle as to which innate strength to follow in any given situation. People with strong Red and Blue tendencies suffer the most from this because both personalities are so controlling. When your secondary color is Yellow or White, there tends to be less conflict because those colors offer a more passive and accepting agenda.

The conflict is even more pronounced, however, when you have innate positive traits in one color and innate negative traits in another. Talk about sending dual messages! Take, for example, a strong blend of Red and Blue (and there are many of you!). The strengths and limitations of these two personalities are dramatically incongruent. Reds can be selfish, while Blues are generally more thoughtful. Blues can be self-critical, while Reds prefer to criticize others. When a person with a Blue core personality operates in the negative Red zone, they send mixed messages and get limited results. Before the People Code they never understood why this happened. Remember, we accept people in their natural core personality, so when they start acting out, especially in the negatives of their secondary color, we become confused and, for self-preservation, we either distance ourselves or attack. The Blue individual who innately seeks intimacy and knows he or she cares deeply for you will become confused when his or her Red negative behaviors are displayed. The Blue may know that he or she cares deeply, but the behavior is bossy, demeaning, or calculated, and it definitely does not feel safe or inviting. Blues must rid themselves of their negative Red traits or suffer a lifetime of sending and receiving mixed messages.

It is far more important to free yourself of the limitations of your secondary color than those of your primary color. People are far more forgiving of our limitations within our primary personality than of secondary color flaws. More important for us, perhaps, is that displaying the limitations of a secondary color does more damage in preventing us from experiencing our driving core motive than displaying our core limitations will.

Let me give you a personal example. I am a Yellow who is driven by the core motive of fun. I travel often for business and have learned that being assertive (Red) gets problems with airlines and hotels addressed and resolved much more efficiently than my innate nature of simply going with the flow (Yellow). However, I have discovered that when I begin expecting others to perform at a higher level, and thus become more critical in my evaluation of them, I become less happy and positive and therefore have less fun. It can be very challenging to develop the gifts of other personalities while remaining true to your own innate core motive.

Motives become the important factor in determining whether it is best to embrace a particular attitude or behavior at any given time. If one's motive is clean, it becomes mandatory for good mental health to act on it. However, if one's motive is dirty (i.e., based on fear or ignorance), it is equally critical that one *not* act on it. We must always check on motives for clarity when selecting attitudes and/or behaviors. Whatever traits we don't have control over will control us. If we allow ourselves to behave according to how we feel, we will soon find that our excuses of "that's just how I am" will forge a lifetime of self-betrayal and produce anxiety for others. We must always be aware of our motives and how they drive our attitudes and behaviors.

Secondary colors can skew our personalities so that we no longer act according to who we innately know ourselves to be. I have worked with Reds who have strong secondary Blue traits, and they appear to be White. Rather than accent the strengths of their Red and their Blue gifts, they abandon the battle and act White. Of course, this leaves no real winners. We don't get their Red or Blue strengths, and they don't experience their core motive of power with Blue accents of compassion and quality. Never let your secondary color drain you of your innate core motive or strengths. The value of our secondary color can be fully experienced only when we remain true to our innate core personality motive.

> People with strong Yellow and White blends
> enjoy the best "people skills."
> If you can't enjoy these people, consider yourself
> the one with the problem.

Secondary colors explain the many nuances of people despite being limited to only four optional driving core motives. While there are only four core motives, there are numerous variables that create unique and diverse personalities, so that no two individuals are ever the same. The gift that *The People Code* offers is an honest foundation of core motives from which we can understand and further develop our own unique personalities.

Chapter Ten

WHAT MAKES YOU HOT?
WHAT MAKES YOU NOT?

REDS

What Makes YOU Hot?

- You love the hunt and making things happen.
- You promote interesting experiences.
- You pay attention.
- You take the lead.
- Your confidence is sexy.

What Makes YOU Not?

- You always have to be right.
- You tend to be selfish and take care of yourself first.
- You don't express your feelings and emotions well.
- You can be cheap.
- You can be insensitive.

WHAT ATTRACTS PEOPLE TO YOU?

Nobody Dates Like a Red

When you are in pursuit of something (or someone!), you tend to go all out. You dress to impress, you get the limo, the tickets, the flowers, the reservations, and the whole shebang. You are—by nature—a very competitive opponent to any other potential dates who may come along, and you take great pleasure in beating them out. With your competitive drive and determination, you will spare no expense as you go to great lengths to woo your love interest.

You Are Highly Protective of Your Companion

When you commit to someone, he or she can feel your protection on all levels. You see your companion as part of you, and are willing to go to war verbally and even physically on his or her behalf. You will not back down or sit back quietly and watch when your partner is being attacked. People love to know that they are being taken care of and that you will be there to back them up and defend them whenever necessary.

You Promote Interesting Experiences

As a Red, you tend to know a little about a lot of everything and enjoy expanding your intellectual horizons. Therefore, you like to conduct activities for your companion that may be a little out of the ordinary or that may require more effort than someone else may be willing to put forth. For example, you may treat your mate to an afternoon at an art museum where you take him or her on a personal tour and explain interesting details about each work of art.

Reds Are Excellent Providers

Reds like to win, and therefore they choose occupations where they can excel, be promoted, and be rewarded financially. You take your business ventures very seriously, and will not stick around if you are not receiving an excellent return on your time or investment. As a result, your partner knows that making enough money to live well will never be a question in your relationship. You are determined to succeed and motivated to make enough money to enjoy life, and that is very appealing in a relationship.

You Tell People Where They Stand in the Relationship

People don't like to wonder about the status of their relationships. That doesn't tend to be an issue with you. You do not shy away from telling your partner exactly how you feel about him or her. The fact is, your love interest knows that if he or she is still with you, you obviously still feel good about the relationship. Because the moment you begin to feel that a relationship isn't going anywhere you will say something. That isn't to say that you readily offer praise when you're satisfied in a relationship. You have a hard time giving credit where credit is due, and, more often than not, if the relationship is going well, you'll enjoy it without indicating its success. In other words, "If I didn't love you, I would have left you a long time ago."

You Provide Natural Leadership

You have a very strong presence and are very decisive and action-oriented by nature. You are always thinking at least five years down the road and always have a Plan B. You conduct your relationships strategically to get the best possible result and readily take charge of every relationship-building decision. Potential partners are attracted to the fact that you are planning for a successful relationship and are willing to put it all on the line for them. You are especially prone to take over when challenges arise. You meet any obstacle to a successful relationship head-on, and can always be counted on to steer your relationship toward success on all levels.

Reds Show Up

When you commit to doing something with your partner, there is no question that you will be there, ready to go. You dress up, you produce, you make good on your promises, and you always leave a good impression on people your partner cares about, because of your high sense of responsibility and strong presence. In other words, you live up to your hype. Your partner will always be able to count on you to be the date or spouse whom he or she expects you to be.

Confidence Is Sexy

Need I say more? You exude confidence in everything you do. You don't like others to see you sweat, which at first is very attractive to others. Just be sure that your confidence isn't a facade for your insecurities. Confidence that isn't just skin-deep will keep your love interest interested even after he or she gets to know you.

WHAT ABOUT YOU TURNS PEOPLE OFF?

You Tend to Be Selfish

The number one reason that marriages fail is selfishness, and unfortunately, as a Red you tend always to think first about yourself and what's in it for you. If you always put your needs before those of your partner, you will foster a sense of resentment that may ultimately cost you everything. The first and last lesson in a successful relationship is putting your partner first.

You Can Be Uncomfortable with Emotions and Feelings

One of a Red's main strengths is logic, and therefore you often feel uncomfortable or insecure when your partner becomes emotional. You see this as a weakness and may become adamant that he or she address emotional subjects in a more logical manner. When he or she does not take a more logical approach, you become very dismissive, when in fact *you* are the laggard in matters of the heart. There is tremendous value in connecting emotionally, and if you cannot learn to do so, you will miss out.

Reds Always Have to Be Right

You tend to be very argumentative, and since you need to look good to others intellectually, you don't like to be wrong. However, if you are creating a relationship with someone and you always have to be right, that means that your partner always has to be wrong—an equation that doesn't yield a positive result.

You Come Across as Harsh and Critical, Even When You Don't Mean To

As a Red, you are very opinionated and sometimes just can't help but noticing what's wrong with your partner. However, even when you are trying to help your partner by fixing his or her problems, you tend to be tactless in the way you say things. This causes hurt feelings, and your partner won't like to be told that he or she is inadequate. You're probably thinking, "If my partner weren't so incompetent, I would not have had to say it." Regardless of whether or not you're right, such tactlessness won't help your partner get any closer to improving.

You Can Be Cheap

It is true that nobody dates quite like a Red, but a problem arises when you have won your significant other over and no longer feel the need to invest in "getting" him or her. This may be especially prevalent if you're married or in a committed relationship. Logically, you may think that since the battle is over, you should not waste any more time or money on wooing your special someone. Wrong! Don't be a cheapskate; it's a big turn-off! You need to continue courting your special someone even after you've won him or her over.

You May Give Priority to Work Over Personal Relationships

As a Red, you are driven and focused on your career and advancement in the world. Because of this, you may cause your partner to feel secondary in importance. If you are not as committed to building your personal relationships as you are your work relationships, you can kiss your romance good-bye.

Reds Can Be Poor Listeners

One advantage of being Red is that you are very analytical and pride yourself on your problem-solving skills. The downside is that when your date or partner just needs to be listened to, you tend to be too busy proposing solutions to his or her problems to provide what he or she really needs—a listening ear. The less well you listen, the less often your partner will come to you for help.

You Can Be Too Controlling and Domineering

Whether you know it or not, people feel intimidated by you. You have a very domineering personality and are quick to put down anyone who dares to challenge your opinion or decisions. Coupled with your attempts to control your environment (and the people within it), your significant other may shy away from you in search of someone who is more approachable and personable. The more you bridle your passion to be in charge all the time and develop the humility to accept that someone else can effectively lead, the happier your relationships will be.

BLUES

What Makes YOU Hot?

- You are a first-class act.
- You think of others before yourself—selfless in every way.
- You have a highly developed sense of quality and order. (Everything has its proper place!)
- You give your whole heart and express your emotions honestly.
- You are a rock—stable and dependable to the very end.

What Makes YOU Not?

- You tend to be self-righteous and think you are on a mission from God to save the rest of us.
- You think *whining* is a good thing and *forgiveness* is not.
- Your mysterious mood swings drive the rest of us crazy.
- You are a perfectionist control freak.
- You can be overly sensitive. (Which is how you are probably feeling right now!)

WHAT ATTRACTS PEOPLE TO YOU?

You Put Your Partner and Relationship First

People like to feel important—especially to their significant other—and you have the natural ability to make that happen. As a Blue, you tend to be very selfless, and your first thought is always "How will this affect my partner?" You would be willing to sacrifice going out with friends or engaging in an activity that you enjoy on your own to do something less exciting with your significant other—not that they would necessarily ask you to—but just knowing you would is a great feeling.

You Make Events Magical

When planning something such as an anniversary dinner or a birthday party, you don't like to go through the same old routine that everyone else does. You have a flair for creativity and a sense of how to create ambience by adding special touches that you know will be perfect for the occasion. For example, you might have personalized gifts or you might re-create something meaningful that happened previously in your relationship. You make ordinary things extra-special, which is very endearing.

Blues Are Unbelievably Thoughtful

You take thoughtfulness to the next level. Not only do you send flowers when your partner's mother is sick, you also remember what her favorite flowers are! You love to deepen your connection with your partner, and do it through remembering specific things that he or she said or preferences that he or she revealed. Your companion will always feel flattered and special when on the receiving end of your thoughtfulness.

You Emanate Quality and Purpose in All That You Do

You have a personal commitment to quality and purpose, which is very attractive to potential partners, because they know that ending up with you would almost guarantee a higher standard in life. You are not into wasting time (in fact, you feel guilty when you do), nor do you spend energy in areas that will not yield meaningful results. Quantity means nothing to you if it lacks quality. In fact, your personal motto could be "If you can't do something right, then don't do it at all."

You Give Your Heart Wholly and Willingly

As a Blue, you have the ability and the desire to open up your heart and give all that you have to your partner. Your willingness to reveal what you're about and to be vulnerable is a great asset in creating truly intimate relationships. This is incredibly attractive, because your companion will know that you are never holding anything back and are giving your all to build the most meaningful relationship of your life.

You Are a Rock—Stable and Dependable

Everyone wants someone who is stable and dependable, which you are. If you say you are going to do something, you mean it. If you commit to a certain path in life (religion, philosophy, code of ethics, etc.), you stick to it. You always pull through and can always be counted on. Not only that, but your strength allows you to be supportive and giving to others as well.

Blues' Capacity for Emotional Depth Is Remarkable

You feel things very deeply, and you are not satisfied with superficial emotions or conversations. That's not to say that you dislike them, but your preference is to go deeper. It is appealing to see the way that you sense things so aesthetically (and even intuitively) and it brings an enhanced quality and perspective to any relationship.

You Are a Class Act

When it's all said and done, you are just classy, period. Remember, not even money can buy class, but you have it. You carry yourself well, you know what's appropriate, and you naturally have a presence about you that is, well . . . classy. Two words for you: *very sexy*.

WHAT ABOUT YOU TURNS PEOPLE OFF?

You Tend to Blame Others for Your Unhappiness

As a Blue, you hold high standards and tend to have unrealistic expectations of yourself, your partner, and how things "should be." So, when things go wrong, you identify others, such as your partner, as the source of your unhappiness. You might say to them, "If only you were more attentive/caring/interested/loving [you name it], this wouldn't have happened." This is obviously not a great way to maintain someone's affection.

It's Difficult for You to Relax (You Require a Purpose to Play)

Blues tend to be overly guilt-prone, so if you are doing things that are not meaningful by your standards, you probably feel guilty about it. Ergo, you tend to require a justifiable reason just to play and enjoy life, which usually defeats the purpose and feels unnatural or forced to others. Your tendency to be high-strung in this way can be alarming to a potential mate who is stuck wondering if you'll ever be able to calm down enough to enjoy a life together.

Blues Can Be Self-Righteous

I once saw a great Blue bumper sticker that read, "Those of you who think you know everything really annoy those of us who actually do." Blues think that they know the best way to handle things, especially from a moral standpoint. If your partner, or anyone else for that matter, steps "out of bounds" in your judgment, they will feel your heavy disapproval. Further, if you do actually say something, you tend to lecture and you come across as being very condescending. Your partner will want to run for cover.

You Tend to Be Moody

You process information with a very analytical but very emotional outlook; therefore, you become inundated with thoughts and other signals that carry an emotional message with them. When you allow this process to control your general mood, it's difficult for your partner to tell if you're going to be up or down or if you'll laugh at a joke or take it personally and cry, and so on. It sometimes makes it difficult to want to be around you.

You Can Be Unforgiving

Blues are generally very loyal and appropriate; therefore, if your partner wrongs you in some way, you will most likely hold a grudge for a long time. You just can't understand why someone would do that to you—after all, you wouldn't do it! You think, "If they truly cared about me, they wouldn't have treated me that way," and your sense of justice wants your partner to pay for his or her wrongdoing before you will forgive. That attitude, coupled with your unrealistic expectations for what a just penance should be, makes it difficult for your partner to win your forgiveness. Your partner, however, may grow tired of begging and move on.

You Can Be Perfectionistic (Untrusting) to a Fault

Your dedication to quality, if overdone, can become a major distraction. As a Blue, you want the job done *right*, no matter what it is— homework, an assignment from your boss, family Christmas cards, organizing your office, and so on. The problem is that you really believe the saying "If you want something done right, do it yourself," and you won't delegate or allow others to contribute. This sends the message to your partner that you don't trust him or her to do simple tasks because he or she is inadequate and can't live up to your standards.

You Can Be Too Controlling

Blues are the most controlling of all the four personality types. Your strong sense of propriety and moral values makes you want to see everyone marching to the beat of "the *correct* drummer" (as defined by you, of course). For a potential or existing partner, this begins to feel very restrictive and eventually he or she will grow resentful.

You May Give with Strings Attached

Often when Blues give of themselves, they have return expectations that people can feel. The return they want may come in the form of anticipated levels of appreciation for what they have done for you, or they may want you to feel obligated to do something of equal value in return. (For example, "When she was sick, I brought soup and took care of her, and now that I'm sick, the best she can do is a lousy phone call?!") This will strain your relationships, because if you make your partner feel as if he or she owes you when you give a gift or do something kind, soon your partner will no longer want anything from you (or perhaps anything to do with you) ever again.

WHITES

What Makes YOU Hot?

- You are so clear and perceptive; you bring the voice of reason.
- You listen—without judgment.
- You are so comfortable in your own skin, that you can let others shine.
- You accept diversity. (Everyone is unique and brings value.)
- You understand the immense gift of kindness, offering it generously and without bias.

What Makes YOU Not?

- You are emotionally dishonest. (Your partner often says, "You don't tell me how you really feel . . .")
- You are notoriously indecisive. (Like where would you like to go to dinner tonight?!)
- You have serious conflict-avoidance issues. (You're no fun to fight with!)
- You rarely express emotional vulnerability.

- You are silently stubborn as a mule—and can be very passive-aggressive in getting your way.

WHAT ATTRACTS PEOPLE TO YOU?

You Are a Superb Listener

Have you ever heard your friends complaining about how their boyfriends or girlfriends don't listen to them, and you don't understand how this could be? It's because you listen so naturally. This is such a turn-on, because your partner will feel your interest and know that you hear even what he or she is not saying.

You Make Others Feel Comfortable

You have a way of putting people at ease. You don't try to intimidate or make things too formal. In fact, you prefer creating a very relaxed and open atmosphere, which works to your advantage, because the people in your life like to know that you are accessible and approachable, and that they don't have to put on a big show to be with you. In fact, they know that they can be *more* real with you, because of your accepting nature.

You Are Receptive to Your Partner's Input

You are open to new ideas and new ways of seeing things in general. You enjoy it when your partner gives you suggestions or constructive feedback, because you like to know how others see things and how they see you. What's attractive about this is that you often do see things their way once everything is explained, and you aren't afraid to adjust accordingly—not necessarily because you want to please them, but because it makes sense, and you are very practical that way.

You See Things Very Clearly and Objectively

When your partner is struggling with difficult decisions and his or her vision becomes clouded with various thoughts, emotions, and so on, you seem to have an amazing ability to see through all of the garbage and can generally come up with what seems to be a very simple solution (as in one of those "How could I have missed that?! It's so obvious!" solutions). You are extremely objective and your ability to reason and give the best feedback possible is wonderful to have around.

You Are Very Adaptable

When life throws you a curveball, you don't panic, you simply adjust your swing. Crisis or sudden change doesn't upset you. You can go with the flow of things and find ways to be very inventive. For example, if your date loses the concert tickets on the way to the stadium, rather than make him or her feel uncomfortable or embarrassed, you just say, "I'm not worried about it, why don't we go to a movie and dinner instead?" What's attractive about this is that you don't make crisis situations about yourself. You just figure life happens, so you make the best of it with those you're with.

You Are Not Judgmental

You are incredibly nonjudgmental and enjoy meeting different types of people with different attitudes about life, dating, religion, fun, or whatever. You seem to understand that if your partner sees things a certain way, then there must be something to it, and before judging or trying to convince of your way, you are always willing to give it a chance. People are drawn to the way that you do not feel threatened by ideas that may be foreign to you.

You Shine When in Your Element

As a White, you don't have ego problems and therefore do not vie to be the center of attention, nor do you require much social interaction and are quite content with keeping to yourself. However, when plugged into your element—your profession, cooking, dancing—whatever it is, when you are doing the thing that you do best, you come alive, to the point that others may see you as being a completely different person. It's attractive to see you doing what you like to do, because your abilities really do show themselves well.

You Are Calm Under Pressure

"Never let 'em see you sweat," really could be your mantra. Under pressure, you are as cool as a tall glass of lemonade on the Fourth of July. Situations such as tense negotiations or the last seconds of a sporting event don't faze you. You don't get frantic or crazy, you just do what you have to do, and it's so sexy to see it happen.

WHAT ABOUT YOU TURNS PEOPLE OFF?

You Tend to Be Too Accommodating

As a White, you have the tendency to accommodate what others want instead of saying no. As a consequence, you get overloaded with what other people expect of you and soon become overwhelmed or end up doing things that you do not enjoy. What happens is that you allow others to take control of the direction of your life instead of you driving toward the life that you and your partner desire.

Your Dislike of Conflict Blocks Honest Conversation

Whites do *not* enjoy conflict in the least. It is the opposite of what you crave through your core motive of peace. Rather than get into an argument with your partner, for example, you pretend that everything's okay. You would rather lie than tell your companion what you really think and risk the potential resulting conflict. So you don't say anything, until it bothers you so much that a month later it comes out. Let's be clear: dishonesty is not attractive, especially when a severe case of "lack-of-backbone-itis," lies at the heart of it, so don't go there.

You Are Notoriously Indecisive

It's great that you're easygoing. It really is. *But* your indecisiveness can drive your partner crazy, because he or she is usually stuck making all of the decisions with little or no feedback coming from you. Your partner will eventually get frustrated and feel like you really don't care about much at all, because you are always fine with doing things "either way." People want you to have an opinion and speak up.

You Are Not Emotional in Intimate Relationships

Many Whites have told me that they have a difficult time connecting what they're feeling to what they're saying or that they have difficulty interpreting their emotional responses to life situations. Since you are uncomfortable in the emotional arena, you simply avoid it. Your partner will at some point (especially if they are a Blue) grow tired of not being able to share an emotional bond with you and will pursue other interests.

Whites Can Be Hesitant to Engage Others Socially

Let's say your date takes you to a party to meet his or her friends and you just sit there all night listening to the conversation—because you really do enjoy doing that—but you never really jump in or sound terribly interested. Or, when someone asks you about yourself, you sell yourself short by saying something along the lines of not being too terribly interesting, just a normal person doing average things. This really doesn't look good for you (or for your date).

You Do Not Voice Your Opinions Well

This commonly happens for two reasons. One, you like to take time to formulate your thoughts completely before you speak, and once you get there, the conversation has moved on and you don't want to interrupt or bring it back to where you started thinking. Two, you know what you think, but you are afraid to say something that could cause conflict or tension. This is a shame, because your partner and others close to you know that you have such valuable feedback— often the clearest and most objective of all—but you don't offer it. This can be a real letdown to a mate or potential mate, because you fail to give one of the best gifts you can offer.

You Don't Communicate Well or Often

People want feedback, especially when they're in a relationship with you, and you often hesitate to offer it. When you do offer it, you tend to withhold important details. You like to live in your own thoughts and don't necessarily feel the need to share them with others. This is frustrating because it presents the message that you don't care enough to spend the time or effort to make the relationship work.

You Can Be Lazy

You can be very satisfied with what you have and the situations that you're in, so that you don't routinely put forth the effort to make things change or to improve the quality of your life. You may just take an "I'll-get-to-that-later" attitude toward the various tasks that need to be accomplished, and you may never get around to many of them at all. Nobody gets anywhere in life being lazy, and your partner knows that.

YELLOWS

What Makes YOU Hot?

- You make every moment magical.
- You are very charismatic, fun, and willing to make a fool of yourself.
- You have a great sense of adventure and willingness to try new things.
- You display wonderful high self-esteem and inclusion of others in life.
- You have a heart of gold and a forgiving nature.

What Makes YOU Not?

- You're so vain (thank you, Carly Simon) and yet undisciplined with life.
- You are so irresponsible and unreliable. (Remember, "Here today, gone to Maui!")

- You lack focus and refuse to commit to anyone or anything long-term.
- You honestly believe the sun revolves around you and your needs. (You can be *so* self-centered!)
- You show poor follow-through and general disorganization in life.

WHAT ATTRACTS PEOPLE TO YOU?

You Are Exciting to Be With

You are not a boring person. In fact, you are often the life of the party wherever you go and whatever you do. You always have something to talk about, and you are constantly getting yourself into unbelievably funny situations. Potential partners love this about you because they know that there will never be a dull moment in the relationship, and that they will never have to worry about a lack of entertainment.

You Have a Heart of Gold

One of the greatest gifts that you have to offer is your amazing heart. You tend to reserve it for those by whom you feel adored, but you give it freely when you find that special someone. Not only do you have a great heart, but you are also able to create romantic moments and memories. You are easy to fall in love with, just as you love easily and openly. Your partner will know that you would do anything for him or her, which is very endearing.

You Are Adventurous and Enjoy New Experiences

You have a sense of playful adventure that makes you want to go out and conquer the world and consequently, you often do. You love new people, new cultures, and new foods, you aren't afraid to risk, and you love having new experiences. The people you date like this about you, because you often open up their curiosity as well, and they feel energized by your passion for life.

You Are Forgiving of Your Partner

You don't hold grudges; you're more interested in getting over whatever wrong has been done, so you can both get on with life. That's not to say you're not tender or you do not hurt (because you definitely do), but you're willing to work things out and forgive mistakes because you don't like time wasted on hurt feelings. You don't like to dwell on things, and you're generally optimistic that things will work themselves out. Your partner will appreciate your lack of emotional baggage.

You Have a Great Sense of Humor

As a Yellow, you love to laugh and find life to be abundant with humorous situations and opportunities. You exploit such opportunities because you were born a comedian and love to make others laugh out loud. You also hate negatives and have the ability to turn crisis into comedy. Potential partners love this about you and love that you are always such entertaining company.

You Enjoy and Promote Physical Contact

Yellows like to touch. They hug and kiss friends and family, and comfortably promote an exciting physical relationship with their significant other. Your partner will never have to wonder how you feel about them because you can be very comfortable holding hands in public or even stealing a kiss or two.

You Like Yourself and Accept Others Easily

You have no problem at all with self-esteem. In fact, you love yourself just because you breathe. The great part is that you are also very inclusive and accepting of others. You like people in general, and are not afraid to engage them. What's so attractive about this is that you don't worry about what others think of you—you know you're delightful, so you don't shut people down or feel that you have to protect yourself against them because of insecurities that they may carry.

You Are Flashy and Charismatic

As a Yellow, you like to do things with flair. You like to dress nicely and look good. You emanate excitement and market your image well. You are also very charismatic and have the ability to make people like you almost instantly (you've never had to read books like *How to Win Friends and Influence People,* because you already do it naturally). Not only is the general public drawn to you, but so are potential partners. You always make a great and sexy first impression.

WHAT ABOUT YOU TURNS PEOPLE OFF?

You Are Irresponsible and Unreliable

You are here today, and then easily distracted and off to something totally different. You operate by the "better offer" principle, which means that you do not always follow through with plans that you make with your partner. You say, "I know that we were going to dinner tonight, but my friend just told me that he has an extra ticket to the U2 concert, so I'll call you tomorrow." What your partner heard was, "Something more exciting than going out with you came up, so I'll call you next time I'm bored." Save yourself some cell phone minutes and don't bother calling.

You Can Be Self-Centered and Inconsiderate of Your Partner's Needs

You tend to look out for "numero uno" far better than you look out for your partner. You think that the world revolves around your schedule and you can be very thoughtless of what others are doing or what their needs are. Your partner will grow tired of this very quickly, because in a committed relationship, he or she wants to be your first priority and not just Plan B.

You Have a Difficult Time Committing

Speaking of commitment, you need to realize that you frustrate people to no end with your inability to do it. I'm not talking only about committing to a potential mate, although if you are looking for love, you'd better wise up in this department. Others also find you difficult to work with because you always leave yourself an escape route or simply do not do what you say you will.

You Are Often Loud and Obnoxious

You are funny. I'll give you that. But here's a little tip that the rest of the world wants you to know: at some point, the joke is *over*. You can get caught up in the humor for too long and then people start to get annoyed with you, so get a clue and move on. Nobody wants to be known as the obnoxious guest's date. It's embarrassing.

You Interrupt Others Frequently and Excessively

You are a notorious interrupter. You freely give yourself license just to jump into a conversation and cut someone off. Usually you do this for a couple of reasons. You interrupt because you can be a poor listener (or you just don't care what the other person is talking about anyway), and you are oblivious to what's going on. You also interrupt because you feel that you are just so delightful and interesting that others won't mind, What you have to say is more important than what they are saying anyway, right? Wrong. You make others (and especially your partner) feel unimportant when you do this, so button it and wait your turn.

You Are Unwilling to Pay Your Dues

You have a bad habit of taking shortcuts through life. You take the easy route whenever you can and always have. Rather than work for something, such as a successful career, you fall victim to thinking that the grass is greener elsewhere and you jump ship. Consequently, you never put in the necessary energy to create a life that is as meaningful or abundant as you would like it to be, and you're always looking for the next best thing to come along and change things for you. Your partner isn't going to buy into this same way of thinking (if they're sharp, anyway), and may move on to find someone with a little more work ethic and a better sense of reality.

You Are Forgetful

You do not remember details very well at all, and you are usually too disorganized or undisciplined to write things down to remind yourself. You forget conversations that you've had with your partner or other minor little things such as birthdays or your anniversaries. This is not attractive at all because it sends the message that you don't care enough to remember.

You Expect Others to Pick Up the Pieces for You

You like people and they like you back. You know that you're charming. As a result, when you mess up or find yourself in a bind, someone comes along to rescue you, or you are let off the hook or out of obligations, because you're so delightful. Here's a little news flash for you: people get tired of doing this (especially significant others) and they will eventually see through your excuses. When they do, suddenly you're not so cute or delightful anymore, and you'll be on your own to pick up the pieces.

Part Three

❋❋❋

CONNECTING YOU
WITH EVERYONE ELSE

INTRODUCTION

Reds and Blues spend their lifetimes
trying to control others.
Whites and Yellows spend their lifetimes
refusing to be controlled.

UNDERSTANDING THE COLOR CONNECTIONS

The next three chapters will focus specifically on what each personality can expect when interacting with another personality. Personality plays a critical role in every aspect of our business and personal lives. **This year 85 percent of the employees who lose their jobs will lose them because of personality conflicts. Only 15 percent will lose their jobs because they lack technical expertise.**

Whenever a child is born, the parents and grandparents check for ten fingers and ten toes. They focus on the obvious physical qualities that will pale by comparison in importance to the innate core personality the child has. It may be a matter of only a few days or, in other cases, many years before the full impact of the personality of a newborn child or a recently hired employee is realized.

Equally intriguing will be the interaction between the newborn child or recently hired employee and the already existing personalities in the family or the company. Some are soothing, while others always stir the pot. Some are accommodating, while others seem to bring multiple agendas with them. Some arrive with a fairly healthy personality already in place, while others struggle an entire lifetime to make sense of themselves.

And how could anyone get married without first knowing the personality of the one with whom they plan to spend a lifetime? Initially, I considered printing on the front cover: "Don't marry anyone until you've read this book!" While any color can successfully marry any other color, *The People Code* will identify specific benefits and consequences of each and every union.

Similarly, the Hartman Personality and Character profiles are used by numerous businesses as tools for interviewing prospective employees and providing semiannual work reviews. Countless hours and dollars are wasted every year by neglecting to screen applicants properly, putting people in the wrong jobs, and failing to properly motivate and reward employees based on their personalities.

Employees see companies differently based on their personalities. I recently asked employees of a corporation to assess the temperature of their company. In reviewing their responses, the most significant factor in determining their answers was their personality color. Even when they gave the same responses on leadership, their reasons for the responses varied with their colors. A Red secretary said, "We have no procedures in place. I've even offered to write the procedure manual, but our president said I have more important things to do with my time, like he knows anyway." The Blue project manager said, "I thought I would feel more connected to upper management. They haven't even introduced me to the owner. How can I be loyal to a business where I am ignored?" The White accountant said, "Well, communication has been a problem in every company I've ever worked for." He went on to explain in very vague, nonthreatening language how it can be difficult to lead people with such opposing views. The Yellow sales representative said, "I think it's great how everyone tries here. We just need to appreciate what a great opportunity working at this company offers us."

If you interact with other people, personally or professionally, these next three chapters are for you. Study them to identify the natural connections and roadblocks you will most likely experience in the interaction of different personalities. In the end, the quality of your life comes down to the relationships you develop. Successful lives are always illustrated by successful relationships. Learn how to make your personality work for you in the various relationships you currently experience.

Chapter Eleven

CONNECTING
RED DOTS

*Red-Red relationships are typically
the most dynamic of all the color connections.*

RED-RED RELATIONSHIPS

"FIREWORKS"

RED RULES OF LIFE (AND THERE ARE ONLY TWO)

Rule 1: Reds are ALWAYS right.
Rule 2: If (and that's a huge "if") Reds are wrong, see Rule 1.

Red-Red relationships are typically the most dynamic of all the color connections. Both people are direct, decisive, and determined. They are such intense people that everything about their relationship is generally bold and high profile.

One close friend told me about her childhood with two very Red parents. Her father came home one evening from working in the fields and became so angry when dinner wasn't ready that he took the uncooked beans from the stove and threw them out in the backyard. This infuriated his wife, who quickly responded by taking his rifle from the kitchen and tossing it out by the beans. They took turns tossing things from the kitchen until it was almost empty and their backyard a cluttered mess. Then they both looked at each other, laughed, and went out to eat at a restaurant, leaving their children to fend for themselves.

This powerful combination can be highly productive. Reds are task-oriented and find little need to concentrate on intimacy or compassion toward each other. Both typically enjoy the leadership role, and because there is usually room for only one king of the jungle, they tend not to attract each other for long-term commitments. Reds are more likely to seek companions with a softer, more compassionate color. Healthy Red relationships often exist and flourish as friendships, in careers, or even between parents and children. However, Red-Red combinations are not generally well represented in marital relationships.

Mutual respect is the key element of a Red-Red relationship. Because of their intense strength, they must learn to respect one another. Respect affords a Red the opportunity to accept the other's point of view. When they value each other's perspectives, they are more likely to alter some of their decisions in order to share mutual dreams. Otherwise, Red-Red relationships merely reflect two separate people living their own lives with little evidence of a shared lifestyle.

When Reds refuse to share decision making or to accept each other's perceptions, they suffer an intolerable stalemate in their relationship. How do two people get anywhere when both of them are absolutely certain that they know the best way to get there, and neither will budge? This dilemma is not uncommon with two Reds in any given relationship. Most Red children are certain that *they* know a better way to raise children than their parents. They are right, and nothing the parent can say or do seems to convince them otherwise. Most Red parents are certain that *they* know the only way to raise children, and nothing the child can say or do seems to convince them otherwise.

Reds demand to control their own lives as well as the lives of anyone who will allow it (including other Reds). Because both Reds in any relationship want control, it often becomes a matter of who has greater power. Typically, Red parents have control over their Red children, and Red employers have an edge over Red employees. I was raised in a large family with a very powerful Red mother who clearly dominated our lives. In developing the color theory, I was initially unable to assess the personalities of my own brothers and sisters. My mother was so powerful that we *all* acquiesced to her. (In our later years, we nicknamed her the "Little General," referring to her dominant manner.) Her dominance so far exceeded the natural power of her children that I initially neglected to see any Red personalities among my brothers and sisters. They were dominated by a more powerful Red and unable to reflect their innate personalities until they left home and developed families of their own. Crossing a Red in his or her own territory is like trying to tell a New York cabdriver that he doesn't know how to drive. Good luck!!

Despite the typical domination of Red parents, society is replete with numerous examples of Red children who assert themselves with their Red parents. Relatively few of the Red youths I have known have survived the teenage years without vowing to leave home before they were eighteen. One Red sixteen-year-old client, Linda, was in direct conflict almost daily with her Red stepfather, Rick. She struggled to comply with his "unreasonable" curfews and numerous parental expectations in order to accommodate her White mother. Her dad's rules seemed impossible to accept. Earning her way in the world seemed far more appealing than continuing to subject herself to his control. She resisted any authority or control. She resented school, so she refused to study. She detested having to grow up.

One day I asked her, "Linda, since you are so unhappy, have you ever thought of leaving home and moving out on your own?" Her eyes seemed to pierce mine with the dullest and yet most defiant stare. Coldly, and convincingly, she said, "I have contemplated that a thousand times." By her tone of voice, I knew she wasn't exaggerating.

She ran away from home two weeks later. She preferred to sleep on a couch at a friend's, work for minimum wage, and put up with an employer's demands rather than prolong what seemed lifetime servitude to her Red stepfather. Note: She returned home within a month with a greater appreciation for her parents. However, she still struggles with parental leadership and authority.

Reds do not like or value anyone who dictates their destiny. Yet they are quite comfortable dictating the destiny of others. (Of course they are. If you had all the answers, wouldn't you feel compelled to design and dictate others' futures for them?) The price they pay for this power orientation and lack of mutual respect is high. Intimacy rarely flourishes with the constant battle cries of debate. Positive energy is often deflected to defend one's position. Sharing feelings becomes a secondary consideration because vulnerability is seen as unproductive in a defensive and combative atmosphere. When two Reds are certain that they are right, and refuse to respect one another, the result can be like the pounding of a jackhammer against cement.

HIGHLY MOTIVATED

Most relationships involving a Red revolve around the Red personality. Reds are so bold and dominant. When they feel strongly about having a family reunion, a family reunion is held whether others plan to attend or not. Two healthy Reds carry their own motivations within themselves. They push each other with strong expectations and become a highly organized front.

One Red parent and Red child were so motivated to work out their differences that they set a record in my office for short-term therapy.

Selfish as Reds tend to be, these two patients had one goal—to escape my office. I never saw two individuals learn diplomacy and acceptance more rapidly than this pair. Their motivation actually promoted good relations within the home until genuine attitudinal changes could follow and further ensure positive parent-child relations.

LACK OF EMOTIONAL BAGGAGE

Reds benefit greatly from how little emotional baggage they allow in their lives. Reds don't require many emotional support systems in order for them to perform well. They are thrilled to share a task with another Red because neither needs to remember to acknowledge the other with "warm fuzzies" and/or repeated statements of appreciation. "Just get it done and forget the feeling!" they shout.

In the early 1950s, a highly successful American Jewish businessman conducted a major business transaction with an individual in Germany. Both were very Red and highly competent in their fields. Upon entering the German's office, the Jewish businessman was stunned to see Fascist memorabilia depicting this man's obvious sympathy for Nazi Germany. World War II had only recently ended, and the fresh memories of the Nazis' brutal extermination of millions of Jews produced a terrible anger within the American Jewish businessman. He was actually sickened to be with this individual whom he instantly hated. However, business was business, and his purpose in being there was to conduct a business meeting. He pulled himself together and successfully completed their transaction, forgetting the painful memorabilia that initially had brought him tremendous personal trauma. Despite his continued anger, he successfully maintained a productive business relationship with this man.

Reds are rarely discouraged. They don't typically drain each other with emotional blackmail—e.g., "Either you spend time with me, or I won't go to your mother's house for dinner." They are generally independent and enjoy their self-sufficient natures. They don't expend a lot of energy trying to make the other feel loved. They are more concerned with productivity and accomplishment.

SHARED VALUES OF PRODUCTIVITY

Reds often push each other to be productive. They enjoy knowing each is highly responsible and will come through on whatever assignments they have agreed to complete. Reds enjoy a shared value of time. They are fast-paced and determined. They enjoy working together and accomplishing a great deal thanks to their strong task orientation.

One Red author was writing a book with a Blue friend. His Blue friend polished every page to perfection. The Red author was furious each week with his friend's lack of productivity. He completed all his sections of the book but was held up by his Blue friend, who was simply unable to produce. "I only regret not writing it by myself or with another Red," he said. He readily agreed that his Blue friend's writing was brilliant, but feared the book would never get published if his friend didn't cut the perfection stuff and just produce. Reds appreciate productivity and are likely to work best with those who share similar beliefs—even if what they produce together falls short of perfection.

PRODUCTIVE GOAL SETTING

One Red married couple was extremely successful in accomplishing goals. They were proud that they both loved goal setting and willingly gave it high priority in their relationship. The woman commented, "We go to Las Vegas or some fun place alone every six months and evaluate our successes and failures. Then we establish a new set of goals for the next six months. I can't tell you how exciting it is to lie in bed with your spouse and feel more challenged than you do with your business colleagues. I often feel like we are cooperatively competing with each other to see who can most creatively produce the most exciting and successful life."

EXTREME COMPETITION

While cooperative competition is highly productive, Red-Red relationships are equally susceptible to extreme competition, which produces negative interaction. This color combination probably travels farther and accomplishes more than most relationships. The question is the quality (rather than quantity) of their trips. Red-Red relationships most probably will arrive first at the top of the mountain. (They are highly task oriented and value completion of any activity.) However, while they are at the top of the mountain, the others may well be farther down the path enjoying a wildflower or an exquisite sunset the Reds missed in their hurry to complete the hike. Reds often arrive at life's end with few moments that really captured their hearts. More often their walls are lined with numerous trophies and conquests. They remind me of the couple who travel in Europe in order to come home and tell everyone where they went. The "going" appears to be less appealing than the "having been." They often live in the future with a sense of triumph for having completed a determined goal. Many Red parents comment on how pleased they are with how well their children turned out, while other personalities reminisce about moments they shared as a family in the growing years. Red-Red relationships often miss the pure enjoyment of the activity they are mutually engaged in, or, perhaps, they simply enjoy it differently from the way other personalities do.

Because of their competitive natures, Red-Red relationships seem to be more prone to obsessive-compulsive behavior than other personality combinations. One Red married couple reflects the common trend in the working world of Reds. They have put off having children for ten years in order to build a successful business. Their entire world revolves around their business. Their social engagements are always connected with helping the business. Evenings spent alone generally focus on business-related conversation. Reading material is typically work oriented. They are financially secure and yet have great difficulty slowing down because of their obsession with the business.

Overeating and dieting are common obsessions with Red couples, as well. Community or church work are noted commitments Reds make in life. They can become compulsive about completing tasks or promoting causes, and hardly notice whether other relationship intimacies (or lack thereof) even exist. Whatever the obsession or compulsion, Red-Red relationships are most assuredly productive. Reds will surge ahead whether the cause is worthy or not. As long as they feel gratified by the relationship, Reds will bulldoze through any obstacles to meet the needs of the relationship.

Competition can be very healthy, when done in the spirit of cooperation. It is difficult for two Reds to maintain a proper perspective on their competitiveness because they tend to see things in terms of winning or losing, with little gray area in between. Red-Red relationships prefer to win and dedicate themselves to that end, but if they must lose, they will often cause others to lose as well.

They are highly competitive and willingly pay whatever price is necessary in order to come out on top of any experience they deem valuable enough to pursue. This style of relationship necessitates a highly communicative interaction. Reds display a remarkable ability and willingness to confront one another. They are equally inclined to express hostility and aggression toward each other.

COMMUNICATION

Red companions tend to be highly critical of each other in a relationship. They are also prone to unite and mock others outside of the relationship. I remember one family with a set of Red twin boys who ridiculed each other mercilessly, and yet they could unite and turn on their parents or other siblings in a flash. They were often negative and dominated most family activities with their critical natures.

Reds generally come to relationships equipped with powerful verbal skills. They are quick with the tongue and can banter with the best of them. When you put two angry Reds together, it is similar to two speeding jets crashing in midair. No one ever truly wins. It is a loss for both. On numerous occasions, I have had to stand up and wave my hands during a therapy session with two Reds just to stop their verbal assaults. Some would spend the entire time attacking each other if there wasn't a referee. Neither wants to give the other one the satisfaction of "winning," so they keep at the same issues long after the issues should be laid to rest.

Reds do not usually listen well. Typically, Reds are very impatient listeners. When they do hear, they selectively hear only those parts of the conversation they agree with or accept. If Reds are not careful, they will set themselves up for living separate, rigid lives because they are unwilling to accept what others have to say. Reds are often poor listeners because they need to be right. They refuse to hear what others say if they perceive that it may force them to accept and admit their own mistakes or limitations and change their behavior.

This unwillingness to listen is demonstrated in the following example of a Red married couple. One night they were playing around and he began biting her (nibbling at first, harder later on). For five years she had repeatedly asked him to stop biting her. He refused to listen and repeatedly said that it was fun and playful. He never really believed she was serious.

This night he was biting her and it really hurt. She told him to stop and he simply laughed, ignoring her requests. She became so angry that she finally carried through on a threat she had been making for years and popped him in the mouth as hard as she could. He couldn't believe it. She couldn't either, but now there was no turning back for either of them. They went after each other physically until their three children were frantic with fear. Imagine the scene. The young children together tried to pull their parents apart. The husband yanked the phone from the wall so no one could call for help and continued to assault his wife and now the kids. Finally his wife forced him out of the house and locked the doors. He spent the night in his car and would hardly speak the next day when she finally let him back in the house.

For years she had asked that he stop biting her. For years he had refused to hear. When we discussed it in my office the following day, he could not see how his inability to listen had played a major role in the conflict. If he had simply heard her requests to stop biting, which had been made over a five-year period, this incident would never have taken place. Unfortunately, he could only see how *she* had over-reacted ("I didn't bite her *that* hard") and unfairly locked him out of his own house. Reds find it difficult to listen without trying to win conversations. They are notorious for wanting the last word rather than hearing the last feeling.

Reds can be very insensitive in conversation. They are more concerned with presenting perceived facts than generating kind feeling. I still laugh when I think back to a comment a Red mother made at a family gathering. Picture all five of her adult male children and their spouses seated at a dinner table. Grandchildren were running around outside. A beautiful dinner had been prepared, and the room was full of enthusiastic conversation. Toward the end of the dinner, the subject of one brother's depression came up. The Red mother boldly stated, "I don't understand what his problem is. I have five boys and they were all perfect when they left my home. I guess it all started in their marriages." The Red daughters-in-law were furious. The gauntlet had been thrown down, and simple discussion would not suffice. Needless to say, a most enjoyable family dinner was quickly, and rather abruptly, ended. Problem resolution and mutual understanding is rarely experienced in Red-Red relationships, because the conversations often lack intimacy. Neither listens nor accepts responsibility.

One of the most positive aspects of a Red-Red communication is their willingness to confront each other on almost all issues at any time. No tiptoeing or walking on eggshells is necessary here. Reds have little regard (and less respect) for dishonest diplomacy. If you have something to say in a relationship, Reds feel it should be said. If the other person has a problem with that, Reds feel the other person has the problem. Reds willingly take the initiative in confronting each other directly, and thus enjoy a rare strength in the communication process. I have often known two Reds to end up laughing at themselves following heated arguments that would have silenced other personalities for days. Remember the two who threw everything out of the kitchen? They have a refreshing ability to look at issues rather than always focus on the personal side of conflict.

LACK OF WARMTH

Warmth is not a word often used to describe Red-Red relationships. They are so intense, critical, and tactless that they do not exude or cultivate a lot of gentleness or provide much accommodation in their interpersonal relations. Most Reds have difficulty sharing positive feelings. Unfortunately, they have little difficulty sharing negative feelings. Of all the personalities, Reds are probably most comfortable with the feeling of anger. They express it often, along with many other critical and negative emotions. However, they are often slow to respond with positive, supportive comments.

ACTIVE

Reds are particularly active people. As a twosome they will generate a lot of energy and involvement. They often find they have to schedule with their two calendars to maintain good communication. Rather than assume a secondary position of support they both head off in whatever directions feel personally fulfilling. This requires a high degree of tolerance and constant feedback from one to the other. One Red couple lists every appointment on the chalkboard by the telephone. Unfortunately, when one feels her activity is more important for both to attend than their previously listed activity, she simply crosses out the first entry and displays her own. Imagine the interesting communication that promotes!

Red-Red relationships can have so many powerful characteristics (positive and negative) that it behooves all Reds to develop their assets and alter their liabilities. The positive values in many Red-Red relationships include mutual respect, high motivation, lack of emotional baggage, high productivity, effective goal setting, willingness to confront issues and each other, and strong activity orientation. The liabilities include lack of intimacy, power struggles focusing on "winning" and "being right," unwillingness to compromise, extreme competition, insensitive communication, and lack of warmth.

> No other combination of personalities
> must work as hard to be successfully compatible
> as Reds and Blues.

RED-BLUE RELATIONSHIPS

"BLOOD, SWEAT, AND TEARS"

No other combination of personalities must work as hard to be successfully compatible as Reds and Blues. Both want to be in control. They are equally strong and determined individuals. However, their motives, needs, wants, and behaviors are mostly opposite. Theirs is a difficult union, and yet the strong sense of commitment and loyalty they share substantially increases their chances for success. They each assume responsibility for various roles and must respect the other's leadership in his or her role.

OVERVIEW

Red Personality	Blue Personality
MOTIVE	
Power	Intimacy
NEEDS	
to be right	to be understood
to be respected	to be appreciated
to look good to others (technically)	to be good for self (morally)
approval of a limited few	general acceptance
WANTS	
challenging adventure	security
leadership	autonomy
to please self	to please others
to hide insecurities (tightly)	to reveal insecurities (openly)
BEHAVIOR STYLE	
highly complex	highly complex
high productivity	strong perfectionism
controlling of others	controlling of self and others
enjoys a high profile	prefers a low profile
welcomes change	prefers stability
logical (unemotional)	emotional (irrational)
insensitive	too sensitive
delegator	doer
manipulative	manipulative
impatient	impatient but long suffering
direct communication (with facts)	direct communication (with feelings)
innovative	creative
intense	intense

Red Personality	Blue Personality
demanding	demanding
unforgiving but moves on	unforgiving and resentful
confrontational	confrontational
strong verbal	strong nonverbal
possessive	possessive
tactless	tactful
rebellious	acquiescent
responsible	responsible
achiever	achiever
gives advice and expects	gives advice and expects
compliance	compliance
does not seek advice	seeks advice from
	knowledgeable people
intimidating	intimidating
critical of others	critical of self and others
arrogant	self-righteous
gives others guilt	gives others and self guilt
conflict-oriented if necessary	willing to deal with conflict
to get own way	for principles
proactive	pessimistic
poor listener	caring listener
difficult to share feelings with	complex and deep when
	sharing feelings
doesn't love easily but	loves deeply and is disappointed
strong commitment	by those who can't love
	(maintains strong commitment)
defies rules	complies with rules
lies to save face	lies to spare others
	embarrassment

RED-BLUE INTERPERSONAL RELATIONSHIPS
(In-depth Presentation)

POWER   *versus*   **INTIMACY**

The greatest struggle for Reds and Blues may well be based in their differing motives. Reds are motivated by power, and Blues are motivated by intimacy. Neither offers the other what he or she wants without first demanding that his or her own needs be met as well. The following conversation reflects their unique perspectives.

Red: Do what I say, and we'll get along just fine.
Blue: Tell me you appreciate me, and I'll walk to the ends of the earth for you.

Typical frustration between Blues and Reds involves perceptions of intimacy.

A national sales manager (Red) for a training company requests telephone calls from each of his thirty trainers to inform him about the results of seminars they conducted. Results to him mean numbers, referrals, and bottom line. One of his top trainers is Blue. Results to him mean successful life changes and connection with his audience, as well as the bottom line.

Prior to Blue's knowing the People Code, their weekly phone calls went like this: Blue trainer calls Red sales manager. Red sales manager is unavailable and prefers message to be left on his voice mail. Blue wants to talk about the seminar directly, so he leaves a message to call him back. Frustrated Red sales manager calls back *because he needs the numbers* that Blue trainer refused to divulge without sharing stories of people connections from the seminars. They play phone tag three times and finally connect. This dialogue follows:

Blue trainer: Had thirty-seven people at the seminar. Two people gave me referral cards for other companies to contact. But the best part was this guy who comes up to me afterward and tells me how the seminar has saved his job. He understands how to apply time-management principles better at home as well. He also wanted me to know—
Red sales manager: Thanks, Tom. I got the numbers and I gotta go!

Both hang up frustrated. The Red sales manager hates having to hear from Tom each week, but he's one of his top trainers. Tom is frustrated every time the sales manager stops him from sharing what really matters to him from the seminar.

After Tom learned the People Code, their dialogue went like this:

Blue trainer: (calls Red sales manager and gets voice mail) Hi. This is Tom. Had thirty-seven people in Dallas. Got two referrals and faxed them to Cindy for follow-up. 'Bye for now.

Red sales manager: (smiles listening to voice mail, transfers the numbers to his report, and calls Tom regularly to check on how he is doing because he wants him to feel connected since he's a top trainer.)

Note: Blue learned to speak Red's language. Red gets his numbers, and Blue doesn't take Red's lack of interest personally. Blue is currently entertaining offers at other companies where he feels more connection. Red offered increase in salary. Blue accepted more money and is still looking.

A Blue wife commenting on her Red husband:

He never really loved me. Twenty-five years ago we went on our honeymoon and ended up staying with his sister whom I had never even met. We slept on their living room couch. He would leave me with his sister while he went hunting and fishing with his buddies every day. One day I became physically ill with food poisoning and when he finally came home that night at 11 p.m., all he said was, "I heard you were sick. Are you better now?" He had a great honeymoon with his buddies, and at the time I thought maybe he needed that after all the hoopla with the wedding. I remember being down by the lake one day and watching a couple walking hand in hand. I wept for two hours over it. I've always built my world around him. He has never done the same for me.

One sixty-year-old Blue woman finally relinquished her struggle for intimacy with her Red husband and became a volunteer for Traveler's Aid at the airport. She realized that he was a wonderful man. She didn't want a divorce, so she redirected her needs for intimacy to other people. It isn't the same as receiving her husband's affection, but it is much healthier than continuing the battle for the intimacy he neither understands nor apparently values.

CHALLENGING ADVENTURE versus SECURITY

Red: C'mon, let's live a little. After all, we only go around once. We've made money before, and we can do it again. Nothing is going to happen and if it does, we'll figure out a solution. We always have before.

Blue: I don't feel good about making lots of changes right now. We should wait until things settle down before we try something else. You're so old. You can't start a new business at this late date. What will I do if you die and leave me with all these bills?

PLEASES SELF versus PLEASES OTHERS

Reds are basically selfish, while Blues enjoy being self-sacrificing. If a family were making banana splits, and there was a limited supply of ice cream, the Red would try to talk one of the others into having something else so he would get the banana split. The Blue would find something else to eat and give the full banana split portions to the others.

TO HIDE INSECURITIES versus TO REVEAL INSECURITIES
(tightly) (openly)

Red: You can't go around just trusting everyone you see. It doesn't matter how I feel anyway. What really matters is the issue at hand. Why do you always end up talking about feelings and garbage no one can do anything about anyway?

Blue: I just want to feel close to you. I need you to know how special and important you are to me. Can't we ever forget business and talk about us? We used to dream about our future together and feel close. I'm scared we won't make it in our marriage. I don't feel like a good parent anymore. And I know I haven't been a good spouse to you either.

Red: You are making mountains out of molehills. Of course I love you. Now let's stop talking about things we can't resolve. You knew who I was when you married me, so what's the big deal?

Blue: I just want to spend more time with you and get to know you better. I want you to know me and understand my feelings.

Blue husband concerning Red wife:

I have come to the conclusion that she either is totally void of feelings or totally insecure and afraid that whoever gets inside her head won't like her when they really find out who she is in there.

Red wife's inward thoughts:

Showing my feelings is a sign of weakness. I am not weak, and therefore I will never show any feelings. Besides, people might use them against me later on.

or

What is the big deal with feelings? You should know how I feel. I must love you. I married you, didn't I?

HIGH PRODUCTIVITY	versus	STRONG PERFECTIONISM

Red: If a job's worth doing, let's stop talking and get it done.
Blue: If a job's worth doing at all, it's worth doing right.

Reds want to complete the task, while Blues want the task to be completed perfectly. This is most frustrating in a Red-Blue relationship, because both people are highly committed to productivity, but they rarely agree on the quality of the finished product or the necessary schedules. Particularly noticeable times of conflict are packing for vacations, having friends over for dinner, or completing a project at work.

Red: (driven by productivity) I feel like my reputation is at stake for every deadline I miss.
Blue: (driven by perfectionism) I feel like my name is on every article of clothing I sew.

LOGICAL (unemotional) versus EMOTIONAL (irrational)

Dialogue between Red employer and Blue employee:

Red: Why you do what you do is totally unimportant to me. Just perform.
Blue: Why would I perform for someone who doesn't care about why I do what I do?
Red: How I feel about you has nothing to do with how well you should perform.
Blue: How you feel about me has everything to do with how well I perform.
Red: Look, just do your job well and everything will be fine.
Blue: Look, just appreciate me and tell me how well I'm doing my job and everything will be just fine.

One couple were distressed when the Red wife wouldn't intercede in arguments between the Blue father and Blue daughter. "If you loved me," he would say, "you would stand up for me. For no other reason than the fact that I'm the parent, you should defend me." The Red wife was furious that he would try to force her to referee between her two emotional "children." Reds quickly tire of others' emotional baggage and their need to be loved and told so all the time.

Blues usually feel emotionally betrayed by Reds. One Blue wife tearfully said after twenty-five years of marriage to a Red husband, "Last night I had the best evening of our entire marriage. . . . My eight-year-old daughter and I went out shopping and to the movies."

Reds typically feel traumatized by Blues taking everything personally. Reds appear insensitive (and often are), but they speak their minds directly and mean no harm with their directness.

"Just remember that if I fire you, your work is unacceptable. Otherwise, carry on and know I am pleased," says the Red employer. The Blue appreciates hearing daily about the quality of her work and the reassuring sense of security on the job. Reds tire quickly of all the emotional needs of Blues. The less the Blues get reassured, the greater their need for it becomes.

INSENSITIVE versus TOO SENSITIVE

An evening out:

Blue: Do you think what I'm wearing will be appropriate for the party tonight?

Red: Don't ask me again whether I like the dress you're wearing. It's fine. If I didn't like it, I'd ask you to wear something else.

Philosophical differences:

Blue: Life's a bitch and then you die.

Red: If you continue to bitch, you're going to die.

Twenty years later:

Blue: I was three months pregnant with our third child. I felt fat and ugly and you still forced me to have sex with you.

Red: This is ridiculous. That was twenty years ago. Are you still whining about that?

Blue: I've never forgiven you for forcing yourself on me when I felt so ugly and fat.

Red: Just because you were three months pregnant and felt ugly and fat didn't necessarily mean my sex drive ceased to exist.

IMPATIENT versus IMPATIENT BUT LONG SUFFERING

Blue parent to child:

I want you to clean your room right now. We are not going to live like pigs. I clean the house every day so we can have a nice environment, and you need to help too. It seems like nobody works around here but me, and I'm sick and tired of doing it all. If you can't get your room cleaned, then don't ask me to do anything for you.

Note: Other personalities call this the "Blue lecture." It usually lasts anywhere from five minutes to an hour, depending on the degree of the Blue's need to be understood.

Red parent to child:

If you expect to be breathing in five minutes, your room had better be clean.

INTENSE

Everything is a big deal in Red-Blue relationships. They care deeply and commit strongly to life. Neither is willing to take a backseat. Both have terrific concentration. Reds exude a more powerful verbal intensity, while Blues use a gritty nonverbal intensity. Reds are usually verbally dynamic, while Blues are nonverbally dynamic. Both personalities are intense and focused.

UNFORGIVING BUT MOVES ON	versus	UNFORGIVING AND RESENTFUL

Blues remember *everything* that ever happened in a relationship. They feel the same joy or anger that they felt twenty years before. They scar deeply and do not forgive easily. They withhold affection and genuine intimacy because of their resentment. In their hearts, Reds don't forgive any more than Blues. Intellectually, their heads simply help them move on and cope more efficiently with life. Speaking of her upcoming thirty-year-anniversary cruise to Alaska with her Red husband, one Blue wife resentfully remarked, "We never had a real honeymoon. So it's about time he showed me a good time. We'll have a great second honeymoon whether he likes it or not!"

POSSESSIVE

Both are prone to jealousy and control. Both love with strings attached. "What's in it for me?" is a common concern they share. Both need to know they are number one in the relationship. Reds are more possessive of things, while Blues are more possessive of people.

REBELLIOUS   versus   ACQUIESCENT

Driving in a car to work:

Blue: The speed limit is fifty-five miles per hour and that is precisely what I intend to go.

Red: Rules were made for people. People weren't made for rules!

Blue: People made the rules and people should follow the rules the people they elect make. Besides, it saves lives.

Red: *Your* driving will never save lives. I have an important meeting to get to on time.

Blue: If no one obeyed the law, think of the chaos we would have.

Red: If people would just use their brains and think a little when they drive we wouldn't need these ridiculous laws. I don't need them because I'm a thinking driver.

In a work setting:

I remember a working relationship I once shared with two men (one Red and one Blue). The Blue would constantly question whether our supervisor would approve the decision we were making, and the Red would constantly suggest we do it first and ask questions later. The Blue personality saw the Red as too rebellious, and the Red personality saw the Blue as too acquiescent. Together they were a terrific balance to the team. Blues tend to see the barbed wire on top of the fence. Reds see the holes underneath.

RESPONSIBLE

Both personalities are highly dependable. They take commitment seriously and act accordingly. Neither tolerates irresponsibility well. Both are highly principled. Reds are fiercely loyal to causes, while Blues are fiercely loyal to people.

ACHIEVER

Both are regarded as tremendous taskmasters. They work hard throughout their lives to succeed. Both give work a high priority. Play is always secondary to Reds and Blues. Reds often achieve best through others, and Blues achieve best through themselves. Both do best when allowed to operate within the limits they set for themselves. They are always stretching themselves professionally, but often for different reasons.

INTIMIDATING

Reds and Blues share the dubious honor of being perceived as intimidating. Each intimidates the other. Blues are so good at what they do that they intimidate Reds. Reds are so logical and verbal that they intimidate Blues. Both recognize their unique skill level and can be highly cooperative or terribly destructive. Choosing to win by intimidation is hardly a recommended style for successful relationships. Reds and Blues are often unaware of how they intimidate each other. Consequently, each blames the other for poor communication. Neither is particularly sympathetic to the other's personality. Both remain somewhat aloof and feel justified in their intimidating style.

CRITICAL OF OTHERS   versus   CRITICAL OF SELF AND OTHERS

When an issue arises, Reds will generally find the fault to lie with others, while Blues tend to look for the fault within themselves. Reds do a lot of introspection, but rarely in public. Blues are more willing to comment on their own inadequacies as well as on those of others. Both personalities are highly critical and blame oriented. Neither is comfortable with mistakes.

ARROGANT   versus   SELF-RIGHTEOUS

Both feel they are right. Both are quick to judge the other. Neither is quick to see his or her own shortcomings despite repeated remarks from others. Reds exude an arrogance that suggests that they know everything and are always right. Blues maintain a daily vigil of moral self-righteousness and piety, which tends to alienate Reds.

ACTIVE   versus   NEGATIVE

Deadlocked in disagreement for exasperating periods of time, Reds and Blues tend to see problems rather than solutions. Reds move more easily through the negative than Blues. However, in their movement, they often dump unnecessary negativity on those around them. Gloomy clouds are often noticeable in the Red-Blue companionship. Neither knows how to play well. They usually depend on others to bring out whatever sunshine life has to offer. However, both are also capable of strong productivity and action, which often pushes them through difficult impasses in the relationship.

DOESN'T LOVE	versus	LOVES DEEPLY AND
EASILY BUT		IS DISAPPOINTED BY
STRONG COMMITMENT		THOSE WHO CAN'T LOVE

(maintains strong commitment)

Reds are amazingly loyal to relationships (personal and professional). They appear to be so distant, and yet they are actually very committed to those they accept into their lives. Reds are not terribly demonstrative with others and often seem quite detached from the world in general. Actually, they can be the finest friends. They can be deeply devoted to their families as well.

Blues share the strong commitment the Reds feel for relationships. Blues love deeply and commit completely to their families, careers, or whatever they deem valuable. Blues are generally devoted to relationships, despite the pain or disappointments the relationships may bring. Reds and Blues value responsible and committed relationships. Regardless of the quality, Blues find terminating relationships very difficult to do.

MAKING THE MOST OF UNCOMPLEMENTARY OPPOSITES

Reds Need Blues:	Blues Need Reds:
To teach them compassion	To teach them honest feedback
To soften their communication	To teach them assertiveness
To point out details	To get the job done
To encourage them	To give them specific direction
To encourage their risk taking	To foster a sense of security
To plan the action	To execute the plan
To confront them directly	To understand them
To listen without taking comments personally	To appreciate them
To approve of their style and direction	To include them in plans
To trust them	To be trustworthy

POTENTIAL CONFLICTS OF UNCOMPLEMENTARY OPPOSITES

Reds	Blues
Power-oriented	Intimacy-oriented
Selfish	Selfless
Wants to look good	Wants to be good
Logical	Emotional

Insensitive	Compassionate
Productive	Creative
Tactless	Beats around the bush
Stubborn	Stubborn
Arrogant	Self-righteous
Direct and self-assured	Indirect and self-conscious

Reds and Whites operate from a logical axis,
while Blues and Yellows come from an emotional base.

Red-White relationships are
one of the most comfortable combinations
found among the personalities.

RED-WHITE RELATIONSHIPS

"FIRE AND ICE"

Red-White relationships are one of the most common combinations found among the personalities. They share many traits (e.g., power orientation, being self-serving, and needing respect). Interestingly, even their differences are often more complementary than distracting. For example, Reds like to lead and Whites enjoy following. The Red says, "Me Tarzan." The White replies, "Terrific. Jane sounds good to me!" The Red is impatient, and the White quite patient, which further encourages the relationship. They accommodate themselves to the other's innate limitations and enhance the other's natural strengths.

OVERVIEW

Red Personality	White Personality
MOTIVE	
Power	Peace
NEEDS	
to be right	to be left alone
to be respected	to be respected
to appear knowledgeable	to feel good within self
approval	acceptance

Red Personality	White Personality
WANTS	
challenging adventure	secure excitement
leadership	protection
to please self	to please self and others
to hide insecurities (tightly)	to withhold insecurities
BEHAVIOR STYLE	
change	stability
high profile	low profile
high complexity	low complexity
controlling	seeks neither control nor to be controlled
unemotional	feels deeply, finds expression of feelings difficult
logical	logical
direct communication (with facts)	direct communication (with facts)
delegator	doer
impatient	patient
demanding	nondemanding
tense	relaxed
possessive	nonpossessive (unless threatened)
confrontational	nonconfrontational
strongly verbal	strongly nonverbal
manipulative	subtly manipulative
can't love easily, but strong commitment	loves easily and strong commitment
high productivity	consistent producer
defiant of rules	compliant with rules
tactless	tactful
gives advice and expects compliance	gives advice only when asked
does not seek advice	accepts advice freely
intimidating	intimidated

Red Personality	White Personality
critical of others	tolerant of others
arrogant	feels inadequate
gives others guilt	feels a lot of guilt
unforgiving but moves on	releases but remembers
innovative	creative
negative	overwhelmed
obsessive-compulsive	dedicated only
	when interested
difficult to share feelings with	easy to talk to, hard to get
	feelings from
poor listener	excellent listener
blames others	blames self
insensitive	too sensitive
achiever	lazy
lies to save face	lies to avoid repercussion
rebellious	subversive

RED-WHITE INTERPERSONAL RELATIONSHIPS
(In-depth Presentation)

POWER   versus   **PEACE**

The different motives of these personalities are effectively illustrated in a scene between a Red wife and a White husband. She was furious with him one morning about a conversation they were having. She wanted to be right in the worst way, and he wouldn't accommodate her. She suddenly jumped up from her chair at the kitchen table where they were having cereal, picked up her bowl of Wheaties, and smashed it to the floor. In order to preserve whatever peace he could at this point, the husband began picking up the broken pieces and putting them into the trash can. Noticing that he was more interested in keeping peace than acquiescing to her superior intellect, she stormed back into the kitchen and poured milk all over the Wheaties on the floor. Then she ordered him to leave the kitchen until the milk and Wheaties had dried on the floor, making them far more difficult to clean up.

She laughed hysterically as she told the story. "Who eventually did clean up the mess?" I asked. "Well, he did, of course," she mocked. I still have visions of this fifty-five-year-old man stooping over a dried mess of cereal and milk and cleaning it up in order to facilitate peace. They both got what they wanted. She felt powerful and he was at peace.

TO BE RESPECTED

Reds and Whites seek respect in different ways. The Reds expect to be accommodated. The Whites expect to be left alone. Both enjoy distinct time frames and work styles, and continually seek methods of protecting their preferences. Because of their own diminished self-esteem, Whites are more vulnerable to feeling a lack of respect than Reds. Whites handle the way Reds show respect better than any other personalities do. They often take Reds with a grain of salt. One White husband told me, "I'm the boss around the house. My wife gave me permission to say that."

CHALLENGING ADVENTURE	versus	SECURE EXCITEMENT

Reds thrive on adventure. They love the opportunity to risk physical danger. My Red daughter constantly tries to handle faster and scarier rides at amusement parks. From an early age she experienced thrills from adventures. Whites also enjoy excitement but want the assurance of support systems and/or guidelines. Police officers tend to be primarily Red and White personalities. They thrive on the adventure and excitement offered by this occupation.

LEADERSHIP	versus	PROTECTION

Remember "Me Tarzan"; "Terrific. Jane sounds good to me"? Both are quite comfortable with the roles of leader and follower in a Red-White relationship. The problem comes if one or the other chooses to switch roles. It typically comes later in life, if at all. A committed couple or parent-child relationship could potentially experience great difficulty with the change.

One White woman let her Red husband give her a list of chores every day for fifteen years, until she decided enough was enough and started ripping up his lists. Despite her change, he couldn't break the habit of list making for six months.

Another individual let her Red husband make all the decisions. She would then quietly determine whether she liked the decisions he made or not. If he hadn't measured up to her standards (big enough house, enough money, successful enough friends), she became disappointed in him. She eventually was able to see how unfair it was to seek his financial protection and social leadership while casting all blame his direction when he performed beneath her standards.

CHANGE	versus	STABILITY

Red adolescents are constantly telling me they would rather be dead than live the boring lifestyle their parents live. Reds are more willing to risk than Whites are. Whites will risk but must first have both feet firmly on the ground. They are less certain of themselves and typically prefer the comforts of safe, familiar surroundings. Whites don't require the constant action Reds do. They offer a comfortable blend for each other.

HIGH PROFILE	versus	LOW PROFILE

Red: I've got things to do, places to go, and people to see.
White: What things, why so many places, and must we see all those people?

Whites make excellent traveling companions because they are perfectly contented to go along for the ride. They are easily entertained. They don't like to be onstage the way their Red friends do. Reds are more driven to see it all and experience everything before they're too old.

CONTROLLING	versus	SEEKS NEITHER CONTROL NOR TO BE CONTROLLED

A classic example of this difference can be found in the world political scene. On one side was Germany, representing the Red. They are a forceful nation with a history of invading other countries and controlling governmental policies throughout the world. Right next door to this powerful Red nation lay Switzerland, equally powerful yet a totally different nation that represents the Whites. The Swiss seek neither to control other nations nor to be controlled by them. They make life very difficult for any nation that tries to control them. They are a peace-loving land with a strong sense of pride. Germany is reflective of the Red personality, promoting its philosophies throughout the world with the obvious belief that they are right and what they believe should be espoused by all. Switzerland represents Whites who never start the war, but they are always quietly counting the money when it's over. So it goes with individual relationships as well.

LOGICAL

Both Reds and Whites have the capacity to be very logical. Both can be very shrewd. Reds are often locked into this mode of thinking, while Whites are capable of operating quite successfully on either an emotional or logical level. Their natural capacity to deal well with logic means Red-White relationships can enjoy hearty discussions on a broad number of topics. Strongly related to this is Reds' ability to communicate directly using facts, while Whites can do it using facts and feelings. They also make a good pair because the Reds stimulate the conversations and the Whites clarify and encourage a feeling tone in the conversations.

DELEGATOR   versus   DOER

Reds are most comfortable in a delegating role. They give orders well. They allow others to do the jobs once they have delegated them. They encourage individuality. Whites appreciate this freedom. Whites accomplish numerous things that others will never know about. They do not broadcast their activities the way Reds often do. They simply carry out assignments and go about following personal interests in a comfortable, casual way. Neither seems to mind the other's style. They respect their differences and appreciate that neither is receptive to changing for others, so why waste the time or energy trying?

IMPATIENT   versus   PATIENT

Whites quietly explain away a Red's temper. It is as if it isn't a big problem for them. They seem to take it in stride, the way a tourist at Yellowstone expects to see Old Faithful erupt on schedule. Though they are not pleased with it, Whites appear to be less concerned with Reds' impatience than other personalities are. Whites believe that everything comes to him who waits.

Reds get the job done. Whites quietly assume the role of friend and supporter. Sometimes Reds are unfairly criticized because of their impatient natures. One Blue woman told me how unfair she had been in judging her parents but couldn't resolve her preference for her (White) father over her (Red) mother. "Dad was so poorly equipped for life," she said. "He couldn't hold down a job, and when he finally landed one, he wouldn't leave on vacation for fear it would be gone when he returned. One summer, my mother simply packed us all in the car and took us to Yosemite for a two-week vacation. Despite her obvious concern for our well-being, I hated her then and I still don't enjoy her company today. It seems that she had no spirit or soul to her. It was all performance and obligation—tense performance at that. Somehow, my father taught me to dream and love and feel. When he died, I lost a very patient, understanding friend. I felt abandoned even though I was left in the very capable care of my mother."

DEMANDING   versus   NONDEMANDING

My favorite quote on Reds' perception of Whites' ability to assert themselves came from a powerful Red lawyer who was frustrated with his passive White wife who was trying to assert herself in their marriage. He was particularly upset one day and commented, "Living with her is like living with a person who has read a book on self-assertion with half the pages already ripped out." Reds initially find it difficult to contend with Whites when they become more demanding in the relationship. However, they quickly learn to appreciate the heightened interaction, and the relationship often improves with this change.

Reds are the most verbally demanding of the personalities. Whites are the least verbally demanding. Red parents have strong expectations of their children. Red employers have strong expectations of their employees. White children and employees are often the best equipped to deal with the strong demands of the Reds. Whites simply tend to accept the relationship as it is and don't demand much of the other person.

It is particularly frustrating for Reds that Whites often don't set goals in the relationship. Reds are so goal-oriented that they expect everyone else to be also. Whites are often comfortable floating through life, while Reds want predetermined action plans. Whites do not see the need to set goals, and rarely follow through as tenaciously as the Reds. This can be annoying to both personalities.

STRONGLY   versus   STRONGLY
VERBAL   NONVERBAL

It is great fun to watch the Red and White personalities in a power duel. Reds verbalize their position, while Whites express themselves nonverbally. In the long run, it is a toss-up as to who is actually stronger. It is often difficult to determine the winner. Most intriguing, however, are their *styles* of presentation. Remember the hunter and the hunted? Which one really gets the best of the other? While the chase is still on, it's hard to tell.

One loving White mother watched while her arrogant Red son ditched school, experimented with the drug scene, and ran away from home. She quietly asserted her position regarding his choices. He continued to verbally lash out at life and all those intimately connected with him. Eventually, he chose to turn away from the drug scene and reestablish himself at school and home. I asked him what changed his mind. He said, "Have you ever felt like you were running in a marathon and there was a guy right next to you, competing with you, but giving you constant moral support and always stopping to get you water from the sideline? No matter what I did, I couldn't shake her. She wore me out until I finally decided she knew a better way to run the race of life than I did."

DOES NOT   versus   ACCEPTS
SEEK ADVICE   ADVICE FREELY

Reds and Whites differ in their approach to advice. Reds do not often seek advice. Whites don't seek advice as much as they accept advice. Because of their quiet ways, Whites appear to be needing advice and protection. Generally speaking, Whites are far more inclined to be receptive to advice than Reds, especially when it is offered in kindness.

CRITICAL   versus   TOLERANT
OF OTHERS   OF OTHERS

Most Reds are judgmental, while their White companions innately find themselves highly tolerant. Very few things bring Whites to criticize, while Reds find numerous behaviors in others to be unacceptable. Reds often voice their disapproval, which drives others away and can make it difficult to develop an intimate relationship, while Whites invite others to share and willingly support differences of opinion.

One White patient was mortified when her Red boyfriend almost started a fistfight with a man who parked too close to his car. She was embarrassed by his public display of anger and felt his criticism was totally inappropriate. She even threatened to leave the car and walk home if he didn't just get in the car and drive away. He felt justified because the other guy had no business parking so close, and someone had to tell him. (Who better than a Red, right?) She felt it was just one more unnecessary confrontation that wouldn't have taken place without his constantly critical eye.

ARROGANT versus FEELS INADEQUATE

One White woman felt so inadequate and immoral (she had a child out of wedlock) that she married the first man she met who loved her and had a strong character. (She was hoping for his noble character to make up for her lack of morality. She was hoping his love for her would increase her love for herself.) She selfishly married this man and dutifully stayed with him for eighteen years, masking all her true feelings and never looking within herself to uncover the real hatred she felt for her "spineless, immoral self." We met in therapy after she had fallen in love with another man and had an affair, only to discover that she no longer could live with her husband because she didn't love him. (Naturally, she had *never* loved him. She had used him to make her feel better about herself.) She wasn't a "spineless, immoral person" at all. She was a wonderful, capable human being who had made some poor choices. Rather than see herself accurately, she found a husband who loved himself and her and would willingly cover all her inadequacies. Three children later, she woke up and saw herself for the wonderful person she truly was, and now the price for originally taking this easier route was a devastated husband, three frustrated children, betrayed extended family and friends—a much higher price than it would have been had she been able to raise her self-image and accept herself and her poor choices earlier.

Reds often distance themselves with their arrogance in this wonderful world of emotions. They often miss true friendship because they cannot be intimate with someone who is better or worse than they are. (Intimacy requires equality.) Arrogance is a shallow defense of a rich treasure that lies hidden in the heart of Reds. Either they discard this shallow, pitiful defense and let themselves know intimacy and vulnerability, or they remain a prisoner for life in their self-constructed cells. At times, I wonder if the passivity of White's patience and acceptance may be the most effective method for eventually enticing the Red's emotions to the surface.

GIVES OTHERS GUILT versus FEELS A LOT OF GUILT

He was one of the kindest men I had ever met in a therapeutic session. He looked so lost and forlorn. He began our session telling me about his precious daughter, Linda, who had repeatedly rattled her crib to get her way starting when she was a year old. She was Red—demanding all the time. Over the years, she rebelled against their standards, got into drugs, ditched school, slept around, and eventually ran away from home.

On one occasion, he and his (Red) teenage son got a call from Linda's therapist's office telling them to forcibly remove her from his office to a treatment center down the coast. They complied. She was furious, and in her rage spat in her (White) father's face as he restrained her in the backseat. He did nothing to retaliate. She turned to her (Red) brother on the other side and prepared to do the same to him. He calmly said, almost hoping to be defied, "Just try it, sweetheart, and you'll never be able to spit again." She was furious, so she turned back at her father and spat at him again.

I asked him why he'd allowed her to behave as she had. He told me he felt so guilty that he couldn't blame her for spitting. I asked him what he had done that made him feel so guilty, and he couldn't come up with anything. Still he felt guilty. She used this on him her whole life. She knew her Red brother wouldn't take it, so she gave it to her guilt-ridden White dad.

At one point she'd shared a bathroom with her brother. She smoked, and he told her never to do so in the bathroom. She ignored him and did anyway. One day he took her ashtray from the bathroom and spread all the ashes out on her sheets and remade the bed. She never smoked in their bathroom again. The father seemed pleased that his son could counter the daughter so effectively but was unable or unwilling to challenge her in the same way. Given the green light by her father, a most immature Linda continued to blame him for her messed-up life.

OBSESSIVE-COMPULSIVE	versus	DEDICATED ONLY WHEN INTERESTED

Reds usually become passionate about everything with which they connect. They resemble a young teenager who hooks up with every new fad that comes along. Whether it's food, sports, religion, or whatever, Reds are known to take extreme stands. It is hard to deter them. They can overeat with the same vigor with which they arise at 6:00 a.m. to hit a little white ball into holes on green grass. Whatever the obsession, they are compulsive about it. Whites are able to commit just as deeply, but feel very little compulsion to tenaciously follow through. They are, however, equally tenacious when they feel the dedication. Former tennis star Bjorn Borg, who appears to be a White personality, reigned as the king of tennis until he lost interest. He didn't even try to regain his desire. He simply quit. Reds are more inclined to reassert themselves and force the desire to accommodate the obsession.

POOR LISTENER   versus   EXCELLENT LISTENER

Reds generally prefer debates to casual conversation. Whites are most comfortable just hearing what others have to say. Reds are so certain they know everything that they don't often deem it necessary to pay full attention to details in conversation. They are more concerned with giving advice and getting results. Feelings are less important than facts. One (Red) father was more interested in the future problems his overweight (White) daughter would have "landing a husband" than in the feelings of low self-esteem her weight condition was causing.

People often seek out Whites for their patience and the gentle manner they use to discuss differences. They are willing to give the time that is necessary to fully understand another individual. Whites are truly interested in others' feelings and life situations. They like being included in others' lives, and freely give the time necessary to encourage warm, communicative relationships.

> Never "do unto others as you would have them do unto you"
> unless they're the same personality color as you.
> Always "do unto others as they would have you do unto them."
> Speak their language.

MAKING THE MOST OF COMPLEMENTARY OPPOSITES

Reds Need Whites:	Whites Need Reds:
To calm them in crisis	To motivate them
To listen to them	To inspire and encourage them
To bounce ideas off	To lead them
To feel safe with	To share risks with
To encourage compromise	To organize them
To delegate responsibility	To establish healthy boundaries
To balance them with perspective	To provide vision
To remind them about quality versus quantity	To keep them task-oriented
To communicate logically with	To set goals and objectives

POTENTIAL CONFLICTS OF COMPLEMENTARY OPPOSITES

Reds	Whites
Too demanding	Too accepting
Arrogant	Self-doubting
Bossy	Passive

Reds	Whites
Too opinionated	Uncommitted
Always right	Easily walked on
Verbally stubborn	Silently stubborn
Often promotes conflict	Promotes peace at all costs
Always telling	Always asking
Tactless and rude	Craves kindness
Workaholic	Lazy

RED-YELLOW RELATIONSHIPS

"FRIENDLY FIRE"

This combination of personalities is a vibrant one. Reds and Yellows enjoy verbal bantering and enjoy freedom from most of the emotional baggage and heavy sentiments experienced by other personalities. They are adventurous and energetic and often amaze and amuse friends with their zest for living and many accomplishments. They often struggle with the self-centeredness of the Yellow and the selfishness of the Red. The obvious commonality is their preference for looking out for number one—themselves.

They are both excited about change and find little need to be concerned with stability. This Red-Yellow combination is the most difficult to sustain among committed, married couples. Each must work to maintain a healthy perspective on the other. They have to mold the playfulness of the Yellow and the productivity of the Red. This personality combination reminds me of a white-water rafting trip—carefree yet productive, filled with adventure, excitement, and passion. However, the Yellow's lack of commitment and Red's demanding nature can prove difficult to combine unless the Red shows great heart and the Yellow develops a responsible nature. On a positive note, they seem to value themselves and feel a commitment to new experiences and challenges in life.

Without question this blend
has the greatest difficulty staying married.
When healthy, this blend suffers no emotional baggage
and experiences life to the max.

OVERVIEW

Red Personality	Yellow Personality

MOTIVE

Power	Fun

NEEDS

to be right	superficial connections
to be respected	to be praised
to look good to others	to look good to others
(academically)	(socially)
intellectual acknowledgment	social acceptance

WANTS

approval by a select few	approval by the masses
challenging adventure	playful adventure
leadership	freedom
to please self	to be noticed
to hide insecurities	to hide insecurities
(tightly)	(loosely)

BEHAVIOR STYLE

likes change	demands change
high profile	high profile
high complexity	low complexity
controlling	craves freedom
logical	emotional
direct communication	direct communication
(with facts)	(with facts and feelings)
delegator	delegator/performer
impatient	good-natured
demanding	obnoxious

Red Personality	Yellow Personality
intense	carefree
possessive	nonpossessive
confrontational	avoids confrontation
strongly verbal	strongly verbal
manipulative	seeks escape
can't love easily, but strong commitment	loves easily, but poor commitment
high productivity	scattered productivity
defiant of rules	defiant of rules
tactless	tactless (uses humor)
gives advice and expects compliance	gives advice, but unconcerned with compliance
does not seek advice	welcomes positive advice from others
intimidating	inviting
critical of others	accepting of others
arrogant	vain
gives others guilt	rarely gives or accepts guilt
unforgiving but moves on	forgiving
innovative	innovative
negative	positive
obsessive-compulsive	lacks discipline
difficult to share feelings with	easy to share feelings with
poor listener	poor listener
blames others	blames others
conflict-oriented	avoids conflict
lies to save face	lies to save face and not disappoint
expects a lot, unappreciative	low expectations, appreciative
consistent	inconsistent
determined	relaxed
focused	scattered

RED-YELLOW INTERPERSONAL RELATIONSHIPS
(In-depth Presentation)

POWER   versus   FUN

She knew he was powerful when she married him. He had enjoyed a most successful career in the oil business. He showered her with gifts and kept her heart spinning with numerous romantic intimacies. She was like sunshine in his life. Full of warmth, she radiated happiness and excitement. She represented everything he had bypassed for his hard-driving career. She felt he was more committed to her than he had ever been to his career, and she was right. However, she forgot just how committed he had always been, and still was, to himself. One day he invited her to take a leisurely drive in their convertible Rolls-Royce and enjoy a picnic on the beach. She was thrilled with this playful gesture. When he began driving in a different direction, she became somewhat suspicious. Before long, his selfish plan became more evident. They were headed for his mother's. This Red man despised his mother but felt obligated to visit her periodically, and did so only with his colorful Yellow wife, who could carry the conversation. He was still looking out for himself. The fun possibilities of the picnic were quickly discarded for the more selfish motive of satisfying his personal obligations of visiting his mother.

Yellows' disorganization often frustrates the Reds as much as Reds frustrate Yellows with their obsession with power. Taking charge of one's life is a cornerstone of personal power. Yellows usually fail to understand the importance of personal power and responsibility. Reds are adept at dissecting problems and making sense out of their lives. They are direct and enjoy having control over everything they do. Yellows infuriate Reds with their casual concern about financial matters, social obligations, and protocol. They are more interested in sharing time with fascinating people who laugh than with people who are in control of their lives. Reds enjoy control and find no personality more impossible to control than Yellows. Like a bird, Yellows simply take off and land when they feel like it. Reds often resent the frivolity and feel their all-important power threatened by the casual mockery Yellows frequently display for them.

TO BE RESPECTED   versus   TO BE PRAISED

Reds are far more concerned with being respected, while Yellows are typically willing to abdicate respect or power in favor of attention. Reds are always looking out for themselves, while Yellows are hoping *others* are looking out for them. The Reds want to produce the movie and earn the money, while the Yellows want to be on-screen and earn the audience's praise.

Reds don't often compliment others well. In fact, they are generally quite uncomfortable with giving and/or receiving compliments. Jobs needing to be done should be done with little fanfare, in a Red's estimation. Yellows couldn't disagree more. They give compliments easily and sincerely. They love to be acknowledged. Perhaps the greatest need Yellows have with regard to interpersonal relationships is that of being praised. They rarely receive it from their Red companions. Numerous unnecessary family arguments actually stem from Red parents neglecting to praise Yellow children. Red employers miss an easy incentive when they neglect to compliment Yellow employees.

Reds only demand respect. For them, respect is more important than praise. Reds ask to be seen as the experts, the leaders, the knowledgeable ones. They will return the favor tenfold. Reds and Yellows have very different needs. Each must learn much from the other if they are to appreciate each other's different styles.

TO LOOK GOOD TO OTHERS (academically)	versus	TO LOOK GOOD TO OTHERS (socially)

Both Reds and Yellows want to look good. Perhaps nothing allies them more than this motive of hiding their inadequacies in order to appear good on the surface. Reds and Yellows struggle with intimacy because they prefer not to risk themselves emotionally in relationships. Reds are more direct in their defensive posture of guarding their feelings. They are not coy or innocent in the refusal to share themselves. Yellows appear innocent and often invite others in with brash openness. However, they also resist true intimacy. Yellows remind me of deer in the forest. They are beautiful to see, but if you come too close they quickly disappear in the foliage that covers and protects them. Yellows instinctively focus the conversation on others. They often find it difficult to talk about their true feelings because they fear the judgment of others. Without a trained eye, people often fall right into the trap and spend an evening or even a lifetime with Yellows discussing intimacies but never actually being intimate at all.

Perhaps the element most lacking in this combination is emotional depth. Neither caters to the needs of others. Both struggle with intimacy. Together, Reds and Yellows have a most difficult time admitting their inadequacies. They must also work very diligently to overlook the other's inadequacies rather than remember them for later debate and teasing. Yellows are more likely to expose themselves, but neither risks freely at the truly intimate level. Both require patience and trust in order to free themselves of their most closely guarded secret—their insecurity.

APPROVAL

It is not surprising that both of the more verbal personalities seek approval, while the more passive personalities seek acceptance. Yellows and Reds seek approval for completely different reasons. Yellows seek approval to know they are socially desirable. They do not appear to value their own opinion as much as they do the opinion of others. Reds are typically impressed with the social skills of Yellows. Reds want approval for their intellectual prowess. They need to know that others approve of them academically. Yellows find it easy to approve of Reds' intellectual capacity. What they struggle with is the arrogant style Reds often use to present themselves.

CHALLENGING versus PLAYFUL
ADVENTURE ADVENTURE

No other personality combination can begin to compete with the adventurous spirit of a healthy Red-Yellow team. They are willing to forgo many of life's luxuries in order to travel the world, risk personal danger, and experience new opportunities. They are known to be constantly remodeling, going back to school, traveling, attending plays, and the like. They are terrifically spontaneous and active.

HIGH PROFILE

Red and Yellow personalities feel secure within themselves and open to new challenges and opportunities. They like visibility. They don't work behind the scenes of life but prefer to be onstage. Both enjoy people and often find themselves challenging each other for the spotlight. Reds succeed in maintaining their high profile through knowledge, hard work, and leadership skills. Yellows succeed in maintaining theirs through their innate love for people, charismatic style, and positive energy.

CONTROLLING versus CRAVES FREEDOM

Picture in your mind a determined Red mother racing after a runaway Yellow toddler who has escaped through the open front door. Reds want to control most people's destiny. Yellows want the right to determine their own destiny. Whenever Yellows feel their freedom is being challenged, they resist. Reds often frustrate themselves trying to channel a Yellow's zest for life. Both are benefited by the other's perceptions of how to live life. Reds offer responsibility. Yellows offer intrigue. They see their roles in relationships very differently. Successful blending requires an acceptance of the other's perspective.

UNEMOTIONAL versus EMOTIONAL

Yellows can live without the depth of emotional connection Blues require, but they are often stunned—unprepared for the limited expression Reds display. One Yellow husband shouted at his Red wife, "I would love to see you just once break down and show your real feelings. You are stoic. It's like getting water out of a stone. I give up! I really do! No human can be that *inhuman!*"

Reds are quite accepting of a Yellow's emotional display, even appreciating their emotional excitement. Upon retirement, one Red employee told his Yellow colleague, "Well, I do have to say this about you. You are definitely one of a kind. I have never met anyone as vivacious and emotionally charged as you seem to be about life."

LOGICAL

Perhaps the saving grace in Red-Yellow relationships from a Red's perspective is the Yellow's ability to reason. Reds are so capable with their reasoning power that they rely on the other person's ability to meet them on their turf. Yellows can do that. Both personalities are skilled at debating issues without necessarily resorting to emotional drama. They share strong verbal skills. Reds and Yellows enjoy the pleasure of boldly debating opposite points of view and remaining personally unscathed. Both are rather direct with their communication. Their relationship is unique in their mutual ability to reason.

DELEGATOR versus DELEGATOR/ PERFORMER

No personality delegates across the board the way Reds do. They are masterful in their ability to see the broad picture and select competent individuals to carry through on the details. Yellows share this ability to pass responsibilities on to others. They, too, are most comfortable with delegation, and trust that others will complete the job. Reds have the edge on vision, while Yellows have the edge on trust. Yellows do not struggle with control as Reds do. They entice others to follow their leadership.

In the long run, it is the Reds who generally remain committed and successful in the position of leadership. They are decisive leaders who willingly focus themselves on tasks. Yellows typically prefer to perform somewhere in the organization or on their own. Managing others can seem too demanding and unpleasant compared to hands-on work. For example, a Yellow university professor who became a department chairman suddenly quit after only two years because he missed being close to students and performing in the classroom. Preparing departmental agendas and fighting university policy held more frustration than reward for him.

DEMANDING   versus   OBNOXIOUS

Yellows are often poor judges of character. They tend to be more concerned about having a good time than the possible negative consequences of running with unhealthy friends. One Yellow sixteen-year-old was acting up and frustrating his dominant Red father so much that the father ultimately demanded that his son change. "Why don't you give up this crazy attitude of yours, and tell your friends you are a businessman now and all you care to worry about is business transactions?" he requested.

With all the diplomacy of a Yellow teenager, the son sarcastically replied, "Yeah, right, Dad! Now I'm a businessman. I only consider business transactions." Turning to me, as if I were one of his peers, he continued, "In the future it will be necessary for you to contact my social secretary to schedule any therapy sessions in order that we not conflict with business. This is necessary in order to prevent any further disappointments for the chairman of the board, my father."

The next evening, he got drunk and fell asleep in his friend's car. The following morning he had to run three miles to be on time to work as a busboy at his father's restaurant. The more demanding the father became, the more obnoxious the son grew. The more obnoxious the son grew, the more demanding the father became.

There is a happy ending to this story. Reds and Yellows share the common need to look good to others. Father and son were able to reach a compromise that enabled them both to save face in the community and with the boy's friends.

INTENSE   versus   CAREFREE

Reds seem to care about everything, while Yellows appear to care about nothing. Reds are very intense (obsessive-compulsive), while Yellows are carefree and often undisciplined. They represent opposing styles. Reds tenaciously attack problems and hang on until they have solutions. Yellows freely release problems, convinced that most things are never truly resolved anyway, so why get upset about something you can't control. Yellows often help others accept that Reds really are wonderful people who just get carried away with their convictions and forget the human element in life. Reds often move others (Yellows included) to action and create a sense of purpose.

Time and again we see how the people skills of the Yellow and the task skills of the Red, given mutual respect, can complement each other.

POSSESSIVE   versus   NONPOSSESSIVE

Reds are typically possessive about material goods and personal relationships. Yellows are the least possessive of the personalities. They love people and feel certain that they will be loved in return. Reds feel love is best displayed by responsible behavior and kept promises. They are typically unsure of others' love for them.

Sometimes the Yellows' lack of possessiveness is construed as a deficiency in caring. Those they encounter who have this perception may get hurt feelings. Yellows tend to feel, "If you love someone, set them free; if they come back, they're yours; if not, they never were." Reds often seem to believe, "If you love someone, demand that they love you back!"

Every color can blend successfully with every other color. However, there are certain "givens" each blend will experience and should accept up front.

MAKING THE MOST OF COMPLEMENTARY SIMILARITIES

Reds Need Yellows:	Yellows Need Reds:
To teach them charisma	To focus them
To converse with logically	To praise them
To accept their leadership	To notice them
To cheerlead for them	To risk with them
To broaden their myopic vision	To give them freedom
To socialize them and idolize them	To allow for their spontaneity
To understand their criticism is not meant personally	To keep them on task
	To accept their boundless energy

Reds Need Yellows:	Yellows Need Reds:
To teach them spontaneity and laughter	To be positive and say "I'm sorry"

POTENTIAL CONFLICTS OF COMPLEMENTARY SIMILARITIES

Reds	Yellows
Intense	Lighthearted
Workaholic	Playful
Rude	Insensitive
Hide intimate feelings	Hide intimate feelings
Have strong verbal argument skills	Have strong verbal argument skills
Seek power	Seek intimacy
Factual and profound	Superficial chatterboxes
Want to look good (intellectually)	Want to look good (socially)
Driven	Lack focused direction
Negative and critical	Positive and accepting

Chapter Twelve

PERFECT BLUE
GENES FIT

Of all the colorful blends
one finds in relationships,
Blue-Blue combinations run the deepest
emotionally and commit the longest.

BLUE-BLUE RELATIONSHIP

"CLOSE AND COMFORTABLE"

Of all the colorful blends one finds in relationships, Blue-Blue combinations run the deepest emotionally and commit the longest. Blues are intimacy-based, and two Blues have twice the commitment. Healthy Blues make the strongest commitment to their spouse in marriage. No other color marries itself as successfully as Blues. Blue-Blue marriages are also the most common same-color marriages.

In the workforce, Blues share perfectionistic tendencies and appreciate other Blues' dedication and commitment to quality work. Blues are loyal to people and respectful of authority. Blues trust Blues. They are reliable and conscientious. There is seldom any power struggle between Blues. The only exceptions to this come with unhealthy Blues who are fearful, hurt, and angry from previous encounters on the job. Bitter power plays and resentful comments often accompany these Blues. Typically, however, Blues focus on their own responsibilities and remain aloof from political maneuvering in the work setting.

This color combination usually enjoys warm, sharing, sensitive relationships. They share many responsible traits important to successful relationships. They are often seen as role models for building meaningful connections with people. Blue-Blue interaction is sincere and committed. They uniquely share the values of integrity and intimacy.

SHARED INTIMACY

Blues value each other. No other color combination comes by intimacy as naturally as Blue-Blue connections. When Blues are dating or married, they do not come to take the other for granted and start seeking personal hobbies that exclude their companion. On the contrary, Blues are more interested in discovering activities they can enjoy together.

Blues understand that intimacy is not just what goes on in the bedroom. They enjoy late-dinner conversations about shared concerns. They appreciate physical touching and romantic glances throughout the day. They sincerely care about loved ones' difficulties as well as triumphs. Blues understand the importance of remembering both special occasions and mundane ones. They are innately thoughtful and take time to demonstrate that they genuinely care.

Shared intimacy is their greatest strength. They feel the quality that comes from giving their relationship top priority. Blue-Blue combinations of all types (spouse, parent/child, siblings, colleagues, friends) value their relationship most, and experience a natural depth other personality combinations must work hard to understand and achieve.

NONCONFRONTATIONAL

A leadership team of a highly successful technical firm was composed of five members. Four members were strong introverted Blue personalities and one was extroverted Red with a big secondary Blue. The Yellow owner of the business was frustrated with their lack of expressed passion and interpersonal communication. Each member was hired as an expert for his or her own specialty and had no desire for team interaction. In fact, they nicknamed the owner the "social engineer" since they could not relate to the value of team building.

They didn't like being exposed or forced to confront one another. They wouldn't challenge another member of the team unless that person was absent. Rather than tell the Yellow owner they didn't want to work with him, some would show up late or not come at all. They resented the owner's positivism and felt he lacked a sense of reality for day-to-day operations, despite the fact that he formerly had run all operations himself. Their emotional immaturity sabotaged any direct interactions with one another that might have created conflict.

At the third meeting the Blue president of the team admitted it was his idea to have the owner come, because the team refused to work together. The predominant Blue group's defensive posture against the Yellow owner diminished significantly when they realized it was one of "their own" who had requested assistance. Creating synergy is difficult with a predominantly Blue team in the workplace. Like cats, they are territorial and prefer to do the work themselves.

LOYALTY

Blues are loyal to each other. They are loyal to law and order. They are loyal to commitments. They are loyal to society's expectations. This shared loyalty makes their relationships very secure. Blue-Blue combinations are loyal to the person in the marriage, family, career, or friendship—not merely loyal to the institution. For example, Blues commit to the happiness and personal development of their spouses rather than to the religious or social obligations that come with wedding vows and a marriage certificate. Blues care about the people in society. They don't just blindly accept and follow law and order or society's expectations. For example, Blues struggle morally with drunk drivers because Blues hurt for people whose lives are affected by people who drive under the influence of alcohol. Blue-Blue color combinations do remarkably well at keeping loyalty to each other in proper perspective and at consciously committing to making it the significant priority in their life.

STRONG COMMITMENT

Whatever Blues commit to will succeed. They are a powerful team and willingly give time and effort to accomplishing everything they value. Blue-Blue parents are often seen as too protective because they appear to overdo everything, from homework to curfew. By the time most kids become teenagers, they no longer suggest that their Blue parents simply overdo. They now refer to their behavior as overkill!

Blues are focused and vulnerable to becoming myopic if they focus on each other too much. One fourteen-year-old Yellow was exasperated with his Blue parents because they supported each other so completely that he felt unable even to present his case before they jointly overruled him. Piety and self-righteousness can also overwhelm genuine commitment, if a moralistic approach is pursued. Blue-Blue combinations must be very careful not to feed each other's shared drive to the extent that other colors feel neglected, judged, and/or abused.

On a positive note, Blue-Blue relationships experience a special sense of commitment to each other. Patrick Henry was one of America's more successful founding fathers. His wife became mentally ill at a time many believed he was about to become the next president of the United States. He forsook it all to remain at home and offer his mentally ill wife the security of a loving and devoted husband until she died. Providing dignity for this woman—who might easily have been abandoned by another in order to pursue his moment in life—was the only acceptable alternative to such a sincerely committed Blue character.

APPRECIATION

Who appreciates a painting more than another painter? Blues give so much to everything they do, that they are most appreciated (which Blues crave) by other Blues. You know the phrase "it takes one to know one." So it goes with Blues. They appreciate the quality in other Blues' work. They see the detail and recognize the time it takes to complete various work projects. They know the sacrifices Blues make to complete projects. They appreciate what few others even identify or understand.

PERFECTIONISM

Blue-Blue combinations do everything "above the call of duty." They believe a job worth doing is a job worth doing well. So how do other colors respond to a unified Blue combination? They often mock them as too perfectionistic and irritating when working on a project. However, Blues find other Blues' concern for detail very refreshing. They appreciate their commitment to quality. They usually value their opinion and expertise. Blue-Blue combinations can be found enjoying remodeling a house or taking classes together. They love to learn and improve themselves and their skills.

> *Of all the same-color relationships*
> *blends, this is the most natural.*
> *However, when one Blue gets down,*
> *the other Blue stabs himself*
> *so they can bleed together.*

CARING COMMUNICATIONS

Blues turn off the television and talk. They enjoy meaningful conversations with one another. They connect emotionally when they communicate. Blues take the time to really listen to each other. They have tremendous empathy for one another and show concern for the other's tragedies as well as triumphs. They are sensitive to each other's moods and will talk into the early-morning hours, if necessary, to understand the other's perspective.

PASSIONATE

Blues live for passion. They want to *feel* life rather than merely exist. Blues need to be involved in activities that count for something. They typically consider family and friends as most important. Unlike some personalities who claim to be very family-oriented and then spend their entire lives at the office or playing with friends, Blues typically spend their time and efforts where they claim their priorities lie.

Obligation is significant but less vital than feelings to Blues. The letter of the law is less appealing than the spirit of the law. Blue-Blue combinations provide each other with reason to be passionate. They care deeply and share intimately. They feel a personal sense of worth in simply being together. Their passion may come in the form of hobbies, career, family, friends, or religion. Blue-Blue combinations encourage passion within themselves by fostering a genuine concern for their partners throughout their lives.

OBEDIENT

Blues are the most obedient of all personalities. Blue-Blue relationships do not struggle as most others do with defiance or resentment of authority. They generally accept law and order as important and follow rules without much difficulty. Both feel strongly about moral obligations and appreciate each other's commitment to high standards and rules.

TRUST

Blues are typically suspicious and lack trust in relationships. Not so with the Blue-Blue color combination in committed personal relationships. Perhaps the reason they trust each other so easily is that neither person gives cause for the other to be suspicious. They usually share their feelings and communicate their goals, plans, and daily activities. Therefore, Blues trust each other and feel secure in the relationship.

DEPRESSION

Blues are not much help to each other when either is severely depressed. They don't have the necessary skills or attitude to demand change or cheer each other up. They typically wait out their companion's depression, which is often counterproductive. One Red once said, "Blues are simply a waste of time." He was referring to their long-suffering patience with each other.

PIOUS RIGIDITY

Blues can be very rigid. This deters their ability to be receptive to other people who see life differently or behave according to different standards. Blues can remain so aloof and smug in a relationship that they get out of touch with others around them. This rigidity limits both growth and intimacy with others outside the Blue-Blue connection.

INTENSITY

Blues are precise and determined in their lives. They approach every aspect of their lives with such intensity that both often experience burnout and distress. They feel so deeply for each other that they aren't much help in providing lighter moments of play or relaxation. Neither plays well or relaxes easily. It frequently becomes necessary for them to look outside of the relationship for a more healthy and proper perspective.

QUALITY

Blues are typically very concerned about the quality in their lives. They maintain high standards and expect the same from others. Blue-Blue relationships enjoy a level of quality few other combinations understand. Blues are generally willing to pay the price necessary for personal integrity. Blues often experience strong bonds of trust, sincerity, and intimacy. They pay attention to each other and see others' needs and concerns. I am reminded of my Blue daughter and her Blue uncle Bill who spent a day at Disneyland together. We were celebrating Uncle Bill's birthday, and after a full day at the amusement park, we sat down for pizza. On her own, my Blue daughter produced a special birthday card for her uncle Bill, complete with stickers she secretly bought at Disneyland. She noticed his need, and he appreciated her concern. They experienced a quality exchange. This awareness, combined with personal

---

integrity, offers Blue-Blue color combinations the possibility of experiencing quality relationships.

BLUE-WHITE RELATIONSHIPS

"GENTLE PERSUASION"

There is a saying that opposites attract. This is true for the most part in committed relationships (e.g., Reds with Whites and Blues with Yellows). The major exception to this rule of thumb lies in the common Blue-White relationships. Perhaps the reason for this combination is the mutual sensitivity and compassion they share.

Blues and Whites are both inclined to be concerned with feelings and are low-key in their approach to each other. Interestingly, my experience indicates that Blue women may become bored with White husbands, while Blue men remain appreciative of their White companions' accepting ways.

The major complaints Blues express in respect to Whites are that they lack initiative, are stubborn, and don't commit. Whites are more likely to complain that Blues are too controlling, emotional, and unforgiving. Blues comment positively on the peaceful nature, kindness, willingness to listen, tolerance, and patience of Whites. Whites appreciate Blues for their sincerity, leadership, tactful assertion, and loyalty.

The Blue-White relationship is an intriguing combination that willingly goes through life unnoticed. Healthy Blues are generally the spark plugs in these relationships, while charactered Whites offer strong support.

OVERVIEW

Blue Personality	White Personality
MOTIVE	
Intimacy	Peace
NEEDS	
to be understood	to be respected
to be appreciated	power and control of self
to be good for self (morally)	to feel good within self
acceptance	acceptance

PERFECT BLUE GENES FIT

Blue Personality	White Personality
WANTS	
security	secure excitement
autonomy	protection
to please others	to please self and others
to reveal insecurities (openly)	to hide insecurities
BEHAVIOR STYLE	
high complexity	low complexity
doer (prefers autonomy)	doer (prefers direction)
very controlling	refuses to be controlled
demanding	nondemanding
highly manipulative	subtly manipulative
stability	stability
emotional	logical
irrational (unrealistic expectations)	rational
too sensitive (verbally)	too sensitive (nonverbally)
achiever	balanced
intense	relaxed
impatient	patient
critical of self and others	tolerant of others
blames self and others	blames self
unforgiving and resentful	releases but remembers
negative	overwhelmed
asserts self when necessary	nonassertive
confrontational	craves peace
willing to deal with conflict on principle	avoids conflict
intimidating	intimidated

*Whites can be abusive in relationships
through their passive-aggressive nature.
Many spouses of Whites tell me,
"I'd divorce him but I have no obvious bruises.
I've just been ignored and bored to death."*

Blue Personality	White Personality
strongly verbal and nonverbal	strongly nonverbal
possessive	nonpossessive (unless threatened)
compliant with rules	compliant with rules
tactful	tactful
well-behaved	well-behaved
obliging	obliging
emotionally responsible	emotionally irresponsible
gives advice and expects compliance	gives advice only when asked
seeks advice from experts	accepts advice freely
lies to avoid hurting others	lies to avoid conflicts and repercussion
self-righteous	feels inadequate
feels a lot of guilt	holds guilt inside
caring listener	excellent listener
direct communicator (with feelings)	indirect communicator (with feelings)
complex and deep when sharing feelings	easy to talk to; hard to get feelings from
loves deeply and has strong commitment	loves easily and has strong commitment

BLUE-WHITE INTERPERSONAL RELATIONSHIPS
(In-depth Presentation)

INTIMACY   versus   **PEACE**

Blues generally make intimacy the most important component of every relationship. Whites place peace at the top of their list. Blues promote activities and opportunities that foster sharing. It is not uncommon for Blues to suggest taking tennis lessons *together,* walking on the beach *together,* or quiet conversation *together.* Whites appear receptive to the Blues' desires, if for no other reason than to keep the peace. Whites are equally content to pass the time alone or to go places with others. Their need for togetherness is typically met long before Blues' needs are satisfied. Generally, their desire to please others and get along is so important to Whites that they cooperate with their Blue companions.

Whites are capable of quietly sabotaging the intimacy needs of

Blues. One Blue woman was furious with her husband's unwillingness to talk much or share in decision making. In desperation, she finally shouted, "I feel like I'm just talking to the wallpaper. Actually, he's not even strong enough to be considered wallpaper. He's more like the stuff inside the wall."

Blues can nag and harass Whites until there is no peace. One White man who loved his fishing trips had finally grown tired of his Blue wife nagging him about his annual fishing trip with the boys. "I don't know why she can't realize," he said, "that after all her shouting is over, I am going to do exactly what I planned to do in the first place. If she would just stop wasting our time by delaying my plans, we would both be better off."

What makes a Blue-White relationship work is the Blue's willingness to accept a White's peaceful style, and the White's willingness to share intimately with a Blue.

TO BE GOOD   versus   TO FEEL GOOD
FOR SELF (morally)   WITHIN SELF

Blues and Whites both need to feel good inside, but for very different reasons. Blues are driven by a moral conscience, while Whites are more concerned with avoiding distress. Blues willingly take on an issue if a principle is involved. Whites are more inclined to ignore a problem, regardless of the principle, if they perceive that discomfort or distress could result from the confrontations. Blues often resent the lack of involvement and moral commitment of White companions. Whites tend to resent the persistent lecturing and moral demands of Blues.

SECURITY   versus   SECURE EXCITEMENT

"All I want is a solid million dollars in the bank, and then I'll be more willing to risk another relationship with a woman," one Blue patient said. He represents the strong need Blues have for security, whether financial, emotional, or physical. Whites are also inclined to seek security. However, they are more concerned with excitement than Blues. This additional twist entices them to pursue numerous risks that their Blue companions forgo. Whites are often very quiet about expressing their need for excitement but often seek situations that afford them opportunities for secure excitement. Blues are generally more comfortable in safe and familiar surroundings, such as the security of known friends and family.

AUTONOMY	versus	PROTECTION

"Do Whites ever say anything without being asked?" a Blue father inquired. "I can't believe how shallow our communication can be at times. I have to literally ask every possible question to get any answers. I would certainly appreciate a little cooperation, a little shared responsibility for the direction of our relationship."

Whites are basically followers. They go with the established direction of most conversations, peer situations, and decisions. Basically, they flow with life.

Whites generally accept being directed and protected by others. Their concern is *how* they are directed and protected. They are terribly resistant to demands or hostile control. Whites resent the *style* of direction much more than the direction itself.

Blues, on the other hand, accept direction out of obligation and other appropriate expectations of relationships and societal pressures, but they prefer autonomy. Blues are typically not good team players. They will not accommodate others the way Whites will. They do not want to lead anyone (including their White companions), which creates leadership problems for the personality combinations. Blues are mostly committed to doing a job right, while Whites are more concerned with simply getting along. Neither personality prefers to lead, although Blues end up doing so in the majority of Blue-White relationships.

TO REVEAL INSECURITIES (openly)	versus	TO REVEAL INSECURITIES

One of the reasons this color combination bonds so warmly is the vulnerability both Blues and Whites bring to the relationship. Throughout their lives, they share information and feelings, which promotes a closeness and trust few other combinations enjoy or understand. One man and woman were so successful in their ability to expose their inner selves to one another, they eventually fell in love because neither of them had ever achieved such openness in other relationships. Despite the fact that both tried dating others, the ability to trust was never the same. Eventually they married, with the foundation of their relationship built on open communication and trust.

Note: Unhealthy Whites are known to appear vulnerable, but they do not verbally share themselves. This presents a particularly frustrating dilemma for Blue companions who seek verbal sharing (including insecurities).

HIGH COMPLEXITY   versus   LOW COMPLEXITY

Typically Blues are perceived to be more difficult to understand. Actually, both have clear needs. The Blues need to be understood and appreciated. The Whites need to feel in control of themselves and be respected. Whites operate on a power base but seek peaceful, accepting relationships. Blues operate on an intimacy base but seek control and understanding. Relationships of Blues and Whites give validity to the saying "Still waters run deep."

DOER   versus   DOER
(prefers autonomy)   (prefers direction)

Whites usually get the job done. They are not particularly concerned with the schedule or exactness of their work. They do quality work and concern themselves mostly with fulfilling the agreement of the contract. They are steady workers who enjoy both doing the job themselves and delegating it to others. They can be lazy and/or overwhelmed when they accept too much work at one time, or they can lack enthusiasm for their endeavors if they have to deal with rigid supervisors or unfulfilling tasks.

Blues prefer doing the job themselves rather than delegating it to others. They love having skilled jobs that require their particular expertise. In fact, one may well find that the artisans of our society are most represented by Blues who enjoy the opportunity of creating and implementing their craft on their own. Therefore, they are more inclined to trust themselves, while Whites are better at delegating the responsibility to others.

CONTROLLING   versus   SEEKS NEITHER
(power play)   TO CONTROL NOR TO
BE CONTROLLED

Blues want to know everything that is going on in their companions' lives. Blue employers tend to be suspicious and keep their eyes on everyone's business. Blue parents are curious about all aspects of their child's life. One White young man, a senior in high school, telephoned his mother from work with a simple request for her advice as to the best brand of floor cleanser to use in mopping up the floor at his job. Watch how the Blue mother extends a simple question into an involved conversation:

White son: Mom, what kind of floor cleaner do we use at home?
Blue mother: Are you cleaning the floor?

White: Yes, Mom, now I have to go, but I just need the name of the best cleaner.
Blue: Is anyone else helping you mop the floor?
White: No! Carl is cleaning the food trays.
Blue: Who is Carl? I've never heard you mention him before.
White: Mother! Just tell me the name of a good floor cleaner!
Blue: There is no need to get upset. I was just wondering how you were doing.
White: I'm fine, Mom. Now could you just tell me the name of that floor cleaner, so I can get done and come home?

Regardless of their age or relationship, Blues tend to try to control Whites. One of my favorite examples comes in the form of a note one Blue thirteen-year-old girl left for her forty-two-year-old White mother, just prior to the girl's departure for a European vacation with her father.

Mom, 'bye! See you July 10th. I love you. Here's a list *I would like* you or Randy to do.
1. Take Rover (dog) for a run *at least* every day.
2. Feed her at night.
3. Feed the fish a couple times a week.
4. Please trim the trees in front and back yards.
Thanks. Please do these for me. Especially the first two because she'll tear up the yard if you don't. Thanks again. It would make me very happy. 'Bye. I love you.

Love, Michelle

P.S. Oh, and Mom, please don't dust the hallway floor. (Just kidding!)
P.P.S. I'll write, don't worry.

(Personally, I don't think her mother has any cause to worry. This thirteen-year-old will worry enough for them both, and then some.)

Another illuminating example of this control issue comes when a White dentist arrives home after a long day at the office. He is greeted with a warm kiss from his Blue interior designer wife, who has just taken a phone message and promised that her husband will call right back when he arrives home.

His initial response is "Thanks for the message. I'll call back in about half an hour." "Half an hour!" she replies. "I promised her you would call her immediately."

Three more times she hammers him while he tries to digest some of the evening paper. Finally, she threatens him, "Bill, either you call her right now or I'll just have to call her back and explain how you and I just don't see friendship and keeping promises the same way. After all, she is your friend and I did promise that you would call." Quietly, he hands her the phone, which infuriates her more. She calls and says, "Louise, I'm terrible sorry to have to call you, but I felt you should know I've given Bill your message and he will return it when he is good and ready." And he did. About half an hour later.

Both personalities are controlling, but Blues are more likely to try to control others, while Whites seek primarily to control only themselves.

EMOTIONAL	versus	EMOTIONAL AND LOGICAL

This represents a strong difference between the Blues and Whites. Blues thrive on emotional interaction. They focus on feelings (rational *and* irrational). Whites are able to work comfortably with both logical and emotional interaction. They focus on logical reasoning.

One couple (White wife, Blue husband) recently divorced and she remarked, "I could probably learn to love him again, but I can't take his excessive emotional behavior. Everything is emotional to him. I thought I had a problem our whole married life until I found out lots of people don't like to constantly deal with feelings. Actually, I was quite relieved to know I was just as normal as he was. I'm seeking a Red personality for my next relationship. I know how difficult they can be, but at least we can move from one issue to another without continually rehashing every negative thing I've ever done to him for the past twenty years."

IRRATIONAL (unrealistic expectations)	versus	IRRATIONAL (timid and fearful)

Blues want everyone to read their minds. They expect everyone to just *know* how they are feeling. They often say, "If I have to tell you, you don't really care." Unfortunately, that irrational thinking creates painful relationships for everyone involved with Blues. Typically, Whites feel guilty when they are unable to decipher the Blues' nonverbal clues as to how to behave and what questions are most appropriate to ask.

Blues fantasize a lot about how things *should* be, and then expect others to share the same fantasy and act accordingly. Whites come close to daydreaming the same way, but their fantasies generally pursue excitement and power rather than intimate relationships. Blues simply can't understand how anything would be as interesting or important to pursue as relationships. One White male said, "She expects me to read her mind because she spends every waking minute reading mine. She tiptoes around the house every morning getting ready for work because she knows *she* would appreciate the quiet. Who cares?! Certainly not me. I'm half deaf and never would have cared what kind of racket she made over the past ten years while she quietly moved in and out of the bedroom."

Whites behave irrationally out of fear. Whites often carry irrational ideas of others and what they are *certain* will happen if they confront someone or make a wrong decision. Some Whites become almost paralyzed and unable to take any risk because they somehow think they *know* what will happen. Healthy Whites readily acknowledge that they wasted many years being bashful or lonely because they perceived and projected problems that had not the least bit of rational justification. Some White mothers are scared to death they may physically abuse their children when no evidence or history of child abuse exists. White men often refuse to date because women will reject them, and yet they have never been rejected. It does become rather ridiculous to continue pursuing such irrational thinking, particularly when there is no historical or circumstantial evidence to support the perceived fear. Blue-White relationships must try not to encourage each other's irrational thinking.

ACHIEVER   versus   BALANCED

Blues are more inclined to stretch themselves in life toward increased productivity, while Whites are more content balancing their lives with work and play. One couple (Blue wife, White husband) found a successful solution with him sailing many weekends with friends while she corrected papers, designed lesson plans, and created new incentives for learning for her kindergarten class. She loved being well prepared for her students, and he loved developing his sailing expertise and friendships.

Blues are more determined to put whatever time and effort is required to be the best. Whites are more concerned with enjoying the total process of living, which includes a balanced support system of friends, family, self, and work. They are willing to sacrifice perfection and high achievement to have it all. However, they are vulnerable to pleasing others. On occasion, you find Whites working longer hours at the office in order to please the boss, until they are chastised by their spouses for not attending to home duties (children, the yard, or other household responsibilities). Then they frantically try to please their spouses, only to be once again drawn into longer hours on the job in order to meet the boss's demands. They are known to feel terribly torn between the components of their balanced lives and high frustration at being unable to satisfy anyone, including themselves.

Blues seem most content with their direction of high achievement. They value their choice of commitment enough to ignore outside influences on their priorities. One Blue woman returned from a slow-paced camping experience complaining about how bored she had been. "There was absolutely nothing to do. I finished my five books the first two days and looked blankly at the remaining five days with rather frustrated eyes. But my husband [White personality] and our daughter had the time of their lives hiking up trails and making new friends." She never suggested, or even seemed to consider, that her priorities might be somewhat limited to high achievement. She simply felt the environment wasn't conducive to her needs.

INTENSE	versus	RELAXED

"I know it isn't right, but I simply can't face my children another moment after we finally get dinner over with and the dishes washed. My [White] husband rescues me by always putting the children to bed. He reads them a story and says their prayers with them, and I sit quietly in my room listening to them ask Daddy why Mommy doesn't want to read the story, too. It kills me, but I really can't take them for one more minute." So goes the common complaint of involved Blue parents. They are so intense that they can easily overwhelm themselves with relationships and have to remove themselves for a while to gather their composure.

Whites seem to roll with life's twists and turns without often losing their perspective. Much of their success lies in their ability to exercise logical as well as emotional control. They are also less involved, and thus less intense, than their Blue companions. Blues appreciate Whites who get involved and share the burdens. When Whites take a more assertive position, Blues tend to calm down.

IMPATIENT	versus	PATIENT

Is it the perfectionism of the Blues that drives them to be so impatient? Is it their dominant personality? Blues tend to play the more patient role in Red-Blue relationships. However, in White-Blue relationships they generally are the more impatient of the two. They appear driven to assume the leadership role and to make things happen.

Whites are typically the most patient of all the personalities. "What difference will a few minutes make?" they say. Blues are usually prompt and expect the same of others. Whites do not give Father Time the power Blues do. They are not as concerned with punctuality. Whites are rarely irritated or distressed when family, colleagues, or friends arrive late. They see little value in getting all worked up over something you really can't change anyway.

| CRITICAL OF SELF AND OTHERS | versus | TOLERANT OF OTHERS |

Two friends were vacationing in Mexico when the White friend had her wallet stolen out of her purse while riding on a city bus. "I felt something tugging at my purse but never dreamed that someone would steal from me," she commented after learning that all their money and passports had been stolen. "We can replace the money, and I'm sure our passports will show up. After all, what would anyone want with them? Let's just drop by the American Embassy and explain our situation to the authorities. Everything will be fine." Her Blue friend remembered looking at her in utter amazement. "Vickie, we have just lost all our money and passports. We are in a country where the national pastime is *not* baseball and they don't speak English. We have no transportation, and we have *no* idea where the American Embassy is located. And you are telling me everything will be fine! Tell me, my friend, do you think it is possible that they took anything else with our money and identification like, for example, your mind?!" All criticism aside, they did locate the embassy, where they got help, and went on to have a delightful vacation. The Blue friend, however, remained terribly suspicious of all Mexicans for the rest of the trip, while the White friend repeatedly invited the local people to join them for dinner and teach them their cultural ways.

Blue parents tend to notice the one C on the report card, while the White parents compliment their children for attending class. Blue employees often notice their boss's lack of appreciation for all their hard work, while Whites accept that the boss deserves longer lunches because he is the boss. Generally speaking, Whites tolerate what Blues criticize.

| UNFORGIVING AND RESENTFUL | versus | FORGIVING BUT REMEMBERS |

For Blues, getting mad is usually not enough. They wait to get even. They will often hold the grudge as long as they feel the other person needs to be punished. One Blue wife came to see me at sixty-five years of age prepared to leave her White husband because she perceived him as "cruel and unattentive." She revealed that he had missed their daughter's sixteenth birthday *and* her high school graduation. He, of course, could neither remember attending nor missing either. The irony, however, was that the daughter saw her father as more loving and supportive than her mother, and held absolutely no resentment toward her father for anything. The Blue mother had made herself miserable for years over an issue that had been long forgotten by the principal parties involved.

Whites are willing to forgive, but only after they have avenged any wrongdoing. Because they tend to be quiet, slow-paced revenge can take a considerable amount of time. One young White swimmer was verbally thrashed by her Red coach in front of all the other girls at an important swim meet. She said nothing to her coach. She simply listened. The final event of the meet was her best stroke. The score was tied. She could win or lose the event for her team. She led the other swimmers all the way to the finish. With a comfortable lead and only yards from touching the wall for a win, she suddenly stopped and stood up, disqualifying herself in the event. Her Red coach was livid. She simply looked up at him with a contented smile, which seemed to say, "Gotcha!" After that, she continued to swim for the team. Neither held the grudge. The wrong had been righted, and all could now be forgiven and forgotten. Blue-White relationships are noted for holding resentments for longer than is healthy. They are also seen as most loving and genuine with their feeling once sincere forgiveness is sought (preferably on hands and knees!).

WILLING TO DEAL   versus   AVOIDS CONFLICT
WITH CONFLICT
ON PRINCIPLE

While it is true that Blues usually assume the leadership role in Blue-White relationships, they are not particularly interested in conflict. Blues are the moral guardians of society and will rise to the occasion when they feel an injustice has occurred. They are often highly principled people who will not tolerate wrong behavior. They will speak their minds and confront anyone when a situation flies in the face of truth and honesty. They are equally verbal when they feel they have been dealt with unjustly. Blues are known to act like cornered tigers, lashing out irrationally at someone they feel has perhaps erred in judgment or crossed them in some unforgivable way. In other words, when a Blue deems another's behavior to be unacceptable, verbal confrontation will generally take place.

Whites are less inclined to create a scene and stir up trouble for themselves. On one occasion, a White mother observed her young daughter being verbally abused by a cruel old man. At the time, she gave no indication that she was terribly disturbed. She did pull a face at the old man behind his back. She also brought the incident up to several other people two weeks later. However, she avoided conflict at the time of her displeasure. Whites do everyone a disservice with their unwillingness to respond.

In order to avoid conflict, Whites are notorious for saying "I don't care." One Blue woman remarked about her White husband, "I get so sick and tired of his 'I don't care' responses that it makes me furious whenever I hear it now. He really doesn't care whether the question concerns seeing a movie, going out to dinner, or even whether to get pregnant and have more children. All he ever says is, 'Whatever you would like to do is fine with me.'"

One day she was so frustrated with his answers that she asked him if they could blow their entire savings and go to Europe. As expected, he, half-listening, replied that he didn't care. She purchased the tickets the next day. They went to Europe, and now he appears to be somewhat more attentive and willing to express an opinion, regardless of the conflict it might create.

COMPLIANT . . . TACTFUL . . . WELL-BEHAVED . . . OBLIGING

Blues and Whites share all four of these traits. They appreciate and value each other for their willingness to extend the small courtesies and appropriate manners that Reds and Yellows struggle to understand or extend to others. These shared values help cement a warm and sincere relationship for Blue-White connections.

GIVES ADVICE AND EXPECTS COMPLIANCE	versus	GIVES ADVICE ONLY WHEN ASKED

Blues tend to make stronger disciplinarians than Whites. Blues feel they have a great deal to offer, and willingly share it with others. When they give advice, they expect others to follow it.

Whites are more inclined to allow others to set their own boundaries. They are not prone to follow up their advice in order to ensure its application. They do not often give suggestions without some prodding by those seeking their advice. They may think a problem through and never say anything unless others specifically request their advice.

FEEL A LOT OF GUILT

Another trait Blues and Whites share is guilt. Actually, I think they have a corner on the market. Both are uncomfortable seeing anyone hurting, regardless of the reason for the pain. Both blame themselves for their inappropriate behavior and hold on to past regrets too long. They are both capable of becoming immobilized if their guilt is particularly serious. I worked with a Blue-White couple who had been separated for years but unable to file divorce papers because they both felt so guilty about dissolving the marriage. Neither could act because of their feeling of obligation to the children and each other. Yet neither was willing to reengage the relationship because of the past emotional scars and dismal potential for future success.

| CARING LISTENER | versus | EXCELLENT LISTENER |

I think the major difference in the listening skills between Blues and Whites is their emotional attachment to the conversation. Both care about people, but Whites are more apt to hear the issues objectively, while Blues are instinctively drawn to the individual. Both are capable of giving their full attention to a discussion and responding with sincere concern for the individual and the content.

| COMPLEX AND DEEP WHEN SHARING FEELINGS | versus | EASY TO TALK TO; HARD TO GET FEELINGS FROM |

Blues' emotions run very deep. They are sincere and genuine when they share themselves with others. They are often insulted when others do not fully understand their complexity and concerns. They are typically left frustrated when there isn't time to finish a conversation. They are always concerned with the emotional content of the dialogue.

Whites are quite easy to talk to. They typically don't display much emotion. They prefer to sit quietly and listen to others. They are not likely to open up unless they are certain of the other's trustworthiness. They do not handle rejection well, and feel more comfortable holding their feelings inside. Many people find Whites desirable conversationalists because they would rather listen than talk. Blues and Whites are known for their sensitivity to others, and appreciate the increased warmth this specifically offers them in Blue-White relationships.

| LOVES DEEPLY AND HAS STRONG COMMITMENT | versus | LOVES EASILY AND HAS STRONG COMMITMENT |

Both Blues and Whites are capable of being highly committed. They value security and find committed relationships the most natural way to enjoy life. They are often traumatized by the breakup of relationships with each other, and neither recovers easily, regardless of who terminated the relationship.

Blues are inclined to feel a deep emotional commitment to people, while Whites find it easy to accept and love those they meet. Blues are known for the lifelong guarantees on their love. While scars may develop with the relationship, Blues tend to feel strong loyalty to those select few to whom they commit. This does not come easily to Blues, but once it does the reward is a deep caring that often lasts a lifetime.

Whites are tolerant and accepting of theirs. Whites commit quietly to relationships. They feel the closest to those Blues who are gentle and kind.

Blue-White relationships are generally characterized by sincerity, stability, and quiet persuasion. Both colors tend to accept each other and yet seek to promote positive changes in the relationship. Unlike most other combinations, Blue-White relationships tend to be gentle in their communication. They represent a most complementary sharing of similar values. They are also fortunate in having enough differences to broaden their capacity for successful enjoyment of each other and life itself.

MAKING THE MOST OF COMPLEMENTARY SIMILARITIES

Blues Need Whites:	Whites Need Blues:
To show them the good in others	To motivate them
To teach them relaxed attitudes	To be kind to them
To listen to them	To help them not to feel guilty
To respect them	To teach them creativity
To appreciate them	To encourage and believe in them
To calm their nerves	To direct them
To minimize their imperfections	To build their self-confidence
To carry out specific assignments	To nurture them
To be agreeable	To initiate activities
To be emotionally responsible	To accept them as they are

POTENTIAL CONFLICTS OF COMPLEMENTARY SIMILARITIES

Blues	Whites
Seek intimacy	Have difficulty expressing feelings

Blues	Whites
Committed	Uncommitted
Judgmental	Tolerant
Perfectionistic	Overwhelmed
Directed	Lazy
Passionate	Doubting
Detail conscious	Unaware
Crave oral communication	Comfortable with nonverbal communication
Unforgiving	Unforgiving
Irrational when angered	Uncommunicative when angered

Blue-Yellow relationships allow for the most intimate combination of different-color personalities.

BLUE-YELLOW RELATIONSHIPS

"HAND IN GLOVE"

Blue-Yellow relationships allow for the most intimate combination of different-color personalities. They represent the entire spectrum of emotions, and together they can experience explosive synergy. Blue-Yellow combinations are primarily concerned with quality relationships (genuine human connection). Blues most commonly represent the depth, sincerity, and compassion of intimacy, while Yellows display the excitement, warmth, and optimism of relationships.

Blues and Yellows tend to value each other but often experience difficulty accepting the other's vastly different perceptions of how life is best lived. For example, Blues believe that play comes after the work is done. Yellows regard work as necessary but play as far more valuable, and tend to give it first priority.

Blues are very steady, while Yellows are rather flighty. Blues prefer stability and Yellows seek change. Once again, the theory of "opposites attract" appears to work. They are as opposite as Red-White combinations, and yet they somehow feel strongly attracted. Perhaps each supplies what the other needs. Perhaps their differences afford them the opportunity to appreciate the other's strengths. Regardless of the reasons, Blues and Yellows frequently seek and enjoy each other's companionship. There is a strong bonding of the heart.

OVERVIEW

Blue Personality	Yellow Personality
MOTIVE	
Intimacy	Fun
NEEDS	
to be appreciated	superficial connections
to be understood	to be praised
to be good for self (morally)	to look good to others (socially)
acceptance	approval
WANTS	
security	playful adventure
autonomy	freedom
to please others	to please others/self
to reveal insecurities (openly)	to hide insecurities (loosely)
BEHAVIORAL STYLE	
high complexity	low complexity
emotional heavyweight	emotional lightweight
purposeful and serious	playful and lighthearted
strong perfectionism	scattered productivity
highly controlling	refuses to be controlled
responsible	irresponsible
attention to detail	what detail?
sincere	superficial
low profile	high profile
stability	change
suspicious	trusting/naive
conscientious	flighty
emotional	emotional
cynical	innocent/naive
too sensitive	insensitive
doer	delegator/performer
creative	innovative
intense	carefree

PERFECT BLUE GENES FIT

Blue Personality	Yellow Personality
impatient	good-natured
manipulative	seeks escape
demanding	obnoxious
direct communication (with feelings)	direct communication (with facts and feelings)
unforgiving of self	forgives self freely
willing to deal with conflict (based on principles)	avoids confrontation
strongly nonverbal	strongly verbal
possessive	nonpossessive
tactful	tactless (uses humor)
behaved	rebellious
gives advice and expects compliance	gives advice but unconcerned with compliance
seeks advice from knowledgeable people	welcomes advice from others
aloof	inviting
critical of self and others	accepting of self and others
self-righteous	unpretentious
feels a lot of guilt	rarely gives or accepts guilt
blames self	blames others
negative	positive
emotionally cluttered	simple
caring listener	poor listener
complex and deep when sharing feelings	easy to share feelings with
gives with strings attached	gives freely
loves deeply and has strong commitment	loves easily but without commitment
lies to avoid hurting others and when embarrassed	lies to save face

BLUE-YELLOW INTERPERSONAL RELATIONSHIPS
(In-depth Presentation)

INTIMACY	versus	FUN

Yellows lighten the hearts of Blues, and Blues enrich the hearts of Yellows. They make a passionate team. Whether they are parent-child, friend-friend, husband-wife, or employer-employee, this combination usually experiences positive bonds of playful creativity and committed caring.

Blues are motivated by intimacy. Yellows are motivated by fun but need intimacy. Yellows are more inclined to seek intimacy than Blues are to pursue fun. Blues typically place little value on playtime, preferring to focus on the more serious aspects of life.

No other personality seeks fun the way Yellows do. Yellows often live to play. When Yellows become pressured at work or at home, energizing hobbies or short vacations replace their haggard looks with youthful vigor. Always reward a good dog with a pat on the head and a deserving Yellow with a vacation. Yellows can't understand why anyone would commit to anything that didn't include fun. They are equally confused by people who don't know how to relax on vacations. Blues have to have a reason to relax and play, while for Yellows, relaxing and playing *is* the purpose.

Blues commit themselves most completely to activities that enrich the Blue-Yellow relationship. They will take swimming lessons if their Yellow companion likes to swim. They give priority to being together in the relationship and schedule their various activities around enhancing intimacy within the relationship. Blue parents typically attend their children's school, sports, and other social functions, regardless of the inconvenience. Blue teachers often empathize with a student who is struggling with assignments. Blue spouses plan business or community obligations around birthdays and other special holidays so they can share memorable celebrations with their families. Blues feel deeply and enjoy committing to intimate relationships, regardless of the numerous expectations or difficulties.

Yellows operate on a superficial level most of the time. They are capable of feeling deeply but prefer a more limited emotional connection on a daily basis. Yellows are often accused by Blues of not really caring because they appear so superficial. Equally frustrating for the Blues is the Yellows' perception that Blues are so controlling. Yellows often remark that the price of being loved by Blues is, at times, too high. When they find a mutually satisfying level emotionally, no other mixed

214

color combination can match their intimacy. They are funny, casual, sincere, accepting, endearing, and vibrant in their connection.

> *Blue-Yellow combinations*
> *are primarily concerned*
> *with quality relationships*
> *(genuine human connection).*

TO BE APPRECIATED   versus   TO BE PRAISED

When a Yellow wants to learn how to get along with a Blue, it's really quite simple. The first thing they must do every morning after they wake up is tell their Blue companion, "I love you and appreciate all you do for me." As long as Yellows are sincere, they will be on easy street for life. Blues thrive on emotional closeness and appreciation. They willingly forgo personal pleasure in order to meet needs of others. It means so much when others, however briefly, forgo personal pleasure to appreciate them. The theme for Blues could easily come from a song in *Camelot*. King Arthur suggests that the way "to handle a woman, is to love her, simply love her." Nothing could be more true for Blues, both men and women. They simply need to know you love and appreciate them in order for their lives to be complete.

Blues give at such a committed level that mere praise would generally not suffice. They are typically unimpressed by social acknowledgment, especially at a superficial level. Blues are more inclined to value a brief handwritten note of acknowledgment from someone who truly understands and appreciates their contribution.

On the other hand, Yellows typically throw things together at the last minute and come up smelling like roses. Appreciation isn't generally necessary for them. A congratulatory pat on the back and public acknowledgment (when appropriate) will sufficiently meet their needs.

TO BE GOOD   versus   TO LOOK GOOD
FOR SELF   TO OTHERS
(morally)   (socially)

Walt Disney's character Jiminy Cricket would call it a conscience. I call it character. Call it whatever you prefer, but in the end it means that Blues are more concerned with their moral obligations, while Yellows need social recognition. I remember consulting with a Blue patient directly after seeing a Yellow patient one day. Both patients had become drunk at their in-laws' twenty-fifth wedding anniversary celebrations. I was fascinated with how differently they approached their concern about their drunken behavior. The Blue patient needed to know if he should apologize for his drunken state. He was concerned that a proper son-in-law would have remained sober and helped host the party. The Yellow patient needed to know if I thought others in the family would think poorly of him. He was more concerned about tainting his social image with his in-laws than the inappropriateness of his behavior. The Blue suffered from moral guilt, while the Yellow suffered from social guilt.

Another illuminating example of the difference lies in the matter of weight control. Blues need to keep in shape so they will like the way they look, while Yellows need to look good for others. Yellows operate from personal vanity, while the Blues are primarily concerned with self-respect.

SECURITY versus PLAYFUL ADVENTURE

Blues are often envious of Yellows' self-esteem. Yellows carry this within themselves (often from birth). They do not seek validation from outside sources. They like themselves and usually feel confident that everything will work out in the end. This confidence allows them to seek adventure throughout their lives, while Blues continually grasp for the elusive feeling of security. Perhaps one reason Blues seek Yellows is the comfort they feel in connecting with someone who exudes confidence and security.

On the other hand, Yellows value the security they receive from Blues. Blues work very hard to offer security to those they love. Yellows intuitively sense the deep commitment that Blues offer, and generally strive to keep Blues in their life. Just prior to leaving on a business trip, a Blue woman discovered that her Yellow husband had worked out a business deal with his father behind her back. She could not tolerate his father. She threatened to leave her husband because she could no longer accept his interactions with his father. This carefree, lighthearted man was heartbroken. The thought of losing his wife became an obsession. He called her every night while she was away on business to the point of harassment. He wanted reassurance that she still loved him and would stay with him. Upon her arrival home at the airport, he met her with roses and a limousine. He read a poem he had written for her. Subconsciously, Yellows may seek Blues because they value security and know that of all the personalities, Blues are not only most likely to seek security, but to *offer* it as well.

Yellows love stretching themselves. They avidly pursue many facets of life. They are primarily interested in playful adventure and find extreme competition unappealing. Yellows risk freely. They will change jobs, residences, and friends more comfortably than Blues. They enjoy the thrill of trying something new and require constant challenges of a playful nature to hold their interest.

AUTONOMY   versus   FREEDOM

The words *autonomy* and *freedom* convey difference in purpose. Blues want autonomy to pursue a task. Yellows want freedom from completing a task as well as freedom to work on their own. In organizations Blues and Yellows find independent work situations very comfortable. Both Blues and Yellows prefer to be given their responsibilities and left to perform them in their own way and time. They accept direction but resist control. Blues enjoy the creative aspect of autonomy and thrive on the possibility of striving for perfection when no one else is able to force them to accept mediocrity. Yellows enjoy social interaction but prefer the freedom to work at their own pace without others setting deadlines and forcing unnecessary meetings. Both tend to find that teamwork often cramps their natural style.

EMOTIONAL   versus   EMOTIONAL
HEAVYWEIGHT   LIGHTWEIGHT

Blues tend to remain committed to the cause of intimacy regardless of emotional scarring, while Yellows are quick to seek refuge from personal disappointments. The animal kingdom offers us two role models. Blues are similar to the dog pursuing a rabbit. He is focused and determined. He is oblivious to any distractions. He tenaciously pursues his goal. Blues are predictably emotional and usually remain focused on the behavior throughout their life.

Yellows are like the butterfly, darting in and out with a look-and-see attitude. They never land anywhere too long and maintain a safe distance from other living beings. Beautiful, gentle, and exciting, they attract everyone's attention but generally make limited connections.

Blues are usually direct and consistent in their emotional intentions. Yellows are more vague and unpredictable. Both value sincere commitments, despite the differences in how they commit emotionally.

PURPOSEFUL AND SERIOUS	versus	PLAYFUL AND LIGHTHEARTED

Yellow: (to wife) Wouldn't it be fun to be in Paris this spring? Just think of how colorful and exciting it would be.

Blue: (to husband) I would love the romance of Paris in springtime. But I want to go when I know we are really in love. Just going to Europe for the sake of traveling doesn't excite me much.

Many Yellows could be nicknamed "the Yellow tease." They motion with one hand to come close and with the other hand to stay away. They seduce with their charm and innocence but are too easily frightened away. They shine like the sun and entice with their very existence, but quickly laugh it all off when the Blues in their lives become serious.

This is particularly frustrating for Blues, who rarely invest themselves lightly (particularly in relationships). They find the Yellows' casual attitude difficult to respect or depend on. Yellows are often baffled by the seriousness with which Blues approach relationships, and consider Blues to be too concerned and overzealous about their commitment. "All I wanted," Yellows explain while dating, "was to have some good, clean fun. The way Blues act, you'd think we were getting married or something."

STRONG PERFECTIONISM	versus	SCATTERED PRODUCTIVITY

Blues go through life noticing all details and maintaining a penetrating concentration. They willingly work out until they are practice-perfect. Blues value people who express the same commitment to perfection, regardless of their profession. They are often admired by others for their devotion to perfection. In relationships, however, this proves to be frustrating for both Blues and Yellows. Yellows become frustrated by the constant need Blues have to do everything perfectly. "Good enough" is exactly that for Yellows—good enough. For Blues, it usually means "settling for less."

Yellows are more inclined to like watching a player like Ilie Nastasie on the tennis courts. This lively Romanian player impressed tennis fans for years with his brilliant moments of tennis play and his equally brilliant childish antics on the courts, which he predictably displayed for the fans' amusement. He was clearly as interested in social approval as technical expertise.

This style of scattered productivity often proves terribly frustrating for Blues, who cannot understand how anyone, let alone this person they love (particularly spouse, child, or parent), can skate through life with little concern for accuracy and dedication to perfection. Blues need to understand that Yellows *will* be hostile and uncooperative, forsaking all their charismatic choices. Yellows, however, will generally balance playfulness with meaningful, productive moments.

CONTROLLING IN ORDER TO GET SECURITY   versus   SEEKS FREEDOM

Blue personalities tend to prefer a conventional, deliberate, and predictable relationship. They have such strong needs for stability that they try to hold everything together in order to feel peace of mind. Blues are so appropriate and exacting that they often elect themselves to be the leaders of Blue-Yellow relationships. Yellows instinctively resist control. They refuse to give control to Blues without a price. Depending on the character of either person, this price could be extremely high.

Blues often appear controlling because they need to feel secure in the relationship, and they think this security comes from always knowing what Yellows are doing and where they are going. Blues also appear controlling because they feel it is essential that they remind Yellows about proper manners and appropriate public behavior. This instruction is typically construed by Yellows as unnecessary and demanding.

Yellows enjoy flexible, changing, and unstructured relationships. They reject hard boundaries ("be home for dinner every night by six") and find little need for stability. Freedom is essential to Yellows if they are to experience life at its best. Yellows prize the freedom to choose whom they will be with, where they will go, and how they will get there. Easily manipulated, they are quite receptive to the Blues, who allow them to choose their own options in life. Admittedly, without healthy character, Yellows do abuse their freedom and may find themselves unable to commit to relationships, pursuing instead a more self-centered (as opposed to cooperative) life.

RESPONSIBLE   versus   IRRESPONSIBLE

"Just tell me if you hear of anyone putting on a production of *The Wizard of Oz*," one Blue mother lamented to me. "I have the perfect person to play the part of the brainless scarecrow—my son!" She was so frustrated with his irresponsible behavior. "Seriously," she continued, "it won't hurt my feelings. Just tell me straight out, is it possible that he will ever get a brain?" Her Yellow son was quite representative of many irresponsible Yellows. Yellows rarely stop and think before they speak or act.

Yellows are more vainly concerned with their physical appearance than the fact that their bedrooms are pigsties. Yellows are notorious for walking on expensive sweaters they may or may not have paid for with their own money. Yellow teenagers seem to epitomize the Yellow irresponsibility, because most teenagers are already that way during this exasperating transition from childhood to adulthood. Yellow babysitters are terrific at playing with the children but then prefer to talk on the telephone with friends rather than clean up the messes their good time with the kids left.

Yellows are more concerned with the speed with which they turn the corner than with the wear and tear on the car's tires. One Blue father was always concerned with the costs his Yellow son incurred. "From sheer negligence," he'd say, "you have cost me more than all your brothers and sisters combined." He always encouraged his son to get a good-paying job in order to be able to survive on his own.

Yellows don't give adequate consideration to the long-term consequences of their behavior. They do not typically take good care of their belongings because they think only of the moment. Blues usually resist loaning camping equipment, cars, and other important possessions to Yellows.

On the other hand, Blues make marvelous companions for Yellows. Like Wendy in *Peter Pan*, Blues constantly work to help Yellows grow up and be responsible. They notice details and constantly acquaint Yellows with reasons why details (like stop signs, high school diplomas, and clothes hangers) exist.

SINCERE   versus   INSINCERE

Blues pride themselves on their sincere and loyal commitment to Yellows. One Blue client, Tom, came in and demanded an explanation for how his best friend John (a Yellow) could leave for southern California for a brief summer vacation and then decide to *stay* in Albuquerque, New Mexico, for his coming senior year in high school. "We were best friends," Tom explained. "I don't think he realized how much I invested in our friendship. And now, on a whim, he just up and leaves me for the thrill of a new environment. If that is all I meant to him, we must not have had a great friendship at all." Tom was devastated to think his friend would consider abandoning him after all they had shared through three previous years of high school.

Tom and John had great times while they were together. Now John was prepared to experience something new. It had just come up as a fluke, and he was game for anything. "After all," Yellows explain, "you only live once." This seems so insincere to Blues, who willingly sacrifice the thrill of it all for their committed relationships. Yellows feel different. They give what they've got while they are in the situation, and then comfortably move on when it changes.

LOW PROFILE   versus   HIGH PROFILE

Picture this: Two people apply for positions with a touring theatrical company. One specifically requests a position designing and sewing costumes behind the scenes, while the other expresses a strong preference to be onstage. Which one is most likely Blue, and which one do you suspect to be Yellow? The odds have it that Blues prefer the behind-the-scenes details, while the Yellows enjoy onstage exposure. One enjoys working with things, while the other prefers people.

SUSPICIOUS   versus   TRUSTING/NAIVE

"My wife is better than the FBI," one Yellow husband explained. "She knows everything I've done wrong since the day we began dating. I would hate to see the Wanted poster she would design if I were a criminal."

"It's true," she agrees. "We just got home from a vacation in Mexico with another couple. One day, our husbands wanted to go fishing. My friend's husband threw his wife a kiss from a distance and told her to eat dinner without him because he wasn't certain what time they would return. I demanded to inspect the boat for seaworthiness and got my husband's life jacket (which I had purchased and packed knowing he might want to go boating). I didn't trust him, the boat, or myself. Can you imagine my husband dying in a boating accident and leaving me to raise two kids by myself?"

Many Blues go through life too suspicious of others. They are rarely free to really enjoy pleasurable moments because they are so busy worrying about what may go wrong.

As much as Blues suffer from their suspicious minds, Yellows may suffer from their nondiscriminating natures. Too often wonderful Yellows allow negative friends to enter their lives and color them ugly. They never believe people could have such negative motives. They naively attach themselves to inappropriate people because, as Yellows say, the people are "fun" or "they really are good people once you get to know them inside."

Yellow innocence causes concern in Blue parents who value their child's refreshing enthusiasm but fear the inevitable consequences of not taking precautions. One Blue mother even sent her Yellow daughter away to a private school in order to break up a budding romance with a negative boyfriend. "Call me controlling or whatever you want," she cried. "I couldn't bear to see this perfectly charming child turn sarcastic, cold, and hardened right before my eyes."

It was a great move. No deception. Right up front, the young girl knew the reasons and, being Yellow, quickly found the exciting possibilities in being away from home and venturing out into the world on her own. She went to the private school and quickly found herself responding positively to new friends and her changed environment and lifestyle.

TOO SENSITIVE   versus   INSENSITIVE

To Blues, everything is personal. They feel deeply responsible for whatever happens in their lives. Their extreme sensitivity can make them unpleasant to live with. If you arrive late, Blues may think you didn't really want to come. If you are angry, Blues typically feel guilty for possibly creating recent dilemmas in your life. Blues take many people and experiences too personally. With Yellows' carefree attitudes and flippant comments, Blues often struggle with Yellows' insensitivity. Blues tend to create many of their emotional traumas with their own hypersensitivity, but their difficulties often seem further complicated by Yellows' insensitivity.

One Blue woman was frightened about an upcoming river rafting expedition. She mistakenly asked two Yellow friends, who had been river rafting, if she would enjoy the experience. They flippantly reassured her, almost mocking her fear. She was furious when they wouldn't take her nervousness seriously. Her friends were insensitive. She was too sensitive. Perhaps nothing short of a violin serenade and a discussion of the need for increased life insurance would have made her happy. (And that probably would have depressed her.)

IMPATIENT   versus   GOOD-NATURED

Blue-Yellow relationships often find their behaviors in conflict. Blues want their families home every night for dinner, and Yellows want flexibility as to what time they will arrive home. Yellows want to be greeted with a smile and a kiss, while Blues want understanding for why they don't always present themselves with a smile at the exact moment Yellows decide to appear at the front door.

Blues struggle with the notion that they know what is best for everyone, especially Yellows. Yellows tend to forget time, people, commitments, and any other hassle that might complicate their lives. Children often adore Yellows for their casual style. This frustrates Blues, who are certain that the only reason Yellows are better loved is because they don't demand anything of anybody. Blues want things done right and done immediately. Yellows also want things done, but freely give allowances when unforeseen circumstances arise. (Unforeseen circumstances can be anything from a friend calling to play golf to a death in the family.) Yellows believe that most things aren't worth getting upset over and let them pass without giving them much thought. Blues notice everything (especially noisy children and late reports), and feel compelled to make everything an issue.

UNFORGIVING	versus	FORGIVING

This represents, perhaps, the best strength of Yellows and the greatest liability of Blues. Yellows do not generally dwell on the past. (They have a hard enough time remembering it, let alone dwelling on it.) Blues harbor tremendous anger, resentment, and bitterness over past negative encounters. They find it most difficult to let go of the feelings that Yellows rarely experience. If Yellows do feel deep anger or hostility, it seems to dissipate without much effort on their part. Their lives tend to be much less cluttered because of it.

One Blue patient told me how she had finally forgiven her ex-husband, who had left her for another woman. "I secretly hope someday to see him bald and fat with his stomach desperately hanging over his pants and underwear hanging out in back." With all sincerity, she then asked, "But don't you think I am finally forgiving him?"

Blues must learn to forgive, or they will frighten their Yellow companions away from any genuine sharing and intimacy. This, in turn, prevents Blues from experiencing their primary motivation in life—intimacy.

WILLING TO DEAL WITH CONFLICT ON PRINCIPLES	versus	AVOIDS CONFRONTATION

There are certain principles that Blues do not consider negotiable. They are willing to lay their reputations on the line for them. They will fight like a mother bear protecting a newborn cub rather than acquiesce in the name of peace. Blue spouses often find themselves angered by Yellows who won't engage in a good, wholesome argument. Blues feel that honest expressions of feelings show that one cares. Blues are more inclined to suffer a stressed relationship in order to make themselves clearly understood on important principles.

Yellows are more inclined to avoid the inevitable confrontation by laughing it off or quickly refocusing the conversation to a less controversial subject. Yellows are often seen as disloyal or "talking out of both sides of their mouths" because of their unwillingness to take a firm stand on issues. Yellows are, perhaps, too easily persuaded to abandon a particular philosophy or principle because it requires too much effort.

DISTANT	versus	INVITING

For many reasons, Blues are more intimidating than Yellows. Yellows have a winning way about them that invites people into their lives. "Everywhere I go, I meet the nicest people," one Yellow patient remarked. Life is much like a mirror, so Yellows seem to find invitations waiting for them wherever they go. Yellows warm up to people regardless of their age, race, or socioeconomic level.

Blues are more discriminating and judgmental. They are reserved and suspicious from a distance. They are most often loved only after a substantial period of time spent getting to know them. Blues feel "to *know* me is to love me." Yellows feel "to *love* me is to know me." Once Yellows feel invited into someone's heart, they willingly become vulnerable and expressive.

BLAMES SELF	versus	BLAMES OTHERS

Blues look inward to explain poor relationships, while Yellows, fearing the rejection created by owning up to their limitations, usually look elsewhere for places to put the blame. This often keeps Yellows from properly developing themselves. If they are not careful, Yellows can spend a lifetime explaining away their failures by placing responsibility elsewhere. Only when they can look within, and see the importance of responding to their limitations, will Yellows ever know the real power that comes from accepting responsibility for one's own actions.

One Yellow child repeatedly blamed his problems of school truancy, sexual-identity crisis, and auto theft on his controlling and demanding Blue father. He actually seemed to enjoy watching his poor father agonize over what he had done to his son, and how he should have done things differently. It took this Yellow child four years of frustration and personal disappointment before he began to see his part in the relationship. Eventually, he claimed some responsibility and began developing more appropriate living skills.

| NEGATIVE | versus | POSITIVE |

Blues seem to zero in on why something can't be done, while Yellows immediately see the reasons why it ought to be tried. Blues ask, "Why not me? I think I'd be the perfect choice!" Blues tend to see all the problems, while Yellows typically see all the possibilities.

| CARING LISTENER | versus | POOR LISTENER |

Yellows are usually out for a good time, and that rarely includes sincere listening. They are not interested in emotional details, and often find it quite boring to sit and share the serious concerns of others. Blues enjoy the idea of deep conversation, and genuinely care about what the other person is trying to say. They are excellent at really listening rather than concentrating on what *their* comments will be.

Blues can be very disappointed in Yellows' superficial style of listening. They may even feel betrayed when Yellows hear only their words and neglect to focus on their feelings.

Yellows are typically frustrated with the storytelling of Blues. Blues tend to overkill their communication by relating every detail several times. You've heard, no doubt, the phrase "to make a long story short"; Blues prefer the other version, "to make a short story longer." Blues want to be understood and tend to keep talking in the superstitious hope that eventually they will be.

| GIVES WITH | versus | GIVES FREELY |
| STRINGS ATTACHED | | |

Blues are more inclined to give of themselves than Yellows are. However, when Yellows give, they give freely without expectation, while Blues often have strings attached. Many Blue personalities become angered at the shabby way they are treated after bending over backward for others. Numerous individuals have shared resentments with me about guests who have stayed with them and been treated like kings and queens without giving back even a word of appreciation. Yellows rarely feel the same depth of disappointment. Either they simply give less, or when they do give, Yellows don't attach any expectations to the gift.

LOVES DEEPLY AND HAS STRONG COMMITMENT	versus	LOVES EASILY BUT WITHOUT COMMITMENT

Blues have a strong loyalty to whomever and whatever they commit to. They are most comfortable in committed relationships and feel great apprehension about abandoning any commitments they make. One Blue colleague of mine experienced deep emotional turmoil while trying to decide whether to stay with her husband, who offered her good fun but no emotional depth, or to leave her marriage for a man she had loved deeply as a friend for years. In the end, there was no real decision. She loved her husband and could never leave him, regardless of the empty moments she endured.

In contrast, I remember heading for the ski slopes one time with a Yellow friend. He reminded me a great deal of Peter Pan, with his incessant acts of irresponsibility and his refusal to accept society's demands that he grow up. He claimed that he felt too restricted, confined, and committed in marriage. He wanted to play more than he wanted the responsibility of a wife and the children he had fathered.

Within a year of our conversation, my friend had abandoned his wife and two children for a more playful life. Yellows tend to be more vulnerable in the long run, because they lack the depth of commitment required to experience earned intimacy.

This exciting combination of opposites offers the possibilities that neither personality could experience on their own. They share a mutual admiration. Yellows prize Blues for their talent, creativity, sensitivity, loyalty, commitment, sincerity, and intimacy. Blues value Yellows for their vigor, optimism, acceptance, forgiveness, spice, candor, and intimacy. Both relish the Blue-Yellow relationships' strong intimate potential, and usually recognize the unique synergy afforded them together.

MAKING THE MOST OF COMPLEMENTARY OPPOSITES

Blues Need Yellows:	Yellows Need Blues:
To keep a healthy "here and now" perspective	To give grounding and direction
To promote creative, playful moments	To teach compassion and sensitivity
To foster optimism and hope	To notice details and specifics
To cherish and appreciate them	To provide stability

PERFECT BLUE GENES FIT

Blues Need Yellows:	Yellows Need Blues:
To remind them of their intrinsic value	To encourage them to complete tasks
To make them laugh	To remember important events and facts
To show them the lighter side of life	To laugh at them
To keep conversations flowing	To praise and notice them
To facilitate social relationships	To provide moral leadership
To share intimate moments	

POTENTIAL CONFLICTS OF COMPLEMENTARY OPPOSITES

Blues	Yellows
Very committed	Often flighty
Too sensitive	Often sarcastic
Generally work-oriented	Prefers playful activity
Controlling	Obsessed with freedom
Detail-oriented	Lackadaisical
Serious	Lighthearted and carefree
Takes on too many responsibilities	Irresponsible
Acts appropriately and properly	Often inappropriate and ill-mannered
Too selfless	Self-obsessed
Requires long deliberation in decision making	Makes decisions spontaneously

Chapter Thirteen

WHITE BLENDS AND YELLOW HIGHLIGHTS

White-White combinations are
very tolerant of each other
and the world around them.

WHITE-WHITE RELATIONSHIPS

"PEACE AND TOLERANCE"

White-White relationships are readily identifiable by their peaceful-ness. White-White combinations are relaxed and patient. They do not expend excess energy on trivial power struggles or concern with details. This combination tolerates differences. They are both more comfortable ignoring irritating behavior than making it an issue. Therefore, what often creates serious conflict for other personality combinations hardly affects the White-White connection.

Whites are not usually drawn to leadership. White-White combina-tions struggle without clearly defined leadership roles. Both typically wait for the other to take the lead. Whites are comfortable living as relaxed and unstructured companions. Neither is driven to plan or create strong goals for the future. Neither is upset if one decides to plan something or commit the other to a future goal.

White-White combinations are very tolerant of each other and the world around them. They are very flexible and accommodating. They allow for each other's independent preferences (personal hobbies or work schedules) and dependence (they listen to each other's con-cerns for hours). This personality combination understands the impor-tance of having a safe port in the storm of life and offers that gift to friends, family, or colleagues.

Though White-White color combinations are not common in marital relationships, they make for very agreeable friendships. Marriage poses leadership-role concerns; friendship does not. As long as the relationship is well structured and firmly established, this combination has little difficulty operating successfully. The two elements this combination primarily struggles with are *motivation* and *leadership*. Charactered Whites work very hard to develop self-motivation techniques and assertion skills. With these acquired skills in place, White-White combinations are more likely to succeed.

PEACE

Whites get along with each other. They are motivated by peace. Each brings the necessary tolerance and patience to relationships in order to ensure peace. This is a clear example of reaping what you sow. World geography gives an interesting illustration of this strong motivation in all Whites. White nations such as Canada or Finland are peace-loving and rarely, if ever, start wars. They are, however, known to maintain strong defenses when attacked by other, more aggressive, nations. White companionships are similar to White nations in their behavior. They strive for peaceful coexistence. They are, however, quick to defend themselves when outside forces interfere with their relationship.

PATIENT AND TOLERANT

This combination is very slow to anger or feel prejudice. They are quietly accepting. They do not demand that other colors be as patient or tolerant. They simply role model their value system consistently and unobtrusively. White-White connections remind us of the lives of Mahatma Gandhi or Martin Luther King Jr. Both men quietly challenged an angry world of prejudice and injustice without need for great fanfare or publicity. White-White relationships are unobtrusive. They live simply and allow others simply to live.

> *White-White relationships*
> *are readily identifiable*
> *by their peacefulness.*

SATISFIED

Imagine a relationship that does not foster unnecessary disagreement or dwell on conflicts. Imagine White with White. These friendships rarely complain of having difficulty getting along with one another. In fact, they rarely even notice problems until other colors point them out. This combination is the least willing to expend energy on negative conflict. They are the satisfied ones.

UNPRODUCTIVE COMPLACENCY

Being unaware of others' faults is a blessing. Being unaware of reality is irresponsible. Many White-White combinations allow themselves to become very complacent in their relationship and ignore the circumstances outside that relationship. They are like the high school students who drop out before graduation and are surprised to find themselves undesirable in the workplace. White-White combinations often remain oblivious of changing external circumstances and end up with the short end of the stick. When push comes to shove, this combination is often too passive and unproductive, which may leave them unaware and vulnerable to a more assertive and changing environment.

This combination is notorious for leaving things that should be done today until tomorrow. They procrastinate and, without someone who is more determined, they are likely to put off important tasks. They tolerate each other's relaxed ways. This could result in a dangerous unproductivity. Hawaii, as a state, experienced the trauma many White-White couples do. Hawaiians remained complacent in their garden paradise until they suddenly realized that outside investors were buying their land right out from under them, leaving them with nothing to pass on to their grandchildren. White-White connections can remain so unproductive that they become victims of other, more determined, color combinations. They must learn to balance their relaxed and complacent preferential lifestyle with assertive productivity in order to successfully endure the ever-changing demands of daily living.

SELF-DOUBTING AND INDECISIVE

This combination suffers most from self-doubt. They are often second-guessing themselves about past decisions and personal capabilities. They tend to foster mutual self-doubt because usually neither is convinced that he or she has made the best choices. Whites are more likely to ask questions about decisions than to take a direct position in support of or in opposition to whatever decision was made. Each waits for the other to react in order to determine whether he himself was right or wrong. Often, neither gives a strong reaction, so questions about decisions remain unanswered. Self-confidence comes from within oneself. Confidence comes from succeeding. Whites either take risks or accept themselves, so self-doubt and indecision often remain stumbling blocks in White-White relationships.

RELUCTANT, TIMID, UNINVOLVED

Whites can be boring or appear to be boring because of their reluctant, timid, and uninvolved natures. White-White combinations can comfortably do nothing for a long period of time, while drive everyone else around them into a frenzy.

One White-White couple dated for years before getting married. Their courtship consisted primarily of television watching and sleeping. One would often call the other late at night on the telephone and talk until one or both would fall asleep. Not to worry! They were terribly patient with each other. They fell out of love shortly after marriage, although they lived together five more years before terminating the relationship. After all, *who* would file the divorce papers? Both were reluctant to make the first move. Neither was involved in other relationships, and so their marriage continued, from a legal standpoint at least, until friends finally pushed the woman to pull the plug. Forcing issues in life can be traumatic to a White-White relationship. Unfortunately, their timidity often promotes unhealthy compromise rather than forcing them both to take a more responsible problem-solving position.

White-White relationships seek a peaceful coexistence. They prefer to float above life's hassles rather than face them directly. They are patient and tolerant of each other and their world. They remain gentle and satisfied observers of life but vulnerable to outside influences. This combination timidly avoids risks and decision making. They prefer a quiet, secure, and unobtrusive existence to a flashy, dynamic, and demanding life. Reflective as the water they represent, they flow deeply and evenly through their shared life experience.

WHITE-YELLOW RELATIONSHIPS

"GENTLE FUN"

This relationship is about the "nice guys" or girls. They are affable individuals, seeking an easy (as opposed to difficult) style of interaction with limited expectations. Neither chooses to hassle the other. Neither is particularly keen about directing the other, either. They can be excellent as friends, colleagues, or parent-child, but rarely find themselves in a committed, intimate relationship. Almost as if there is no compelling magnetism, they instinctively recognize the limitations of their companionship in surviving the rigors of daily living.

I was engaged twice to a wonderful, gentle, delightful girl but could never sign on the dotted line. I realize now that while there was a strong physical chemistry and an emotional comfort, our relationship felt incomplete. I am Yellow and she is White. At the time, I needed someone stronger and bolder to commit to me. Having developed my character over the years, I am certain we could now successfully complete the puzzle, because I've added new pieces that were not there in my innate personality.

Whites and Yellows accommodate each other. They do not generally motivate each other. Perhaps they lack the ferocity or drive Reds and Blues innately have to light each other's fires. As children, similar values and preferences for playful activity invite a natural blend. As friends in adolescence and early adulthood, their gentle natures make for a positive connection. As charactered adults, they appreciate each other's accepting and easy style. Theirs is a casual blending of two comfortably independent people.

OVERVIEW

White Personality	Yellow Personality
MOTIVE	
Peace	Fun
NEEDS	
power and control of self	superficial connection
to be respected	to be praised
to feel good within self	social acceptance
acceptance	approval
WANTS	
independence	playful adventure
protection	freedom
to please self and others	to please others and self
to withhold insecurities	to hide insecurities (loosely)
BEHAVIOR STYLE	
stability	change
low profile	high profile
refuses to be controlled	refuses to be controlled
boring	exciting

White Personality	Yellow Personality
passive	active
reluctant	engaging
loner	involving
tenacious	easily distracted
plow horse	racehorse
feels deeply, finds expression of feelings difficult	emotional and expressive
logical in direct communication (with feelings and facts)	emotional, direct communication (with feelings and facts)
doer	delegator/performer
likes backstage	likes front of stage
patient	good-natured
nondemanding	obnoxious
relaxed	carefree
nonpossessive (unless threatened)	nonpossessive
craves peace	avoids confrontation
strongly nonverbal	strongly verbal
quiet manipulation	seeks escape
loves slowly, with strong commitment	loves easily but without commitment
consistent producer	scattered productivity
compliant with rules	defiant to rules
tactful	tactless (uses humor)
gives advice only when asked	gives advice but unconcerned with compliance
seeks advice freely	welcomes positive advice
aloof	inviting
tolerant of others	accepting of others
feels inadequate	high self-esteem
holds guilt inside	rarely gives or accepts guilt
lies to avoid conflicts and repercussions	lies to save face and to keep from disappointing others
releases but remembers	forgiving

233

WHITE-YELLOW INTERPERSONAL RELATIONSHIPS
(In-depth Presentation)

PEACE	versus	FUN

Whites can't understand why Yellows must go to all the trouble they do in developing relationships and meeting personal commitments (mostly playful activity), or why they overextend themselves in the community, at school, or at work. Whites are more inclined to go with the flow and become frustrated when their Yellow friends over-book and/or try to drag them into all their unnecessary commitments. "If I had known life with you would be this hectic," one White woman exclaimed to her busy Yellow roommate, "I would have taken fewer classes and hired on as your personal secretary. This is absolute madness, with the whole world constantly calling us and men always tramping through our house. Do you suppose we could start charging rent or at least retain an answering service?" Whites try very hard to uncomplicate their lives, while Yellows keep committing, connecting, and conversing in order to make their life fun.

Whites are more interested in getting along with others than in having the last laugh. Whites quietly accept many of Yellows' limitations, while Yellows tend to tease White and poke fun at their limitations.

POWER AND	versus	INTIMACY
CONTROL OF SELF		

Whites are concerned with developing a safe environment, while Yellows risk more freely for an intimate relationship. Yellows are more outgoing, and their White companions remain more reserved. Whites are like cats, able to come and go comfortably on their own. Yellows are like dogs, always seeking to be noticed, petted, and played with.

TO BE RESPECTED	versus	TO BE PRAISED

Whites need to have their wishes respected. They resent being pushed into decisions they find uncomfortable. Whites appear (behaviorally) to need constant praise and attention. In reality, they want you to respect their pace in life and their preferences. Because Whites are not a verbal group, they resent always having to speak up in order to secure their right to be left alone, be with certain friends, or whatever else they want. Yellows generally couldn't care less about respect. They want to be noticed and praised. They become frustrated with their White friends who don't talk but expect Yellows to know their desires and respect them. Perhaps one of the most difficult interactions for the White-Yellow combination is their differing needs for respect and praise. Whites are not known for their skill at or interest in praising others. Yellows are often disrespectful of others and typically overstep their acceptable boundaries with Whites.

PROTECTION versus FREEDOM

Yellows tend to be more confident than Whites. Yellows risk more freely, and therefore seem more comfortable with the unknown, while Whites prefer safer surroundings. Yellows often challenge their White friends to reach out and try wild and crazy experiences. Whites are more concerned with what will happen after the wild and crazy experiences. Yellows are more inclined to leave Whites hanging emotionally while they recklessly bound through life. Whites want to know they are secure and safe in the relationship.

STABILITY versus CHANGE

Whites and Yellows do not often see life through the same window. Whites want to see the same scene, and Yellows keep changing the picture. Whites appreciate the many opportunities Yellows bring to them but don't find it necessary to experience them all so rapidly or inconveniently. Yellows thrive on the fast pace and seldom feel inconvenienced as long as they're having a good time.

BORING versus EXCITING

Clearly, Whites are more inclined to fall into a rut. Whites are often plagued by the *sameness syndrome*—same car, same books, same friends, same house. Yellows struggle with the exact opposite tendency—the *differentness syndrome*. Everything in their life is in a constant state of flux. They are always trying new foods, traveling to new places, meeting new friends, and buying new cars. Each can be quite beneficial to the other when they allow their differences to provide a positive balance. On the negative side, both can feel constantly harassed by the other's lifestyle.

RELUCTANT versus ENGAGING

Whites often need coaxing from their Yellow friends to try new experiences. Yellows willingly involve Whites in their activities. Yellows are so engaging and undemanding that Whites find them difficult to resist. If anything, Yellows get tired of having to convince Whites to stretch and risk a little more.

TENACIOUS	versus	EASILY DISTRACTED

Whites are like plow horses. They are consistent and tenacious in their efforts to complete a task. They allow very little to distract them once they are committed to a cause. Yellows are less likely to commit over any length of time to relationships or activities. They float like butterflies, staying briefly in one place before they dart off to a more appealing location. Whites can become frustrated with the flighty, unreliable nature of Yellows but generally tend to remain tolerant despite the irritation.

FEELS DEEPLY, FINDS EXPRESSION OF FEELINGS DIFFICULT	versus	EMOTIONAL AND EXPRESSIVE

Yellow teenage girl: (frustrated and pleading) But why won't you come and have dinner with my parents? They want so much to meet you!

White teenage boy: (frustrated and quiet) I really don't feel comfortable meeting them yet. Maybe next month.

This White young man confided in me that he was afraid that his girlfriend's parents would ask him about his grades. He felt frustrated because they would be disappointed in him and in the future resist their daughter's decision to date him. Rather than be honest with her or them, he chose to avoid any communication and stay away.

Whites often think deeply but choose not to say much because they feel awkward in their verbal skills. Instead, they ponder their feelings and share very little. Yellows get upset and emotional and say what they feel regardless of how eloquent it may or may not be. Yellows need both to express themselves and to hear what their White friends feel.

Yellows must learn to be patient with Whites. Whites appreciate Yellows just spending time with them, without expecting the Whites to speak. Whites require time. When they feel accepted, they are more likely to express themselves.

DOER	versus	DELEGATOR/PERFORMER

Whites are Indians rather than chiefs. They are not interested in great fanfare and complication. They generally feel more comfortable doing the work than delegating it to others. Whites are not strong verbal communicators, which typically limits their managerial skills. However, when Whites feel comfortable with these skills, they make excellent delegators because of their patience, tact, and tolerance for other employees.

Yellows like center stage. They enjoy opportunities to perform (no routine housework, please) and willingly delegate mundane work and details to others. Yellows are charismatic leaders with poor follow-through. They are dynamic motivators and often find themselves in the spotlight regardless of their actual job title. Whites and Yellows usually work well together because their role preferences lie in different directions.

PATIENT   versus   GOOD-NATURED

Two best friends spent a lot of time together throughout their college careers. They were roommates and would often get together on campus to eat, see a movie, or study at the library. The White roommate would typically arrive up to one hour later than they had agreed upon. His Yellow friend would usually find a quiet place and study or share some good laughs with someone while he waited. They never became angry with one another. They simply ate later or took in a later movie. If Yellow became bored, he would go ahead alone, and neither was upset or concerned.

Yellows and Whites enjoy a rare capacity for tolerance and acceptance that no other mixed color combination shares. Both are slow to anger and quick to move on when slighted.

NONPOSSESSIVE   versus   NONPOSSESSIVE
(unless threatened)

Neither personality is usually driven by a need to possess people or material things. Yellows live for the moment, rarely save money, and just need enough to survive. Yellows can always make new friends and, therefore, rarely feel threatened by losing people in their life. They can't really imagine losing friends, spouses, or children because so many people are so easily drawn to them throughout life.

Whites are gentle in their approach to other people. They are sometimes overwhelmed if they feel rejected and don't know how to respond. Whites typically have little concern for monetary advantages. They are easily satisfied and usually unwilling to expend the energy necessary to beat the competition and climb the ladder of corporate success.

White-Yellow combinations are very relaxed with each other. Neither places much demand on the other. Both are willing to live with less because their relationship is often comfortable without the pressure of always having to *be* or *have* more.

COMPLIANT WITH RULES   versus   DEFIANT OF RULES

Whites tend to obey laws, rules, regulations, and authority figures. Yellows often disobey laws, rules, regulations, and authority figures. This disparity can create tension between White and Yellows. However, Whites are so tolerant and tactful that they can often convince Yellows to rethink their unacceptable behavior. Yellows are sensitive to social approval. Despite their zest for doing wild and crazy things, they are open to positive social influences from those they value and respect.

FORGIVING BUT REMEMBERS   versus   FORGIVING

Both personalities are very forgiving. They tend to accept that everyone makes mistakes. Neither wastes much energy on holding grudges. Whites, however, are more likely to remember when they were crossed and steer clear of any similar situation that appears to be potentially dangerous. Whites are also known to feel transgressions against them deeply, but generally they find their desire for peace so dominant that it overrides any need for retribution.

Yellows forgive quickly. One Yellow woman confided a very personal problem to a White friend. The friend told others. The Yellow was terribly hurt but acknowledged not more than a day later that she would most likely confide in the same friend again.

Whites and Yellows rarely burden their relationship with emotional baggage. They focus on the positive aspects of the other's personality and appreciate his or her unique contribution.

OVERWHELMED   versus   POSITIVE

When crises arise Whites often feel overwhelmed. Yellows typically see the silver lining in the dark clouds. Whites tend to see only a few options when seeking solutions. Yellows often find unlimited possibilities. Whites *seek* magical rescuers (the white-knight syndrome), while Yellows *feel* magical in problem resolution. Usually, Whites are pessimists, and Yellows assume the role of the optimist.

DEDICATED ONLY WHEN INTERESTED   versus   LACKS DISCIPLINE

Whites are particular about their commitments. They can be lazy and do not necessarily feel any compulsion to be productive. With this relaxed attitude, Whites find it difficult to commit themselves to people or to activities that have little or no interest for them. Whites are often difficult to motivate and keep motivated. Yellow parents and spouses are often frustrated trying to get White children and companions to take responsibility for themselves or stay interested. However, once Whites connect with some activity or work assignment, they are generally dedicated and loyal.

Throughout their lives, Yellows have trouble with discipline. Consistency is a foreign concept to Yellows. They tend to stay with something as long as it is fun. Most achievements in life require a commitment of consistent effort and pain. Fun is not generally a major ingredient in the initial stages of achievement. This explains why many Yellows settle for the simple life. They prefer to play and often lack the desire and commitment of stretching.

EXCELLENT LISTENER   versus   POOR LISTENER

Yellows are restless, and Whites are calm. Listening requires patience and a willingness to put others before oneself. Yellows tend to do neither well. Whites are comfortable sitting with another person for hours while they discuss details of how they feel. Yellows constantly interrupt. Yellows hurry the conversation along, often finishing the speaker's sentence. Whites enjoy a slower pace and encourage the speaker to move at his pace, accepting long pauses without questioning or rushing the thoughts. Whites find Yellows quite abrasive in this behavior and tend to stay quiet until (or unless) the Yellow learns to appreciate and practice the art of listening.

BLAMES SELF   versus   BLAMES OTHERS

When something negative happens, Whites usually blame themselves, and Yellows blame others. The following example reflects their styles.

White: How could I have been so stupid? I would have handled it differently.

Yellow: Why didn't you take care of the problem? You should have handled it differently!

Neither response is positive. Whites often struggle with low self-esteem because they assume responsibility for creating (or at least contributing to) most problems. Yellows are naively overconfident and tend to be limited in their emotional growth because they assume no responsibility for creating or contributing to most problems.

TOO SENSITIVE   versus   INSENSITIVE

Whites tend to feel bad easily. They are especially vulnerable to Yellows' flippant criticisms and overall naive insensitivity. Yellows do not think of others' feelings when they make rude or playful comments. Whites are not inclined to respond. They are more likely to hold the pain inside and quietly shy away from further social interaction. Often Whites silently blame themselves and simultaneously feel hurt that others don't understand their pain. Yellows typically misread Whites' behavior as, "They're okay. They're always quiet like that." Yellows do not pay much attention to others' needs or behaviors as long as Yellows are having a good time. They are often totally surprised to find out later that they have offended Whites.

MAKING THE MOST OF COMFORTABLE OPPOSITES

Whites Need Yellows:	Yellows Need Whites:
To excite them	To calm them
To encourage them	To listen to them
To accept their low profile	To praise them
To be kind to them	To play with them
To be intimate with them	To be tolerant of them
To keep confidences	To share confidences with
To promote activities	
To share a peaceful relationship	To share a peaceful relationship
To be sensitive to their self-doubts	To accept them

POTENTIAL CONFLICTS OF COMFORTABLE OPPOSITES

Whites	Yellows
Nonverbal	Crave praise
Directionless	Directionless
Passive	Passionate
Enjoy private time	Like social scene

Whites	Yellows
Lackadaisical	Lackadaisical
Quiet	Loud
Softspoken	Obnoxious
Boring	Exciting

*Yellow-Yellow relationships
are as striking as neon lights
on a street corner at night.*

YELLOW-YELLOW RELATIONSHIPS

"SPARKLE AND SHINE"

Yellow-Yellow relationships are as striking as neon lights on a street corner at night. They sparkle and shine for everyone to see. People rarely mistake this combination for anything else. Like two playful pups, they chase each other through life, oblivious of the rest of the world around them. They are playful and fun. This combination definitely knows how to have a good time.

Yellows enjoy their mutual friendships. They are not typically drawn to each other in committed marital relationships. Friendships are generally convenient, while marriage is not. As long as two Yellows can get themselves to the same place at the same time, they will always enjoy a good time together. Marriage requires much more than merely agreeing on a place and a time. Someone has to tell the playful pups when the work needs to get done. When there is no one but the playful pups, they rarely have a healthy balance between work and play.

Yellows live on raw energy. They can go for hours without needing to revitalize themselves. They travel well together. They party well together. They laugh well together. What they don't do well together is work—homework, housework, or detailed deadline work. They are easily distracted from labor and easily find numerous reasons why it is an excellent time to take a break from the rigors of work. They focus their energy on playful productivity such as recreation, conversation, and creative exploration. They prefer to use their energy in twos or more and rarely opt to be alone.

Yellow-Yellow combinations draw people to them like magnets. They are leaders and yet tend to be overwhelmed once they attract the interest of others. They lead most comfortably in play activity. Therefore, their greatest influence on others is most often expressed in the playful world of fun.

FUN

Yellow-Yellow combinations generally agree that the more, the merrier. They want to share their fun with everyone as long as others don't demand too much of their time. They also struggle with people they think are too conventional in their thinking. Yellow-Yellows rarely place limits on the fun zone in their relationship. As long as everyone is having a good time, everything else can wait. This relationship shares the fantasy that all roads eventually lead to Disneyland, a ski resort, or the beach.

NEEDS ATTENTION

Each requires a lot of the other's attention. Actually, this works out because Yellows seek instant and simple praise rather than deep appreciation. They are naturally optimistic and praise each other easily. They can accommodate each other's needs by pausing briefly in their self-centered monologues to notice the other. Neither is generally offended or concerned by this limited attention. A good time and praise is usually enough to keep Yellow-Yellows from feeling neglected in the relationship.

FREEDOM

This combination regards freedom as a sacred principle in their relationship. Neither tries to attach strings or commitment (a less than sacred word). Yellow friends accept whatever time they have to share together and share it to the fullest. Neither wants or intends to commit to much beyond the present. Yellows can drop out of each other's lives for years and easily pick up where they left off when they get together again. They don't feel neglected or particularly frustrated by losing touch over the years. Both value the freedom to move in and out of the relationship and don't attach strings to their relationships. They are more likely to simply accept each other at face value.

HIGHLY VERBAL

Talk, talk, talk! Yellows can talk about anything or nothing equally well. They appreciate superficial as well as serious discussions. Put them at a party, a funeral, or in their kitchen and they will find things to converse about. Neither is strong on listening skills, which doesn't seem to deter their interest in conversation. However, it does preclude much depth or meaningful direction in ongoing relationships, because their poor listening skills often make them miss many important insights.

Constant dialogue is not lacking in their relationship, and both willingly share responsibility for promoting and sustaining positive chatter.

UNCOMMITTED

This color combination promotes play and fears commitment. They have the perception that freedom and playful activity are necessarily incompatible with commitment. In light of this dilemma, Yellow relationships typically choose freedom and neglect commitments. This attitude makes interaction of an intimate or responsible nature unlikely. They typically wear out, which is disappointing in relationships that require a long, enduring commitment.

IRRESPONSIBLE

Yellows expect others to handle the details and loose ends. When the other person is another Yellow, the details are often neglected and loose ends never tied together. Neither takes his or her role very seriously, so their relationship is often burdened with last-minute mixups and other problems that reduce the quality of their shared life experience.

This is well illustrated by two Yellow friends who were babysitting together one evening. The girl fell asleep at 5:00 p.m. and woke up at 7:00 p.m. Meanwhile, her friend had made popcorn. He and the kids were enjoying popcorn and a movie when she awoke. She assumed they had already eaten dinner because they were eating popcorn. He assumed popcorn was enough. Needless to say, neither was asked to babysit again. Ignoring details is not always serious, but repeated negligence can be dangerous, if not life-threatening.

OPTIMISTIC

This color combination believes most anything can be accomplished with time or help or something—perhaps just hope. They are eternal dreamers and optimists. They always seek the silver lining in the cloud or find some value in the pit in a cherry. Pollyanna times two is tough for anyone. Yellows don't get depressed easily, and if they do, they don't stay depressed for long. In a Yellow-Yellow relationship, each supports the other with hope and positive reinforcement.

CURIOUS AND INQUISITIVE

Yellows ask the darnedest questions at the darnedest times. They simply want to know things and usually forget important social protocol when asking. The answers are not as important as the process of discovering the answers. Yellows find it great fun to look for clues to explain human behavior. They enjoy each other's free-spirited (often bordering on the obnoxious) pursuit of insight and understanding.

ENTERTAINING

Yellows love to entertain and be entertained by each other. They are performers. They entice each other with spontaneous surprises (show tickets, weekend retreats, cards, or flowers). They enjoy carefree experiences and light moments of laughter and intimacy. This combination is far more inclined to spend money and time on action-filled opportunities (trips and recreations) than on material possessions (expensive gifts and household fixtures). They live for the present, and both appreciate experiences that offer immediate pleasures.

Yellow-Yellow combinations adore each other. They value their relationship and find each other spontaneous and refreshing. They enjoy their freedom, and struggle with necessary commitments and responsible behavior. As they are living for today, they have little interest in yesterday's regrets or tomorrow's concerns. Yellows gravitate toward each other and often remain playful companions for life. They casually enter and exit each other's lives with little concern for the long term.

This combination loves life best when it is shared with others. They appreciate each other's positive and hopeful natures. They are fun and superficially attentive to one another. Intimacy remains an important, yet fleeting, concern in a Yellow-Yellow relationship. They value their connection to other people and particularly enjoy sharing special moments with other Yellows.

Energetic and highly verbal, Yellows ignite each other with constant chatter and inquisitive interaction. These shared behavior styles make this combination enjoyable to observe. In the long run, Yellow-Yellow connections are enviable playmates but unlikely marital companions. Whatever relationship they experience together will never be dull or lack excitement. They are a fun, dynamic duo who vigorously pursue the good life with refreshing curiosity and optimism.

Chapter Fourteen

THE RAINBOW CONNECTION: BUILDING SUCCESSFUL RELATIONSHIPS

Each of us is 100 percent responsible
for the quality of relationships we create.

There you have it. It doesn't matter whether we are discussing personal or business relationships. If you are engaging a certain personality, you now have a clear picture of what natural strengths and limitations you will create and face in your relationships.

I have always told businesspeople who are recruiting new staff to apply the People Code so they will know generally what they can expect from the relationship. And anyone getting married or rearing children without identifying their core color must prefer high-stakes gambling to a sure bet. Knowing who you are and the personality you are engaging with offers you tremendous advantages in making your best possible connection.

You always deserve what you get when you marry or when you work for the same company more than one year. Great managers and positive business relationships are not created by sheer luck. They require hard work and equal partnership in providing essential personality gifts for success. They seek (albeit often subconsciously) someone to balance them and fulfill their needs. Bad managers and poor business relationships aren't just bad luck, either. Someone looked the other way rather than focusing on the negative truth about why they engaged each other. We must take 100 percent responsibility for our relationship choices, or we can never feel empowered to experience the tremendous magic that healthy relationships can bring in completing our lives.

We understand that Reds enjoy power. We accept the sincerity of the Blues, the gentle touch of the Whites, and the charisma of the Yellows. Furthermore, we have discussed how daring Reds interact with reluctant Whites. We see now how committed Blues and carefree Yellows work together.

We established that each color represents natural strengths and limitations. We reviewed the desirable and undesirable traits that come when a person of one color interacts with someone of another. Each combination offers a unique blend. For example, two Red individuals interact with one another differently than a Blue and Red couple does. A business composed mostly of Yellows and Whites will operate differently from a business composed of Yellows and Blues.

Let's investigate the fascinating world of relationships a little further. There are some general themes that may prove helpful in understanding specific dynamics of the rainbow connections. These insights will save individuals countless hours of emotional grief or financial waste in needless hiring and firing of employees if they understand how the concepts play out in relationships.

HEAVYWEIGHT VERSUS LIGHTWEIGHT PERSONALITIES

There are general similarities and differences that we should delineate before focusing on specific combinations. For example, Reds and Blues are the heavyweight personalities, while Whites and Yellows reflect the lightweights. They represent the hunters and the hunted in nature. The lion pursues the antelope. The wolf pursues the lamb. There is an offense and defense in sports. The tackle pursues the quarterback in football. In tennis, the person at the net attacks the person at the baseline. In business, the sales representative pursues the customer.

In life, the Reds and Blues assume the roles of lion and wolf. They are the football tackles and tennis players who charge the net. They are the sales representatives. The Whites and Yellows are the antelope and lamb. They are the football quarterbacks and tennis baseliners. They represent the customers and the consumers. Each role is invaluable.

We could not be as successful without both types. Each requires the other. Both have strengths and limitations that enable them to survive as well as contribute. *Opposites do, in fact, attract each other.* Each enhances the other's life. Each would be lost without the other. They give credibility to each other. Each serves as a role model for the others for specific areas of character building. Each color gives balance in the full spectrum of relationships.

INTIMACY

Blues and Yellows are intimacy-oriented. Blues and Yellows are motivated by intimacy and prefer an emotional connection in securing a strong bonding with others in life. Celebrating romantic occasions, holding hands for no apparent reason, and remembering early days of intimacy between a couple are most common for Blues and Yellows. Both colors want to be told often of their romantic allure. In business, they appreciate being noticed, and often decide whether to stay in a particular job based on the shared intimacy at work.

Blues and Yellows understand their needs for intimacy at a much more subconscious level than they realize. For example, one major reason Yellows are so demonstrative is their inner desire to be touched. Many Yellows never understand why they are so physical, but, in truth, they may be simply reaching out for what they need.

POWER

Reds and Whites are power-based. Reds and Whites expend a lot of energy preserving the balance of power in the relationship and other practical issues. One White woman demanded that her Red husband immediately repay her the money he had borrowed. I suggested that her timing was not the best for the relationship. She said, rather blandly, that it needed to be done since it was already overdue, and, besides, she was trying to learn how to be assertive. Actually, she was striving to balance the power.

Reds and Whites want the conveniences of companionship without all the complex emotional strings attached. Subconsciously, they understand each other's style and often position themselves to maintain control of their relationships. Reds are far more direct in their pursuit of power than Whites. Whites often use a passive-aggressive approach. (Passive-aggressive behavior refers to accepting certain slights without negative reaction and then later aggressively getting even under a totally different set of circumstances.)

An example of passive-aggressive behavior is the mother who tells her son he can go outside and play football, *but* he can't get his clothes dirty. When the son comes home filthy, she gladly tosses the clothes in the washer but neglects to fix his dinner until much later than usual that evening. She is terribly upset by his behavior, but rather than confront him at the time, she gets even later in an unrelated situation.

COMMUNICATION STYLE

Methods of communication differentiate styles. Reds and Yellows are more inclined to tell people things to do, while Blues and Whites are more likely to ask people for their opinions. Whites and Blues are comfortable seeking advice, while Reds and Yellows prefer to give the solutions. Reds and Yellows tend to blame others. Blues and Whites blame themselves. Reds respond best to direct, logical communication. (Whatever you do, don't cry!) Blues prefer a softer, emotional style of feedback. They tend to be hardest on themselves with their perfectionistic tendency. Negative feedback offered empathetically is most effective for Blues. Whites cannot be yelled at. They prefer a profile with gentle honesty and low conflict. Yellows enjoy a casual (even humorous) style when receiving feedback. They appreciate warmth and reassurance.

SELF-ESTEEM

All colors seek self-satisfaction and self-esteem with a unique flair. Self-esteem has become a particularly interesting component of personality in this century. Parents want to know how self-esteem and productivity are connected. Teachers want to understand how learning and self-esteem interact. One of the most significant findings in the People Code is the difference in how each personality reflects self-esteem.

Reds and Yellows appear to be born with higher self-esteem than Blues and Whites. Blue and White children tend to have self-defeating attitudes. They criticize themselves and feel inadequate. Most Red and Yellow children tend to project themselves, criticize others, and openly display more positive self-regard. All personalities, however, come with some positive self-regard and some negative feelings of insecurity.

Reds appear to the the most self-assured of all the colors, and yet they tend to be the most insecure. Perhaps they are not originally less secure, but since they work so hard to disguise their insecurity, they often delay character development, which can come only by exposing oneself emotionally (being vulnerable) and taking responsibility for one's insecurities. Unfortunately, Reds hide their insecurities so well that few people recognize that they need to grow up emotionally. They are often allowed to slide emotionally because they are so stubborn. Most people are unwilling to invest the energy necessary to deal with them. Reds willingly dive from the highest diving board and scale the most difficult mountain in order to maintain their competent and secure image.

Yellows often manage to maintain a superficial social snobbery, thus protecting themselves from real, intimate exposure of their insecurities. Whites and Blues are far less likely to make the effort to hide their insecurities.

Consequently, when we look at self-esteem, we consistently come up with the supposition that Reds and Yellows appear stronger than the Blues and Whites. Perhaps the Reds and Yellows maintain strong self-images because society (especially parents and teachers) perceives the initial behavior of Reds and Yellows as strong and treats them accordingly. As a result, Reds and Yellows theoretically develop even greater self-regard. The Blues and Whites openly reveal their insecurities, and society often responds with a protective, coddling, or condescending manner. This encourages a potential lifetime pattern of self-degradation and/or martyrdom.

Unfortunately, Reds and Yellows often fall prey to a "self-satisfaction syndrome." Perhaps they feel so good about themselves that they simply slide through life rather than working to earn a deeper self-respect. This self-respect only comes from confronting personal inadequacies and choosing to contribute to others. On the other hand, Blues and Whites may develop deeper self-esteem later in life because they recognize and acknowledge their deficiencies and put forth the effort necessary to feel better about themselves. Unfortunately, some may feel overwhelmed by their feelings of inadequacy and live their entire lives with fear and guilt complexes.

All personalities find true self-esteem only after honest self-analysis followed by a loving commitment to promoting the well-being of themselves and others. Self-esteem is gained slowly and often painfully by risking exposure to others. Many individuals are willing to have shallow relationships in order to avoid disclosing negative personality traits and/or character flaws. Charactered people value self-esteem enough to continue to risk it throughout various phases of life.

INVOLVEMENT VERSUS ISOLATION

Reds and Yellows are alert and focus directly on practicalities and tasks. (Remember, for Yellows *task* often means *play*.) Blues and Whites tend to think in terms of the past and the future, while Reds and Yellows concern themselves predominantly with the present. Blues and Whites are the daydreamers and are often preoccupied.

We need to allow Reds and Yellows their task orientation. Blues and Whites deserve time for creativity or quiet reflection. We enhance relationships when we encourage opportunities for individuals within the relationship to pursue their style of life. It might be more destructive than productive to demand that a Yellow reflect quietly for too long if the individual isn't prepared for such an experience.

Educators (typically Blue) can hinder Red students if they refuse to afford them task leadership opportunities. Most Blues will feel frustrated if they are not allowed their time to meditate and plan prior to taking action or making a decision. Whites typically become silently stubborn when they are ordered to move faster or to act too aggressively on a project. Each color responds most effectively when allowed, within reason, to use his or her preferred style.

THERAPEUTIC INTERVENTION STYLE

Every psychotherapist has the opportunity to serve in the role of a "change agent." In order to be effective, the approach should match the specific needs of the patients. There is a high correlation between the patient's personality and the style of intervention. Reds and Blues are far more resistant to change, while Yellows and Whites are initially more receptive to the change process. Resistance is less direct and abrasive for Blues than Reds. The intensity of the resistance is, however, fairly equal. On the other hand, Yellows are more likely to say they are receptive to change than the Whites are. However, both generally appear receptive and willing to adapt their lifestyles.

Just the reverse is true of these personalities when it comes to follow-through and completion of the change process. Reds and Blues are far more likely to successfully commit themselves to the changing process once their resistance is removed. Yellows and Whites are more inclined to slip back into old behavior patterns or feel unmotivated to complete the change process.

Therapeutically, Blues and Reds demand answers. They want specific methods, solutions, and direction once they decide to change. They request behavioral therapy that focuses on specific homework assignments and expectations. The most frustrating aspect of therapy for them is coming to the realization that the therapist will not and cannot necessarily design a specific behavioral process with long-term success for them. What they actually need most is an attitudinal adjustment.

Attitudinal therapy forces them to examine their motives and clear up unhealthy perceptions. Reds suffer most often from inaccurate emotional messages such as hidden insecurities, blocking communication, or layers and years of denied anger. Blues suffer most often from irrational thinking. They have usually relied so heavily on their "emotional muscles" that their ability to think rationally is seriously impaired. This process of attitudinal readjustment takes much longer and requires more patience than the behavioral process. Consequently, Reds and Blues often become frustrated with psychotherapy.

Conversely, the therapeutic approach for the Whites and Yellows is more direct and behavioral. It is the kind of therapy Reds and Blues would really prefer. Generally, Yellows and Whites have positive and receptive attitudes, but their discipline and motivation often leave a lot to be desired. They require constant support with new techniques for effectively tackling life. It is particularly challenging to work with a couple requiring different approaches (e.g., a Yellow-Red couple). The Red often complains that the therapist attacks him or her too much in the session. The Yellow complains that he or she has more homework than the Red after the session is over.

Yellows and Whites need to see themselves completing goals and disciplining themselves consistently over a long period of time in order to increase their self-esteem and to develop healthy lifestyles. Giving a Red or Blue more hobbies or tasks will do little to increase self-esteem. They are already driven to achieve and produce, and probably don't feel that what they do is good enough. They need to increase their awareness of self-flagellating (Blue) or arrogant (Red) feelings and thoughts in order to be more accepting of themselves and others.

To sum up, Reds and Blues want immediate action and behavior modification. They most often get a time-consuming attitudinal adjustment and must struggle with it. Yellows and Whites want a relaxed, attitudinal approach. They get a direct process, requiring commitment and behavior modification, and they find it taxing to endure. Once they accept a "no pain, no gain" philosophy, they can modify their behavior.

Blues and Whites are less verbal, while Reds and Yellows generally share strong verbal skills. (The strong, silent type is a White.) Reds and Yellows also tend to think very quickly on their feet, while Blues and Whites spend a lot of time kicking themselves for not having had the best retort at the time of the conversation. Their creative wit often lets them come up with great lines. Unfortunately, the thought is two days too late.

It has been suggested that *an unexamined life is hardly worth living*. Knowing ourselves makes our journey through life much more meaningful for ourselves and others. It also enhances our opportunities to change those limitations that inhibit our ability to contribute. It enhances our opportunities to develop the strengths that define our uniqueness in how and what we contribute. With luck, you will be receptive to learning about yourself and understanding those around you as we look at specific color combinations.

IT IS IMPORTANT TO UNDERSTAND THE CHARACTERISTICS OF *ALL* THE PERSONALITIES IN ORDER TO APPRECIATE HOW WE AND OTHERS SEE THE WORLD. Nothing in nature operates well in a vacuum. Each personality relies on the others to fully experience its true color. Learn about the personalities without judgment. Seek to appreciate the unique strengths and limitations in others. Strengthen your inherent limitations in order to get along better with others. Limitations can become strengths. Strive to recognize the natural bonding or resistance that various personalities experience. In accordance with the prayer of St. Francis of Assisi, "Grant that (we) may not so much seek to be understood as to understand."

The following diagram illustrates the similarities and differences among the personalities in the total color spectrum.

PERSONALITY CONNECTIONS

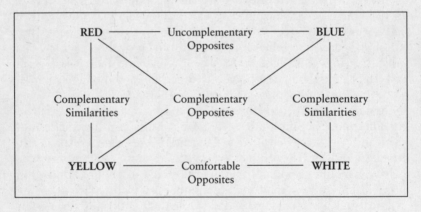

Let me explain this diagram. By definition, *complementary* suggests "an adding to the effect of" or "supplying what is lacking." By the literal definition, then, each color complements every other color with its innate strengths. However, this diagram presents a looser definition in order to help us understand the realities of color combinations, rather than simple theory.

Some colors are more alike than others. Reds and Yellows share strong verbal skills, insensitivity, and positive-action orientation. Blues and Whites are similar in their nonverbal preference, sensitivity, and desire to accommodate others. When an individual's personality is a combination of Red-Yellow or Blue-White, they find the blend very comfortable.

Some colors are opposites but appeal to each other for a sense of completion and to make them feel whole. Reds and Whites enjoy a practical orientation to relationships and rely on facts and common sense to light their way. They share similar perceptions of power, excitement, and leadership. Blues and Yellows mutually seek intimacy, romance, and fantasy. Both sets of colors offer a natural balance within themselves. Consequently, Reds-Whites and Blues-Yellows are most inclined to find themselves in committed relationships with each other. However, when *one* individual has either of these blends within himself/herself, he/she finds a perpetual split in focus and must commit to the dominant motive in order to find harmony within his/her attitudes and behavior.

Some colors do not find their blending naturally complementary and/or innately comfortable. Red-Blue and White-Yellow combinations find themselves in this category. Reds and Blues generally experience the greatest conflict because (1) they are such strong personalities, and (2) their innate impulses, one to power, one to intimacy, provide an awkward blend. People with a Red-Blue personality experience the same awkwardness within themselves as two individuals with Red and Blue personalities feel in their relationship. They must work harder on their character in order to facilitate the potential strength of this uncomplementary connection.

White-Yellow combinations do not offer each other completion. They are both easygoing and unlikely to commit to business or to marriage because without a lot of character development, both lack the necessary strength to be successful in a shared, committed relationship. As uncomfortable as Red-Blue combinations are, they are far more likely to connect than Whites and Yellows. However, an individual with the White-Yellow blend enjoys strong people skills and rarely feels much inner conflict because each personality is innately gentle.

The film classic *Gone With the Wind,* derived from the equally enduring Pulitzer Prize–winning novel, offers us a vivid presentation of the colors in relationships. The leading characters represent the different personalities and provide us with a visual portrayal of how the colors interact.

Scarlett O'Hara was a Red. Influenced by power and a strong will to be right, she brilliantly orchestrated her survival during the Civil War. Her great love was Rhett Butler, whose charismatic and flamboyant lifestyle illustrated the Yellow personality. His attraction to

Scarlett was eventually doomed because she would never give the emotional connection he craved.

Ashley embodied the loyalty and high moral standard of the Blue. He consistently rebuffed Scarlett's romantic overtures, despite his attraction to her, because he sensed her emotional insecurities and that she would be inadequate to his needs for genuine intimacy.

Melanie, on the other hand, offered peace and support to all three characters. She represented the White. She never suspected Ashley or Scarlett of anything less than moral and proper behavior. She defended Scarlett against her enemies. She warmly received Rhett into the family. She loved Ashley to her dying breath. Interestingly, Rhett and Ashley (Yellow and Blue) were quite compatible despite their different backgrounds.

Each character embodies the essence of personalities within relationships. Their colors defined their preferences, limitations, and motivations. Their relationships were decided before they ever met.

Now let's look at specific relationships. The following comparisons offer a quick guide to how the different personalities interact in their most raw and natural forms. If you have a developed character, you may find that some of the statements no longer completely reflect your current style. Simply make a note of how your character development has replaced innate personality limitations and added new dimension to your life. With rare exception, the *motives*, the *needs*, and the *wants* remain in place. What you are trying to do here is to identify how you (and those you care about) are *motivated* and what style you should choose to use while interacting with others.

This is your opportunity to see yourself and the way your relationships connect. Review the motives, needs, wants, and behaviors and determine your own compatibility.

RAINBOW

Look for the various combinations you encounter in your life. Ask yourself why you seek the combinations you do. Consider how the color combinations of your parents and yourself affected your life. Reflect on the relationship between your employers (or employees) and yourself. Seek to understand how your personality influences and is influenced by others. How do the different combinations affect you? Which combination do you find most intimidating and why? Which combination feels most comfortable to you? Why do you respond to certain colors more than others? Why is a clean home so important to one individual and relatively meaningless to another? Does your yeller and screamer really mean the awful things she or he says? How do we accept or redirect laziness in others? Why do I link up with people who spend money lavishly, while I save everything I earn?

Consider the wonderful possibilities you can use these insights for in your life. Whether you are selecting a candidate for a job or trying to make sense out of a parent-child relationship, the rainbow connection is invaluable. Determining the depth of one's character is important to understanding people as unique individuals. However, we can rest assured that everyone operates best within his or her own personality. Therefore, despite the obvious limitations each color has, we can generally trust that we will behave, at least to some degree, in a manner consistent with our defined personality color group.

Each personality combination brings with it a unique set of strengths and limitations. Developed character and an understanding of innate personalities allow us to deal with the specific needs of each possible combination, whether it be in the role of friend, lover, parent, employer, or child. Learning to facilitate relationships without jeopardizing our integrity is essential to our success in life.

Part Four

❧❧❧

APPLICATIONS

Chapter Fifteen

BUSINESS APPLICATIONS

"People are definitely a company's greatest asset.
It doesn't make any difference whether the product is cars or cosmetics.
A company is only as good as the people it keeps."
—Mary Kay Ash

Business is about making a contribution while creating a profit. Winning in the business arena is great fun, but requires a unique balancing act of strategy, execution, and people. What many people don't appreciate is the creative juggling act that successful business leaders perform on a daily basis. Ultimately, they must piece together a rather tricky puzzle that provides bottom-line results with top-line growth. All of this necessitates paying attention to people. Both top and bottom lines in business are strongly tied to the people factor.

So how does motive-based training positively impact the top and bottom lines in business? How will this process improve your competitive advantage? You have a thousand other pressing matters to resolve, so why should you be concerned with this?

People make or break a business. Whether internally (employees) or externally (customers), no business is ever better than the quality of people it keeps. Learning what motivates you, your employees, and your customers lies at the core of your success. Nobody knows people better than Hartman Communications. We tell you not only what they will do, but also *why* they do it. You can trust the *whys* that we find behind people's behaviors.

Consider three of the most critical components that every successful business venture must address.

Like a three-legged stool needs all three legs to stand, all three components must exist in order to win at business. There are so many moving parts in business that anything you can do to create a compet-

People

itive edge is important. Hartman Communications is committed to the success component of people.

People are every company's greatest asset or liability. Jim Collins made this poignantly clear in his book *Good to Great* when he delineated five crucial elements for determining company success. Each of the five elements touches the human factor and two of the five are focused on solely the human factor. Simply stated, people matter! So *why* are so many leaders reluctant to pay attention to this critical component of their business?

1. Leaders often fail to see themselves accurately. They don't *get* themselves. They play to their strengths while ignoring their limitations. When their limitations impact how they handle people, there can be serious consequences. Before Hartman Communications ever signs a contract to consult with a client, we meet to determine if the leader is willing to do his/her own personal work as an integral part of the process. As consultants, we recognize the powerful primary role that key leadership plays. We participate by taking an important supportive role. With your leadership and our process skills, together we create a legitimate, high-performance culture. In order to succeed, though, we need your commitment.

Remember, *no* team is better than its leader. If leaders are not congruent within themselves, they will never be able to read incongruence in others. Every leader on a team is ultimately responsible for creating effective or dysfunctional teams. Leaders alone create promise or poison through their decisions and actions. Whether it is eventually realized through their employees' performance or their customers' loyalty, *people generally get what they deserve.*

This is often a very hard pill to swallow when a leader is particularly effective with other critical elements of running a successful business, such as strategy or execution. However, the three-legged stool will not stand long without getting the people factor right. Few people are truly self-aware, and honest self-awareness becomes even harder to achieve the higher one climbs on the leadership ladder. It requires both humility and trust to invite our process in, but your company will always produce better top and bottom lines if you do your work and lead out in this process.

2. The people side of business can prove rather dicey. Sometimes leaders simply don't *get* people. They don't understand them, so they focus on other areas where they have expertise—strategy or execution. Leaders may have little interest in the human element or find it too unpredictable for their comfort level.

The People Code diagnostic tool (the Hartman Personality Profile) is a powerful gift for every leader to use in reliably assessing their employees and their customers. *Why would anyone* not *want to know the driving motivations of someone with whom they are establishing a long-term relationship?* The beauty of color-coding is simply this—it works!!! Once you have experienced its penetrating insight, you won't consider entering negotiations or managing others without it.

Color-coding becomes your compass and will always point you in the right direction. With its accuracy, you can easily assess an individual's internal legitimacy. It frees you to correctly place the best candidate in the best position where both the company and the employee win. It specifically delineates how the various color personalities will interface with each other, which is important for every team, sales, management, or customer service interaction.

Many companies prefer the Hartman Personality Profile to other long-established instruments such as Myers-Briggs and DISC (Dominance, Influence, Steadiness, Compliance), because it provides them much richer information. But other instruments (by their own confession) can measure only behavior, while the Hartman Personality Profile measures motive, which ultimately drives behavior. It is a much deeper diagnostic tool that provides rich layering of insights about people.

3. Training requires time and money. Perhaps a leader's most challenging juggling act comes with keeping an eye on the future and developing a long-term foundation for success while dealing with immediate demands of the day. Today versus Tomorrow. Urgent versus Important. Treatment versus Prevention. This is always a tricky piece of business success and requires a leader with keen perspective.

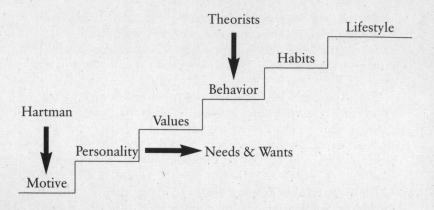

Fortunately, what used to be guesswork about the cost of the human factor is no longer a mystery. What leaders are unwilling to prevent today will need expensive treatment in the future. The following statistics offer a brief but critical reminder about the high cost of ignoring the people factor in the workplace. Industry experts claim that it costs 150 percent to 200 percent of an employee's annual salary to replace him or her (includes both direct and indirect costs). Sixty percent of employees' unsatisfactory performances can be attributed to workplace conflicts (Dana Mediation Institute: www.mediationworks.com/gov). Exit interviews reveal that chronic unresolved conflict acts as a decisive factor in 65 percent of work performance problems and at least 50 percent of all involuntary departures (Greg Hessel, "The Cost and Management of Organizational Conflict," *New Hampshire Business Review,* July 14, 2003). Managers spend at least 24 percent of their time resolving conflicts at work (Volunteers of America—Mediation Services: www.voaww.org).

Perhaps the reason Hartman Communications' process leads in providing longevity is that we get at people's core motives rather than dealing with merely behavior. We teach transparency, congruence, and accountability. All principles are central to helping the various personality types become legitimate and effective interpersonally. Since our early beginnings, we have been a vital resource to many diverse companies. Together we have created remarkable results. The people factor is never simple. Developing a legitimate culture of respect and accountability requires our mutual commitment to true principles and people. Our process blends our unique understanding of people with consistent focus on sound principles.

Just as water seeks its own level, employees rise to the established cultural values and expectations of the company. New hires are screened against the established culture in assessing congruence between the new applicant and the developed culture. Key assessment observations are:

- First, are candidates legitimate within themselves?
- Second, are candidates right for the job they have been hired to perform?
- Last, does the candidate synergize well with others?

Company leaders tell us that once they have established cultural congruency and raised expected levels of performance, the quality of new candidates is always substantially higher than prior to going through our process. Furthermore, many of them tell us that they could not have hired themselves against the congruency standards the company has created with this process.

Hartman Communications knows people. We understand their driving core motivations. We see both their strengths and limitations. We know everyone's innate wants and needs. We teach individuals how to play to their strengths while working on their limitations. People can and do change as they become charactered.

TESTIMONIALS

Color-coding provides you with a consistently reliable tool for assessing your employees' real potential for congruence in all three areas: personal legitimacy, specific job match, and team interaction. A business professor at a university recently relayed that she requires students to take the Hartman Personality Profile on-line and purchase the business application printout as their class text. She said, "This has revolutionized my success with my business students. I cannot even imagine teaching my courses without the motive-based business application ever again."

The president of one company in Florida always has both internal candidates and clients take the Hartman Personality Profile in order to map out the best future relationship. His company considers this the primary component of hiring and customer relations, secondary to no other. He claims that using the color code is their secret weapon. "It has clearly enhanced our success in outperforming all competitors," he said.

An executive at a California company stated that color-coding allows him to appropriately fit employees in positions where they are more likely to excel. It has dramatically improved his retention, which has freed him to pay more attention to positive career development as opposed to endless hiring and firing of personnel.

A leadership team at a sales company in Colorado asked us to help them create congruence in their hiring procedures. They wanted Reds but hired Blues. We rewrote their job advertisements, created an interview format that invited a check on all three critical elements for congruence, and saved them thousands of hours and dollars by simply applying the profound principles of motive.

We teach a course entitled The Sales Code, which combines revolutionary sales strategies with color-coding awareness. One major insurance company tells us the course has transformed sales in the insurance industry. Matching universal principles of genuine sales strategies with core human motivations makes this combination a phenomenon all on its own.

Many companies display each employee's color code wheel, which visually displays the percentage of each color in an employee's personality. It shows what an employee's core color is, and also the amount of other colors his/her personality contains. It has been remarkably helpful for internal dialogue, because people remember what kind of personality they are working with and get much better results in their communication.

This is a tool businesses love, because it is so easy to apply and generates results. Business leaders know that they must play to win. When something comes along that enhances their bottom line *and* simultaneously enhances employee and customer relations, they quickly become devotees. The concepts of *The People Code* free them to pay more attention to other pressing matters, which also affects bottom-line results.

That said, color-coding is not a one-dimensional instrument. Its beauty comes with both its simplicity and complex depth. It's like climbing a mountain—you see new vistas the higher you go. With color-coding, you will find immediate application, which invites you to seek further applications. The deeper you delve, the more you'll find that the applications are endless.

Hartman Communications finds its strongest partnerships with companies who are committed to doing the right thing by their employees and customers. Motive-based training requires long-term commitment. Businesses engaged with Hartman Communications must do their work and remain committed to the central principles, which are essential to finding success with the people element. Commitment to this process promises clarity and confidence. The process is specifically described in my upcoming book *Playing Life to Win,* which provides both personal and professional illustrations on how to implement motive-based training in your life.

One company that has been extremely successful at building the three-legged stool is MASYC. I asked Russ Stenquist, the owner, to share his story so that business leaders could see the dynamics of this process we offer from a business perspective.

The story of MASYC is one of a small company that went from being comfortable, to nearly ceasing to exist, to wildly successful. It's a story about people—our people—and the way they met the incredible challenges and changes that took place in MASYC. **As in our business, it's all about the people!**

In many ways, there are three versions of MASYC as a firm. In the first version, there were only two of us; we minded our own business and had little competition. By the end of this version, there were four employees in our firm, and we are all still here and part of our leadership team. The second version of MASYC started after we were in business for about seven years. Great opportunities arose, but they required more than the few consultants we had. The demand for our services well outstripped our resources and as a result, we grew. Our revenues increased over six times, our organization grew over five times, and—best of all—we never lost an employee. Morale was high and we were busy.

Before the third version of MASYC, we took quite a hard fall. We hired poorly, and because we took good care of our employees, some new hires came for the money. Several folks in our organization became bitter. We were way overextended, which nearly put MASYC out of business. We lost 50 percent of our organization and over 30 percent of our revenue, and we had zero profits. We were working in an organization that had poor morale and it was miserable to come to work each morning. My partner and I felt we could do better working on our own than keeping MASYC going.

As the dust settled in early 2003, we had nowhere to go but up. Unfortunately, we had no idea how to get there. Enter Dr. Taylor Hartman and The People Code. The change has been dramatic. We nearly tripled our size and have the most impressive, productive consultants in our field. Our retention is extremely high, because we've learned to council employees out of our organization who don't fit our unique culture and grow those willing to commit.

The process of change started with getting to know who we were, identifying the motives behind our actions, and taking responsibility for our surroundings. We created MASYC College, where the whole team comes together four times a year. Things had to change. Four years later, there are dramatic differences in the way we deal with each other, our clients, and people outside of work. We have learned an entirely new language including concepts of 100 percent Responsibility, legitimate congruence, and clean motives. We created a mentor program and a 360-degree feedback system, which keeps us mutually accountable to ensure each other's success.

As a Red leader, I am always looking at bottom line results and return on investments. There have been tremendous benefits from our investment in this process. Our recovery time from internal and external miscommunications is much less—in the old days those events would have blown up into huge issues. Mutual understanding, trust, and respect are at an all time high within the organization. Also, we've invited clients into our meetings to provide us with constructive guidance about our organization, how we approach them, and how we could grow with them. This is truly priceless to our group. Constant feedback is now open and welcomed. This process has completely changed the quality of our internal dynamics with each other and our external dynamics with our clients.

Today MASYC is a strong, positive culture, focused on our people and driven to be the best at what we do. We work as a team, help each other, and produce a truly outstanding product: our consulting services. Was embracing Taylor Hartman's bold process worth it? In an industry where consultants are often viewed as a commodity and there are many independent players in the market, MASYC is in the greatest demand. We are able to command the highest rates and pay our consultants at the highest level. At the same time, we are constantly seeking to grow the organization in an effort to catch up with the demand for our services. Our profits are above the industry norm. We have doubled in size over the last three years and will do so again over the next three years. Our clients value our new culture and how it delivers for them.

This process, like anything worthwhile, takes time, energy, and commitment over a period of years. Many executives may not be willing to make the investment today for the returns tomorrow. We paid a large price when we first brought Taylor on. We lost people. Change creates discomfort; plus, this was hard work. Finding the right people—legitimate people—who match our new culture requires a huge commitment. However, since we've paid that price, our success has skyrocketed. I look back now and wonder how I ever ran the company without the knowledge and understanding I have now. There is no doubt that the price we paid is well worth the rewards we now enjoy.

As Russ said, applying *The People Code* and principles of motive to a business requires paying a price. There is always a downside. I often compare it to losing weight: at first, it is terrible. Exercising and dieting are painful. Losing weight takes time and it's difficult to change your habits. However, once it starts happening, you find yourself asking a question similar to the one Russ asked himself, "How did I survive before?" Once you experience the clarity that comes from knowing *why*, you'll wonder *how* your company ever ran before.

Chapter Sixteen

EDUCATION AND
THE PEOPLE CODE

"The only thing more expensive than education is ignorance."
—*Benjamin Franklin*

There are few things in life that are more rewarding or challenging than educating our youth. Every year teachers are presented with a sea of new faces for which they must create connection and meaning. The students behind the faces represent tremendous variety in their personal histories and family cultures. Even so, teachers must make sense of the students' individuality as well as create a community wherein they can work together and learn.

We have high expectations for what teachers must accomplish in order to be considered legitimate in society's eyes. However, none of our expectations can equal those set by the teachers themselves. For many, teaching is their passion and mission in life. They want nothing more than to make a difference in the lives of young people. They have curriculum they want to share and lives they want to touch. They welcome any tools that will assist them in accomplishing their goals. They are eager to make the type of relationship with their students that allows them to successfully teach their message.

Nothing provides greater clarity about individual students' personalities than the Hartman Personality Profile for youth. This profile is geared to grades 4 through 12 and uses vocabulary that students are able to easily understand (unlike the adult profile, which is longer and more challenging). The process of taking the profile provides each student with an active, important voice in assessing who they believe they are at their core. They are much more receptive to this process than merely being assessed by others and told what color personality they are believed to be. While there is a natural bias for young people to see themselves as Yellow, the discussion that ensues between parents, teachers, and peers with the young people provides tremendous dialogue and clarity about who they innately are versus who they might wish themselves to be.

We have to remember that each color is valued differently at various stages of age, life circumstance, and a myriad of other variables. For example, the "in color" to be in youth is Yellow, while the business world drives Red preference. Home life promotes Blue, while international diplomacy invites Whites. While our personalities are innate, we remain vulnerable to the cultural, gender, and many other biases that surround us.

Once administered, the Youth Profile helps both students and teachers connect with a mutual understanding that enriches both their personal and professional connection. Young people are especially open to discovering new insights about themselves. They feel far less threatened than adults by the prospect of looking inward at their inherent strengths and limitations. They freely challenge each other and seek feedback from their peers about how they are perceived. For many, this awareness is extremely positive because it provides an identity separate from their family and cultural foundations. It frees them to see themselves at their raw, innate core.

> *"I finally felt like I was somebody I could accept. I had tried all my life to be what my parents were like—who they wanted me be—and this gave us all permission to like me for who I really was inside."*
>
> —Lisa, California

Furthermore, the concepts of color-coding provide powerful tools for understanding other students. We recognize that humans are social beings and spend much of their lifetime in groups or some form of human interaction. We rely on each other throughout life in so many varied ways. This diagnostic tool, the Hartman Youth Personality Profile, educates everyone about their peers' basic wants and needs. It gives understanding about why people behave differently from each other and makes allowances for our differences.

> *"We rely heavily on The People Code for teaming purposes. Once students have taken the Hartman Youth Profile, we discuss how each color personality brings different gifts that enhance and limitations that may block the process. They are challenged to bring the best out in each other as a team. We do four integrated projects combining technology and color-coding throughout the year. This process has made a huge difference in student success!"*
>
> —Pam, Michigan

For the teacher, it is content rich in application. *The People Code* provides a framework for meeting individual student learning styles. How can you effectively teach someone you do not understand? How can you present a message you care deeply about to someone who cannot hear you because of how it is presented? Consider the value of grouping students into teams that enhance their individual learning rather than detract from it!

Many teachers who currently use the system provide the profile during the first week of school and use the results in numerous forms to assist in student learning—everything from teaming to leadership opportunities, seating charts to project partnerships. This awareness of students' personalities greatly enhances teacher effectiveness. Knowing the strengths and limitations of each personality, they are able to develop a structure that enriches the educational experience. Color-coding is simply a tool that works. It is easy to administer yet provides amazing depth in understanding.

> *"I have a 90 percent effectiveness rate in bringing students from failure at the University with Hartman's work. This has made all the difference in the world."*
>
> —Joyce, Pennsylvania

Imagine the excitement generated by *The People Code,* with its ability to identify for every individual in the classroom an awareness of what motivates them at their most inner core! Consider the value this body of knowledge provides in making strong connections with the various personalities. For example, when you are teaching a Red student, you know he is looking for results and will challenge you directly. It frees you from personalizing his challenges and enhances your more assertive approach in earning his respect. When you are working with a White student, you know she is highly introspective and logical. She sees far more than she expresses. Yellows seek to be entertained, while Blues seek to please the teacher and do the right thing. The knowledge of color-coding frees teachers to engage their students far more effectively than when they were unaware of driving core motivations.

Another critical aspect of teachers' effectiveness is their understanding of themselves and their own personal biases. Before teachers entered the classroom, they were human beings. Teachers are as unique and human as their students. When teachers understand their own wants and needs, they can begin to see how they enhance or detract from their students' success.

"I was a mentor teacher and ready to quit my profession. I had been teaching fifth graders for many years, but this class almost put me over the edge. Dr. Hartman recommended that we profile the students to see what personalities we were dealing with by percentages. I'm very Blue and the class turned out to be 60 percent Yellow core personalities. We completely revamped my teaching strategies for the rest of the year and it literally saved my teaching career as well as at least a few students' lives to be sure!"

—Kris, California

Both teacher and student bring their personalities to the educational experience. Blending personalities and preferences for learning may well be the most daunting challenge yet also the most magical achievement in the entire educational process. For example, a Blue teacher who believes that students should always act appropriately and be well-mannered may struggle with Yellow students. Yellow teachers, on the other hand, may cause stress for Blue students who are looking for structure and clear directions. Red teachers can be heavy authoritarians, which causes White students to react with passivity rather than challenge the educational learning process. Neither benefits the other if this relationship is not well understood.

On the positive side, Blue teachers can provide the structure that enhances learning possibilities for Yellow students, and Red teachers can provide leadership and direction for students with a White personality. All colors can enhance or detract from one another depending on their own natural preferences *and*, what's more important, their character.

Character education has stepped to the forefront of education, which is a good thing. We must educate the whole person, not simply the intellect.

In Daniel Goleman's work on emotional intelligence, he states that EQ is far more critical to an individual's success in life than IQ. He suggests that self-awareness is the foundation for effective emotional intelligence. *The People Code* provides this vital piece to the puzzle of every individual's self-awareness. Knowing oneself with the clarity of innate driving core motives, needs, and wants is pivotal to success in developing legitimate self-awareness. Trying to foster emotional intelligence without the foundation of *The People Code* would be like requiring students to study calculus without their first learning basic addition and subtraction.

The four basic tenets of character education are outlined in my upcoming book, *Playing Life to Win*. Successful people *get* themselves (self-awareness), *get* truth (universal principles), *get* over themselves (resolve internal selfishness), and *get* others (connect with and serve others). Each personality intuitively struggles with different tenets of becoming charactered. Learning why we struggle is the first step in overcoming our resistance to living legitimate lives.

> *"Character education is becoming a critical component of the college experience. Faculty across the country are seeking ways to enhance student learning by including concepts that raise self-awareness and increase people skills. Utah Valley State College has found an incredible tool that does just that! The People Code is used in a variety of courses across the curriculum. From the First-Year Experience Course for freshmen students to the Business Management Capstone course for seniors, Dr. Hartman's work contributes to student learning by providing a critical introspection for students to discover their strengths and limitations and then make a plan to improve upon their strengths and get rid of those traits that hold them back from being successful in life. We have used this program for more than 10 years and find that when the students are asked about which college concepts have most impacted their life, invariably they mention The People Code experience. If you are looking for a program to build self-awareness and teach positive values that will enhance your students for life, you should definitely look into The People Code."*
>
> —Phil, Utah

Educators can bring this powerful, life-affirming process to life for every student with the tools provided by Hartman Communications. Educators know that their work goes far beyond the classroom and are often eager to make a long-lasting impact with students. They simply must be armed with the tools to do so.

Hartman Communications is dedicated to improving the educational process for teachers, students, parents, and administrators. We have sponsored a nonprofit organization that focuses specifically on providing tools and support for enhancing education with our products and services. You can contact this organization directly at www.hartmanei.org.

Chapter Seventeen

CHARACTER:
HOW TO BECOME
YOUR BEST COLOR

If you want to be all you can be, like a finely tuned athlete,
you must choose to commit to the whole process,
not just the convenient parts you like.
Becoming your best self means becoming charactered.

Picture this. You have arrived at the airport and identified the correct gate where you will board your flight. (We have correctly identified your innate personality.) You have surveyed the other passengers and flight crew. (We have clarified the roles that various color combinations offer in relationships.) Now it is time to take off and fly. This is where becoming your own best color begins. It's like taking off and completing your flight. Why else would you come to the airport if not to complete the journey to your final destination?

However, as odd as that seems in the airport metaphor, it is not uncommon for people to show up for life and never complete the experience they came here to have. Some never gain an accurate self-awareness. Others figure themselves out but never apply their awareness to their business or personal relationships. Still the majority of people fail most often to complete the process of becoming fully human—fully alive. They never become their best selves.

The People Code offers you a very clear structure for identifying yourself correctly, building successful relationships, and becoming a legitimate, fully actualized person. All you have to do to begin the final process is accept 100 percent responsibility for yourself. This section is not about anyone else but you. If you want to become all you can be, like a finely tuned athlete, you must choose to commit to the whole process, not just the convenient parts you like. Becoming your best self

THE SEVEN MOST COMMON CHARACTER STRENGTHS OF EACH COLOR

RED	BLUE	WHITE	YELLOW
loyal to tasks	loyal to people	tolerant	positive
committed	committed	patient	forgiving
visionary	quality-oriented	cooperative	friendly
logical	sincere	accepting	optimistic
leader	honest	objective	trusting
focused	purposeful	balanced	appreciative
responsible	moral	excellent at listening	open

THE SEVEN MOST COMMON CHARACTER LIMITATIONS OF EACH COLOR

RED	BLUE	WHITE	YELLOW
proud (arrogant)	self-righteous	timid	uncommitted
insensitive	judgmental	silently stubborn	inconsistent
poor at listening	easily depressed	emotionally dishonest	obnoxious
tactless	controlling	lazy	irresponsible
rebellious	unforgiving	uninvolved	rebellious
critical of others	suspicious	dependent	self-centered
impatient	irrational	directionless	permissive

means becoming charactered. It means developing muscles (strengths) you never realized you had before and accepting pain (stretching, risking, getting out of your current comfort zone) as inevitable.

People behave in four basic patterns. They are charactered, healthy, unhealthy, or psychologically sick. While we may operate in all four patterns at any given time, most people commonly find themselves in one of three blends of these basic patterns. They live predominantly in the realm of charactered-healthy, healthy-unhealthy, or unhealthy-sick.

The *charactered* pattern refers to people who identify, value, develop, and embrace the positive strengths outside their innate core color. *Healthy* describes people who exude the positive strengths that come within their natural and innate core personality. *Unhealthy* defines people who live their lives out predominantly in the negative limitations that are natural to their innate core personality. *Sick* patterns refer to people who embrace negative limitations that do not innately come with their personality but have been developed in their lives. People in this pattern are terribly difficult to deal with because there is absolutely no rhyme or reason to match their personality with the attitudes and behavior they display.

Though we can never change our innate driving core motive, we can develop any strengths of any of the other colors. This is becoming charactered. In order to free ourselves of our innate limitations and become our best selves, we must develop strengths from the other colors. Simply staying within our own personalities will not suffice. Building character is the only way to override the innate limitations that already exist in our personality (unhealthy pattern) or the limitations we learn through unfortunate life experiences and/or dysfunctional relationships (sick pattern).

Character is a powerful phenomenon with complex beginnings. We can explain personality as innate, but character defies such a simple explanation. Our understanding of character begins with an accurate definition.

Personality is a gift.
Character is a victory!

It takes character for a Red personality to *tolerate* differences, or a Blue personality to take time to *play,* or a White personality to *assert* himself or herself as a leader, or a Yellow personality to *commit* to an intimate relationship. When we push our Override button, these behaviors go against the natural grain of our innate personality and require developed character in order to exist.

Individuals develop character strengths and limitations, just as they are born with personality strengths and limitations. Furthermore, it appears that some character traits are most innately compatible with certain personalities. Every individual has obvious strengths and limitations that he or she must deal with from birth. Though we may not be born with a particular character trait, we do appear to be more receptive and/or vulnerable to one or another depending on our given personality color.

We have defined character and linked common character flaws with each personality. Personality limitations are capable of inhibiting others' character development. Notice particularly those areas where *your* personality may be inhibiting another's character development. Look for any specific behaviors in any colors that are currently inhibiting your character-building process. The following list delineates common and specific ways each personality inhibits the character development of others.

INHIBITING BEHAVIORS

REDS

1. Have a tendency to be overbearing and inflexible (which limits depth of shared feelings and/or perceptions in conversations).
2. Often have exaggerated ego needs (which may create an unnecessary power struggle).
3. Known to make sarcastic and unkind remarks in order to maintain control (which drives others around them into a defensive posture).
4. Typically are too task-oriented. They forget the spirit of living and remain too strict in their orientation to life. (If I suggest that a Red patient buy flowers for his wife, he may do so, but rarely for the enjoyment—he completes the assigned task rather than feels the spirit of the giving process.)
5. Often are judgmental of others' weaknesses (which causes others to hide their insecurities for fear of rejection or ridicule). Doesn't bring out the creative best in others.
6. Tend to resent being questioned and need to always be right. (Typically others learn to lie or pretend they agree with a Red to his face and mock him behind his back.)
7. Often are unappreciative of others. They don't give compliments freely, which frustrates others who crave their approval and/or acceptance. This also backfires on Reds who would enjoy intimacy but rarely get it because they don't generate it themselves.

BLUES

1. Tend to take things too personally (which often causes others to lie in order to protect the insecure and overly sensitive Blue).
2. Often have too many unrealistic expectations (which makes others feel inadequate, unnecessary, or unloved).
3. Typically place themselves last on their list of priorities, presenting bad role models for self-esteem.
4. Often are too critical of others who choose to live life with a more relaxed or aggressive style (which causes others to feel unable ever to please them).

5. Tend to be too demanding of others' manners (which causes others to rebel against manners altogether).

WHITES

1. May be too easily overwhelmed by life (which causes others to pity Whites).
2. Can be too fearful of expressing themselves honestly (which causes others to lose respect for them).
3. Often are too timid to take a stand (which causes others to feel a need always to protect them).
4. Tend to be too insecure to set goals and pursue them (which causes others to resent being held back by their lack of initiative and cooperation in accomplishing joint endeavors).
5. Can be too independent to promote teamwork.
6. Often are too silently stubborn (which angers others and often causes them to ignore Whites and go their own way).
7. Appear to be too helpless and inadequate (which causes others to want to rescue them).

YELLOWS

1. May appear to be too flighty and uncommitted (which causes people to feel Yellows don't really care about them or anything).
2. Can be too flippant and make rude comments (which hurts feelings and/or causes others to not take them seriously).
3. Often are too irresponsible with jobs (which causes others not to trust them to come through).
4. Can be unwilling to learn many living skills (which causes others to lose respect for them or become overly protective of them).
5. Sometimes refuse to accept committed leadership roles (which causes others to carry more than their fair share).
6. Can be emotionally dishonest in order to avoid conflict (which causes others to believe things that aren't really happening and/or keeps intimacy on a superficial level).

We have briefly reviewed how the personality limitations of each color actually bind the character development of others. We can easily see the value of building our character. Now we can choose a healthy character-building process that will enable us to balance ourselves and experience the greater meaning life offers to those of us who are willing to reach out and stretch.

HOW TO BUILD YOUR CHARACTER

It is predominantly character, not personality, that ultimately determines the quality of our lives. Character is essentially anything we learn to think, feel, or do that is initially unnatural and requires an effort to develop. Character is reflected in the changes we make in our values and beliefs through our lives.

There are several components that are essential for character development. The first component is *free will*. The second component is *selecting positive influences in our lives*. The third component is *identifying positive life principles*.

FREE WILL

If free will were not at the very core of our human existence, we would be trapped within the limitations of our innate personalities. There would be no personal development or possibility for change. Developing our character is a way we can balance our personalities. Unless we build character, we must remain unfulfilled and limited. Developing our character allows us to most fully enjoy an exciting and productive life.

Character is usually shaped best in an atmosphere of free will, which lies at the root of every healthy character-building program. One young woman was forced by her father to practice piano every morning for two hours before school. She appeared very charactered to those who witnessed this daily ritual. However, healthy character is reflected by consistent commitment to positive life principles. This young woman grew to hate the piano. She also hated her father for demanding that she practice so much. She even hated herself for allowing him to control her life. Unfortunately, she had developed an unhealthy character by committing to the negative motive of pleasing others at all costs and resenting and blaming everyone for her miserable life. Similarly, her father had erred in demanding that his daughter develop character by working on his values rather than her own. He was shocked when she voiced her hatred for him, confessed that she was bulimic, attempted suicide, and vowed never to play the piano again. Neither the father nor the daughter had effectively identified positive life principles and consistently committed themselves to them. Both had accepted unhealthy character.

> *If free will were not at the very core of our human existence,*
> *we would be trapped within the limitations*
> *of our innate personalities.*

SELECTING POSITIVE INFLUENCES IN OUR LIVES

We are often told that we preach our greatest sermons by the lives we lead. Example is often all a child knows for its first few years of life. As we continue the aging process, we choose examples to follow. After years as a psychotherapist, I am convinced that with the exception of self, the most influential factor in childhood character development is the example and influence of parents. As teenagers, we are highly influenced by our peers. As adults, we are most influenced by our spouses. Playing a strong supporting role, however, are siblings, extended family, and friends. We must continually ask ourselves whom we seek as role models and who may be looking to us for mentoring.

IDENTIFYING POSITIVE LIFE PRINCIPLES

Life principles are those positive principles common to everyone. They may include living and being loved, the need for food and shelter, or the importance of feeling there is purpose in our lives. They may be theoretical or philosophical in nature. They help us to become more effective and charactered. They include the knowledge that:

- Every person can offer unique strengths to a relationship.
- Individuals who have personal confidence feel little need for power plays with others.
- People who like themselves find it easier to like and accept others than do those who feel inadequate.
- When we spend energy belittling others and blocking their development, we limit our own growth.

Life principles enhance our color by giving us insight into how others perceive things. These same life principles assist us in overcoming our inherent personality limitations by developing initially uncomfortable, yet positive, attitudes and behaviors based on principles that apply equally to all people.

In order to build character, we must identify and commit to those life principles that will maximize our color strengths and minimize our limitations. Regardless of our color, these life principles will guide us through the challenging process of character development.

Character building requires attitudinal and behavioral commitments. In order to be effective, character building must become specific and personal. For some, it may include the act of letting go or forgiving another for something that was said or done. For others, it may require a physical act such as refusing an alcoholic beverage. It may mean initiating a physical embrace with another person, or it might be as simple as giving a compliment to a deserving family member or a co-worker.

> *We must continually ask ourselves*
> *whom we seek as role models*
> *and who may be looking to us*
> *for mentoring.*

The character-building process requires us to *identify healthy life principles; accept them into our lives; commit to living them consistently; and share them with others.*

Life principles will benefit all colors in their own development as well as in becoming less inhibiting of the relationships they encounter with other colors. Key life principles include:

Life Principle 1

Personal truths must be identified, pursued, and blended with universal truths if we are to have a balanced life.

Life Principle 2

Charactered people take responsibility for their own attitudes and behaviors.

Life Principle 3

We must stretch and risk personal discomfort in order to make alien attitudes and behaviors become natural.

Life Principle 4

Charactered people actively love themselves and others.

Life Principle 5

Our strengths must be shared with others in order to benefit us fully.

Life Principle 6

Everything has its price. Charactered people choose wisely and pay their debts.

Life Principle 7

Trust is vital to the positive human experience. We are all interdependent in varying degrees.

LIFE PRINCIPLE 1

Personal truths must be identified, pursued, and blended with universal truths if we are to have a balanced life.

Personal truths differ from universal truths in their focus. Personal truths may include careers we choose, friends we enjoy, hobbies we pursue, or the amount of sleep we require. Personal truths are those unique and healthy lifestyles we individually prefer, regardless of our personality color. When we think *everyone* should drive fast or slow on the freeway, we cause accidents. When we think *everyone* should be academically educated, we deprive our skilled laborers of earned self-respect.

Some of us would be miserable if we were psychotherapists or medical doctors. Others would be miserable as plumbers or auto mechanics. Unfortunately, we may disguise our own professional and personal insecurities by criticizing the occupations of others. We think this enhances our occupations. Personal truths suggest that one occupation is not necessarily better than another as long as both render an honest service. *Charactered individuals understand this concept. Simple, innate personalities do not.* We can waste so much energy trying to force personal truths into universal truths. We develop character when we identify universal truths and embrace them. We also foster effective human relationships when we understand and accept others in light of their personal truths.

You love to ski. I prefer tennis. You relax by reading novels. I relax with music. You prefer living single. I want children in my life. One person works in order to play, another individual thrives on the work itself. These are all examples of personal truths that simply suggest that each of us has our own road in life. We're not right or wrong for having different preferences. Personal truths are directly connected to our personal preferences. They do not necessarily apply to humanity in general. Being true to oneself often means valuing oneself enough to pursue the lifestyle of one's choice.

In order to build our character we decide on many personal truths and commit time and energy to developing them. Personal truths range from wanting better communication in our family to wanting to take a step up the career ladder. Only we know what is true for us.

We must keep revising some of these truths in order to stay current with our changing life situations. We may want to make a list of at least ten personal truths we want to utilize in our lives. We should pay particular attention to our specific needs and values when we design our lists. This list is most effective when it focuses on our "wants," rather than our "musts" and "shoulds."

All of us want to feel loved and to be valued by others. We appreciate our lives more when they include a sincere element of purpose. Friendship is a mutual experience for two sacrificing individuals who willingly give priority to their relationship. These statements reflect some feelings and realities that are *universally true.*

The charactered person seeks a healthy blend between his/her personal values and the values of the universe. An individual may love his/her free time but forgo some in order to comfort a sick friend. Another person who values peaceful relationships may be forced because of integrity to confront a situation. Life is a series of choices. It is motivating and thus productive to maintain a proper perspective about our life. Balancing personal daily commitments with universal ones remains the most challenging and creative high-wire act any of us attempts.

We should seek help with our balancing act from within ourselves and from others. We are advised to listen to our internal intuitive senses. We also benefit by listening to sound suggestions from others who may have greater life experience than we do. Setting up positive support systems of family and friends, and keeping ourselves emotionally healthy so that we are receptive to intuition, are essential for successfully balancing on the high wire in life.

> *Unhealthy judgment of others*
> *comes from one's personal inadequacy.*

LIFE PRINCIPLE 2

Charactered people take responsibility for their own attitudes and behaviors.

Character building requires that we take responsibility for our attitudes and behavior. The emphasis for *charactered* people is in the action word *take.* They take responsibility while others passively accept or even deny it. Immature people often say, "I'm just that way. I've always been that way, and I will always be that way." *We must be cautious that we never use the colored personality labels as a way to excuse ourselves, to judge others, or to limit or trap anyone.*

If we hope to be charactered, we must be able to present ourselves with a given personality (style) but simultaneously accept responsibility for healthy attitudes and behaviors that may not be associated with our given personality. For example, I am a Yellow *personality*. We Yellows present ourselves as fun, full of optimism, and playful. However, as a *charactered* Yellow I recognize our tendency to be irresponsible. I try to pay equal attention to our optimism, our playful personality, *and* our irresponsible nature. A spontaneous, friendly Yellow who also commits willingly to an intimate relationship with sensitivity and honesty is a wonderful blend of a healthy *innate personality* and *developed character.*

Charactered people don't use personality color labels to limit themselves or others. They simply use the labels to help them understand and accept basic differences and similarities in all of us. They use these insights to build rather than block human relationships.

LIFE PRINCIPLE 3

We must stretch and risk personal discomfort in order to make alien attitudes and behaviors become natural.

Some individuals say they are unable to identify their personality from the available options. One individual was confused as to whether his personality was Red or Blue. We briefly discussed his dilemma. Suddenly, he said, "I have always been a strong, dominant man. My wife has been dead for several years. I'm just beginning to realize how she influenced my life. My wife was an invalid for most of our married life. Twenty years before she died, she had a serious stroke that limited her physically and forced me to shoulder many of the burdens usually shared by a couple. She had been so good to me that I initially felt obligated (admittedly resentfully) to take care of her. Through the years, however, my feeling turned to devotion, and I genuinely cared for this special woman. Her handicap allowed me to stretch. Eventually, I actually learned how to love."

This charactered man is innately a Red personality. He exemplifies many of the strengths we admire in Reds. However, he was able to replace his innate Red limitations with positive Blue attributes, giving him the enviable combination of Red and Blue strengths. Charactered individuals either rise to the tasks placed before them or honestly acknowledge their inadequacies. This man rose to his task with success. Charactered people learn to grasp every opportunity (positive or negative) encountered and to give the best that is in them.

Charactered people invite risk into their lives. They want to experience change. Their self-respect is heightened as they face life's discomforts with sincere purpose and clear motives. They do not passively wait for life to test their strength. They seek the opportunities and confront complacency in their daily lives with personal integrity. They are deeply committed to stretching themselves regardless of the inconvenience or discomfort.

LIFE PRINCIPLE 4

Charactered people actively love themselves and others.

Recently, an article in the newspaper caught my attention. The article mourned the loss of a school crossing guard. She was killed by a car only seconds after pushing seven youngsters to safety. Many remembered her for her unselfish love of children. Giving her life for them made a remarkable statement about her commitment to the children she had loved for so many years. However, one child captured a far more endearing expression of her love. The child said, "She'd ask how our classes were going. She was so nice, never grumpy or grouchy."

I once asked a group of parents how many would be willing to die for their children. Every parent raised a hand. Then I asked how many of them would be willing to commit to a daily expression of love for their children and mates with declarations of love; positive comments; quality time for social activities, reading, or games; and by touching them with their hands, their voices, and their eyes. No one raised a hand. "Are you kidding?" one man asked. "I have to earn a living too, you know!" "At least you are honest," I remarked. "But it appears that your perception of being a husband and father is somewhat typical. Many of us may be saying we would rather die than live for our mates and children!" The crossing guard remembered by the children had captured the total picture. In her daily living she had communicated her love before she had died expressing it.

There comes a time in life when the children leave home, and some mothers find themselves at a loss for meaning in their lives. This is referred to as the empty nest syndrome. Actually, dads are often left in worse shape. Mother had expressed her love daily. Dad had been busy earning money to pay the bills and missed opportunities to develop his relationship with the children.

"I should have seen it coming when they were teenagers," one father lamented. "That was my first clue that they were more interested in friends and clothes than they were in me. Instead of thinking about some creative options for getting closer, I retreated to my work and television. I think I was scared of them. I didn't understand them. I refused to go to parenting classes. I wouldn't even take up a mutual hobby with my kids.

I just expected my wife to handle them. Now they're gone and I can't bring them back." Then he shrugged his shoulders and asked rhetorically, "What am I saying, bring them back? How can they come back to a place where they have never been? I mean, they have never been with me, and I've never been with them. Not really. We're strangers who shared most everything life offers except ourselves."

It's interesting that men are more affected than women by the empty nest syndrome. Many men actually break into tears during interviews as they recall the lost opportunities for loving their children. Parenting requires a commitment to daily expressions of love and to being a quality role model for children.

We may limit the lives of those we love by expecting them to love us the way we are. We limit the character building of those we love when we tell them what they must be and how they should perform because we don't trust them to make the right decisions. Some husbands and wives want to change each other. Some employers hound employees. Some parents overprotect children because they haven't learned to trust either themselves or their children. We may restrict and monitor the lives of those we feel responsible for. This is not love.

Love is accepting and encouraging others. Too many of us think we are especially wonderful lovers because we love others the way *we* would like to be loved. Unconditional love is always expressed in the language of the receiver, not of the sender. One woman shared her grief in realizing that all her life she had loved on her terms and simply ignored the needs of others. For example, when she was giving a dinner at her home, she was more concerned about how beautiful the house looked and how delicious the food was than about her guests. She almost canceled a dinner party one evening because she was so worried about herself and her performance. Fortunately, just prior to the event, we had a counseling session. We discussed her dilemma, and she agreed to pick some things up at the local delicatessen and simply enjoy her guests. The evening was a smashing success, and she began to realize how her entire life had been dedicated to looking good rather than loving others.

She also told me that she had not given her best friend a Christmas gift the previous year because she couldn't find the perfect gift. Rather than try to look good and be perfect, she could easily have invited her friend to a special dinner or suggested they meet at a fast-food restaurant just to get together. Something personal would have been appreciated by her friend. Unfortunately, she was concerned only with her needs and never realized that being concerned with only her needs would never allow her to genuinely say "I love you" to others.

Our love is most helpful when we accept and encourage others as *they* need to be accepted and encouraged. It is critical that we recognize the importance of *accepting* each individual as he or she is. Remember, we did not select our personalities. They came with us at birth. Each of us is struggling to identify, understand, and accept ourselves. Perhaps the most valuable gifts we can offer our friends, children, and companions are acceptance, approval, and appreciation of their unique expressions of self. We can also help by having patience with them as they go about the arduous task of character building.

Any discussion of acceptance immediately brings up the issue of self-esteem. How well you accept and appreciate yourself has a direct effect on how well you *can* accept, approve of, and/or appreciate others. Unhealthy judgment of others comes from one's personal inadequacy. This is perhaps best illustrated by teenagers. Teenagers are known for their cruelty to peers. Who can't recall being on the hurting end of an unkind comment during those years?

Ask most junior and senior high school students what they value most. The two most commonly stated attributes are looks and athletic ability. *Looks and athletic ability?* Is there a more awkward, acne-attacked, body-changing time in life? They value what so few of them have at that time.

We are most likely to criticize the very thing we crave most. For example, if I am an individual who needs emotional stroking, I am more likely to expect others to provide what I lack than would another individual who feels relatively secure and doesn't require excess emotional support. We often criticize others for our own inadequacies.

We have often been told that in order to love others, we must first love ourselves. Loving ourselves means we value and accept ourselves as we are, with the understanding that we are endeavoring to improve our faults. When others misunderstand or mistrust our love, it is our self-love that allows us to continue loving them because we know our motives are pure. We can genuinely accept that while we may choose to love, others may not yet be willing to be loved. Loving ourselves frees us from attaching strings to our caring for others. When we are too needy, we may be kind and caring toward others, but the underlying motives are selfish. We are trying to control the behavior of those we are being good to. We may appear to give freely, but there are actually conditions that others must meet in order for us to continue to "love" them.

For example, arrogant people and people who grovel for approval are all suffering from the same need. They are insecure. At times they may seem to be loving by taking care of others (arrogance) or by telling others how they only wish they were as bright or attractive or rich as they are (groveling). Arrogance and groveling come from insecurity. Neither is an example of humility. Self-respect produces a humble (teachable) nature that allows us to love unconditionally.

Humility requires an accurate perspective on ourselves and others. It requires that we value ourselves enough not to need validation from others. It suggests we are receptive to others' feedback as a way of maintaining an accurate perception of ourselves and our interpersonal relationships.

Seeking feedback constantly from our children, co-workers, employees, and friends regarding our motives is a growth process. Only insecure individuals fear the answers to "How am I doing as a parent, employer, or friend?" Secure individuals appreciate truth and opportunities to correct any misunderstandings.

We cherish friends who accepted and approved of our awkward self-discovery, who believed in us and shared that belief without reservation. We value those parents, teachers, friends, and children who taught us and nurtured us in the skills of living and the art of loving. We value those who offered us the numerous opportunities that have enabled us to build a strong platform to leap from childhood into adulthood.

In all these experiences we are often simultaneously restless and at peace. We love ourselves, yet we seek further life challenges to deepen our ability to love. We have wisdom, yet we feel terribly ignorant about the mysteries of life. We are heartened by meaningful friends who remind us there is always time for those who love us and for those who are willing to be loved.

> In order to be effective,
> character building must become
> specific and personal.

LIFE PRINCIPLE 5

Our strengths must be shared with others in order to benefit us fully.

Developing a character begins with desire. The desire is expressed with an action. Character begins with what we think and do when no one else is around, but true character goes beyond personal commitment. *Fully developed character inevitably expresses itself in the giving of service to others*. It may begin as a mental battle, then proceed to an outward search for more knowledge and understanding. Character is not what we have, nor what we do. It is what we are that determines our worth.

Personality can be expressed without reference to others. Character must eventually affect others' lives as well as our own. We may be able to practice in the privacy of our homes, but we cannot fully develop our character alone.

Do we not have a mutual responsibility to love and accept love from everyone we encounter? How we model love for others often has a significant impact on them and their ability to love others. As we express our love, others watch us and learn from our ways.

We may ask, "Who are our role models? Who are the individuals we most admire?" We find them historically and when we are open and honest. We find them in our current everyday lives.

Florence Nightingale forsook wealth and physical comfort in order to pursue a need she felt deep within her soul. She felt driven to try to care for thousands of men, to share their emotional devastation and fear while they died with her at their side. She became the mother of the profession we know and appreciate today as nursing.

Father Damien, the Catholic priest who gave up everything to minister to the lepers on the Hawaiian island of Molokai, fully embraced the principle of sharing for character building. He fought numerous battles with the church bureaucracy to acquire supplies for his congregation. Eventually, he contracted leprosy and died with the people he had lived for and had loved.

Mahatma Gandhi gave over his entire being to the cause of freedom. His theory and example of nonviolent revolution eventually allowed him to break the bonds of English subjection for millions of Indians. When he was repeatedly encouraged to write about his life, he gave his greatest statement of character: "My life is my message."

These historical examples of charactered role models, who shared their strengths for the good of others, may help us identify and appreciate those individuals (including ourselves) in our everyday lives who share themselves for the benefit of all humanity. Recently, some historians seem determined to discredit public figures by dredging up all their character flaws. I have little doubt that we could find fault with any public role model if we looked hard enough. This merely verifies my contention that character building is no easy task. However, we must celebrate the wonderful contributions these charactered individuals made to their fellow man, despite their obvious human limitations.

LIFE PRINCIPLE 6

Everything has its price. Charactered people choose wisely and pay their debts.

The price for reading this book can be calculated in various ways. It may help change aspects of our lives. For example, it may encourage an individual to address existing problems in a relationship that have previously been ignored. It may cause pain with the realization that we have been ignoring the development of our character. It costs us time to read when we could be engaging in other activities. It may directly influence our relationships with those we love. Remember Amelia Earhart's challenge, "Courage is the price you pay for peace"? If you are not at peace with yourself or your relationships, this book may cause significant shifting in how you courageously challenge the status quo. Any movement on the part of one individual will always impact others around them.

Similarly, there is a price for those who may choose not to read this book. They may miss helpful insights that would enhance their personal and professional lives. They may miss learning about concepts that would open doors for future relationships. One can only imagine the prices we have all paid with our decisions in life. The prices we pay, good or bad, are not ours alone. Everyone connected with us gains or suffers as well.

One individual has been involved in an extramarital affair for many years. He says he wishes to leave his wife and yet continues to live a double life. His lover explains the price she pays: "I can't continue to live like this. We can't go any further with true intimacy because we are living a lie. I want memories of us sharing the holidays with family and friends, but I have to settle for a phone call after his wife goes to sleep." The man's wife necessarily suffers as well. She experiences the loneliness that comes when one's companion is psychologically withdrawn from a relationship, whether he or she ever acknowledges it or not. Everything has a price. We never pay the price alone.

The effect of our character is much like the ripple effect caused by throwing a pebble in a lake. The intensity of our impact increases with greater character. We are rewarded when we commit to integrity. A scattered life offers mixed messages and little intensity, because it lacks identified purpose. Likewise, we must recognize the high price of a charactered life. It necessarily prohibits a totally carefree and peaceful existence.

LIFE PRINCIPLE 7

Trust is vital to the positive human experience. We are all interdependent in varying degrees.

I have often asked students at the university to guess how many lives touched them prior to our 8:00 a.m. class. The answers usually range from zero to three. That's when the fun begins. The eyes light up and the minds grasp for answers as we consider the clothes they put on (who raised the animals, processed the chemicals, sewed, and sold their clothing?). Who directly and indirectly furnished their breakfast? Who drove with them or against them in traffic? Who designed, built, and repaired their cars? Who set the stoplights, paved the roads, and painted road signs? And we've only just begun! Somehow we typically perceive ourselves as independent agents and seldom recognize that we are connected to others. When we have agreed to sincerely see ourselves as we are and develop a vision of what we hope to become, taking classes, risking new friendships, seeking therapy, reading books, and learning new hobbies can assist us. By appreciating our own contributions to humanity and those positive additions others make to our lives, we can see the value of the life principle known as *interdependence*.

It is not enough simply to choose our *preference* of interest. We commit to a broad spectrum of character development, or we suffer the consequences of a limited life. We will find certain areas easy and inviting. Others may require assistance from people we meet throughout our lives. Typically, the most common categories of interdependence are social, intellectual, emotional, financial, physical, and spiritual. Spirituality has received an unfortunate rap in its association with organized religion. Spirituality runs far deeper than religion. Spirituality is the light in our eyes reminding the world that we are well rooted and "at home" with our purpose in life.

The character-building process begins within us. We are the ones who allow ourselves to feel guilty, arrogant, uncommitted, or withdrawn. We are responsible for choosing the friends we keep and accepting the life we live! Uncharactered parents, siblings, teachers, and/or other role models may have been teachers who taught us limitations rather than strengths. They may have shown us disappointment rather than creative optimism. Our lives may have crossed one of those tragic souls who, in fearing themselves, taught us to fear our potential. However, all of us can seek and find examples of healthy, charactered role models. Choosing positive role models is crucial to charactered living. Becoming a healthy role model is equally essential to our own personal success.

The power of pure motives and healthy life principles is phenomenal. We can never underestimate the value of clearing our energy sources in order that we become free—free to love, free to change, free to accept ourselves at our worst as well as at our best. We can set our goals and commit to a charactered life congruent with those goals. As highly charactered people, we have pure motives. We examine our reasons for behaving or thinking in a particular way. We accept and encourage the best in everyone we encounter. We are emotionally and spiritually alive. We are mentally alert and physically disciplined. We honor our commitments.

Examples of charactered individuals are: the parent who promotes opportunities and independence but accepts and approves of each child's preferences; a busy parent who freely gives her own vacation and/or play time to children; a student who risks a lower grade point average to try a more difficult course; a lawyer who defends a client he or she believes in regardless of fee or notoriety; a corporate president who fosters excellence in his or her product and remains equally concerned about employee morale; a teacher who seeks alternative ways of learning in an attempt to reach struggling students.

We can broaden our vision. We can sacrifice life's trivial distractions in order to remain focused on our true purpose in life. *When we seek with pure motives, we can balance our lives by developing all strengths expressed uniquely by each personality.* We can exchange our limitations for strengths and enrich our own lives as well as the lives of others we touch. It is an interesting irony that often highly charactered individuals' personalities are difficult to decipher because they have so artistically and skillfully blended the strengths of others with their own innate strengths. In other words, when our character and personality are blended, our innate personality is no longer always easily recognized.

Character is one of the three major aspects we must balance in our individual lives and relationships, along with passion and personality.

Passion expresses feelings we have no control over. It comes from deep within our subconscious mind. We may feel passionate toward ourselves, another person, or toward a particular hobby or course of study. Passion reflects an unusually strong bonding of emotion. It feels clean and unencumbered. It just feels right and good. This explains why some people are so hard to let go of in relationships, whether they are right for us or not. It explains why some of us may be attracted to certain hobbies and careers that others do not find particularly inviting or worthwhile.

Character represents the responsible attitudes and behaviors we select for our lives. Healthy character is always rooted in truth. We can continue to develop it throughout our lives by striving to adhere to various life principles essential to successful lives, regardless of our culture's influence.

As we balance these three components of relationships, we will feel the confidence that comes from expressing committed, quality lives.

Truth lies within all of us. Nothing and no one can release truth within us without our consent. Even if we are arrogant, critical, devious, or uncommitted, we can ultimately seek, hear, and accept that truth. (Our innate personality, or style, is not undesirable. The unique qualities in each personality offer us opportunities to mix and blend with each other. There are many variations of successful living. It is quite natural for a person to continue developing his or her life with unique preferences.) We must learn to recognize our true motives and commit to healthy life principles. In our quest for truth and character, we feel the ultimate joy known only to those individuals who are willing both to risk pain and accept happiness. As we work toward developing a life built on both a *positive personality* and a *developed character,* we experience the most passion.

ADVANTAGES OF BUILDING CHARACTER

Character defines the type of positive or negative connection we make with ourselves and others throughout life. It is developed over years by personal design and commitment to life principles. Once established, it cannot be easily altered. We must be patient with the process. Character development often changes and takes numerous twists in its process. However, once the various aspects of character are established, they become as solid as our given personalities at birth. In the follow-up book, *Color Your Future,* more specific steps are provided to assist you and enhance your character-building journey.

Knowing that our character will eventually become as solid as our personality should motivate us to enrich ourselves by balancing our life experiences. With luck, we will seek those positive attributes we observe in others. The search for this balance eventually provides greater meaning to our own lives.

> *As we work toward developing a life*
> *built on both a positive personality*
> *and a developed character,*
> *we experience the most passion.*

Personality is the style we use to present our thoughts and actions to others. Character is the core of life principles behind those thoughts and actions we present. Many naturally vibrant individuals have allowed themselves to put their best "personality" foot forward rather than take a more balanced stance on one "personality" foot and on one "character" foot. We are much stronger and more valuable when we add to the color of our innate personality by developing the best character traits we observe in others. Once we have identified our existing personality and character traits, we can begin to work on designing whatever image we prefer. We can't alter our innate personality. It is, however, tremendously important for us to keep striving to develop our character.

Character allows us to recognize our flawed human nature. We recognize the many times we have made poor decisions. Yet we continue to pick ourselves up and try, with renewed determination, to overcome our limitations. We want our lives to count for something— to matter. We want others to know we have lived for a greater purpose than merely to have survived this existence, after all. This feeling can come only with developed character. Personality alone can never offer such a powerful sense of destiny.

COMMONLY ASKED
PEOPLE CODE QUESTIONS

How do you know someone's color?
Have them take the profile! If they haven't taken it, listen to the words they use and pay attention to the way they interact with you. However, remember that behaviors can sometimes be deceiving because of cultural influences. Treat people as the color you think they are, and if they don't respond positively, you've probably assessed them incorrectly.

Which colors are most compatible?
Every color is compatible with every other color. Each color combination comes with innate strengths and limitations, much as each individual color comes with innate strengths and limitations. However, any two colors can have a meaningful and healthy relationship, whether it be personal or professional. *The People Code* becomes an invaluable tool in learning ourselves, owning our strengths, overcoming our limitations, and understanding and speaking the language of someone else's personality.

Why are there only four colors?
Some people find it unsettling that I categorize personality into only four groups. What needs to be understood is that *The People Code* doesn't categorize *people* into four categories, only what motivates them. In thirty-plus years of research, I have yet to come across someone who is motivated by something other than power, intimacy, peace, or fun. Think of it this way: the human face, which has only a small number of variables (eyes, nose, chin, ears, hair, etc.), has never produced exactly the same look. The same is true

of personality. While core personalities are "limited" to only four core motives (or colors), no two people are exactly the same.

What is motive?

Motives are our innermost reasons for doing what we do at our most raw and basic level. They explain why we think and behave as we do. They are the driving force behind our personalities, and the principle means of identifying an individual's personality color. Motives are to our personalities what engines are to automobiles.

Can your color change?

Our core personality is complete at conception and comes in the soul of each and every one of us. Therefore, our core motives are innate and will always be a part of us. We are not, however, restricted to living in the strengths and limitations of only our core color. Secondary colors can influence our core personality to our benefit or our detriment, and at times can make it seem as though our color has "changed." Regardless of our behavior at different times in our lives, our core motive came with us at birth and will never change.

Why is it best to take the profile as if you were a child?

Because your personality is innate and comes with you at birth, this will provide a more accurate perspective on who you innately are, as opposed to who you have become.

How is the Hartman Personality Profile different from other personality tests, such as Myers-Briggs or DISC?

Other personality profiles are based on behavior. They offer a snapshot of how you currently behave, but they admittedly offer no insight into *why* you behave as you do or who you are innately born to be. The Hartman Personality Profile is based on motive, which is what determines all behavior. Categorizing personality by motive provides a much more complex and accurate picture of ourselves and of those around us. People who use the Hartman Personality Profile are forever changed by the depth of their new-found awareness.

Why Power, Intimacy, Peace, and Fun?

In nature, there are four essential elements required by all humans to live: earth, air, fire, and water. In human relationships, the four essential elements are power, intimacy, peace, and fun. After thirty years of in-depth interactions, I have discovered that all people are primarily driven by a single innate core motive. While some are most clearly identified by one sole color personality, others may have strong secondary (and even tertiary) colors. Still, everyone has a solitary driving core motive.

Why does knowing your core personality color matter?

When a child is born, the first thing we look for is ten fingers and ten toes. Far more critical to their life experience, however, is their innate personality. Personality impacts every aspect of our entire lives, especially relationships, far more than physical features do. It is critical for you to know yourself so that you can align congruently with your natural preferences. It gives you the creative edge in life. Furthermore, if you don't know yourself—your driving core motive, your strengths and limitations—how can you expect others to relate effectively to you?

How do the color code and birth order impact each other?

Many factors influence our personalities, but none of them can change our driving core motive. Motive comes first; birth order is just one of those variables that has an influence. An oldest child will most likely have more responsibilities and feel more weight on his or her shoulders; however, being the oldest will *not* change the child's color. All it will do is influence the type of Red, Blue, White, or Yellow the child already is. A youngest child will probably be allowed more freedom than others. This will enhance a Yellow's natural tendencies toward irresponsibility, while being the eldest will help a Yellow child overcome that limitation.

How should *The People Code* be used in hiring employees?

Any color personality can do any job. However, there are certain fields that enhance each color's strengths. Reds excel in leadership positions, Blues do well with detail-oriented work, Whites shine in supporting roles, and Yellows feel very comfortable in public relations.

What role does color-coding play in team building?

No color is better than any other color, and there is no better illustration of that fact than team building. The beauty of a team is diversity. The members of the best teams learn to value one another's strengths and compensate for each other's limitations, covering all their bases. Forming a team of only one color personality will ultimately come back to haunt you.

How does color-coding enhance my dating success?

Without question, the biggest decision you'll ever make is whom you marry. While chemistry obviously plays a large role in making that decision, it is color-coding that allows you to see what your future will be like. A relationship will hold far fewer surprises if you know your partner's color from the very beginning. It will come as no surprise when your Blue partner is critical, or when your Yellow partner is late for every date. Color-coding tells you what you'll need to do in order to make a relationship work. And while any two colors can have a healthy, successful relationship, it is true that opposites (Red/White and Blue/Yellow) do attract.

How does culture affect personality?

The many different cultures we come in contact with (business, family, social) all play powerful roles in molding who we are and what we deem acceptable. Knowing the color a particular culture values helps you know what is expected of you, what the norms are, and what you must do to be successful. The blending of your core color with the color of a culture will help you feel comfortable. On a world stage, South America is a Yellow culture, North America is a Blue culture, dictatorships are Red cultures, and island nations are White cultures.

How does color-coding relate to politics?

From the time Richard Nixon was impeached until 2008, America has never elected a Red or Blue president. George W. Bush is a classic Yellow who lost his way and became a bad Red. We have had exceptional and terrible presidents of every color. It is interesting to examine the reasons why different colors become involved in politics: Reds to get something done, Blues because of an injustice they want to correct, Whites to be diplomats, and Yellows for social reasons.

How does color-coding influence parent-child relationships?

There is nothing more critical in a parent-child relationship than how effective the parent is at valuing the child. Certain personalities, by nature, may find other personalities difficult or easy to relate to. As a Yellow boy, my Red mother adored me while my father struggled to understand and appreciate me. Therefore, I was much more responsive to my mother, because Yellows love to be adored. Blue children seek a parent who is understanding, Reds need parents who respect them, and White children need a parent who is kind and accepting. What children want in a parent is not always what they need (a Yellow child rarely loves being taught morals by a Blue parent). However, parents need to look past what their children want and give them what they'll need in the long run.

AFTERWORD

Look at your journey
as the ultimate purpose of life.

Life is a series of mountains to climb. *The People Code* is simply a beginning. It may, however, represent a significant step in your life's journey. Your new identification as a Red, Blue, White, or Yellow may encourage further questions and insights about your life. You have identified how your color fits in the puzzle of relationships. You may want further help addressing concerns you struggle with in the process of mixing colors and creating your rainbow connections.

During every mountain-climbing experience, there are wildflowers and beautiful sunsets. They are available for every climber to see and enjoy. They represent truths in all of our lives. Whether we choose to see them or not, they exist. Truths in life, like wildflowers and sunsets on our mountain climb, can be pointed out—taught. If we refuse to see them, however, we will remain ignorant and blind. Yes, we will still climb the mountain, but the quality of our mountain-climbing experience remains limited and disappointing.

As we go through life, superficial people may ask us to lead them up the mountain, knowing we have been there before. Limited by our own choosing, we can only take them directly to the top. We are unable to see and point out the wildflowers and beautiful sunsets because we have neglected to see them ourselves on previous climbs. Until we choose to see and hear quality truths in life, we necessarily remain unable to offer them to others.

Quality people (whether in the role of parent, child, friend, lover, or employer) demand a more balanced mountain-climbing experience. Yes, they desire to reach the top. For them the climb must include the truths and available beautiful aspects they instinctively know or have been taught can be experienced on the climb as well.

Merely surviving the ordeal will never fully suffice. They expect to live their lives, herein symbolized by a mountain climb.

Our personal happiness and our success at building our character will be determined by our willingness to observe, conceptualize, and apply what we learn. Depth, breadth, and height are gained accordingly. Limitations are placed on us primarily by ourselves. If our goals are flexible and our expectations are reasonable, we can attain and maintain a positive self-image.

Look to your journey as the ultimate purpose of life. We can never again live our lives quite the way we do today. As we look within ourselves and identify who we are, we can feel joy in knowing we have substance and value. We can commit to replacing personality limitations with charactered life principles. We can commit to relationships with passion, and feel the strength expressed in the rainbow connection. The first step is being able to say, "I know who I am and what I am, and I know who and what I want to become." These perceptions may change as we grow, but the essential attitudes of humility and positive goal setting remain healthy catalysts in our life journey.

A common sign of an unhealthy person is defensiveness. Insecure people get stuck on the mountain, refusing to seek higher levels of awareness. Consequently, having to deal with a new color (one with explicit limitations as well as strengths) often overwhelms a weaker person and causes him or her to resist any new and challenging input. These are *frightened individuals* who refuse to be labeled or to see themselves as flawed in any way. They may react to new information about themselves with any number of attitudes and/or behaviors. Common defenses include: attacking the presenter of the material, ignoring the material, quickly pointing out a friend who could really use the information, pretending to accept the material but having no intention of pursuing it in their lives, or suggesting the timing is somewhat difficult and they will get back to you when there is a better time to discuss it.

Unfortunately, they are reacting the only way they know how. They are simply protecting the little self-regard they feel is left them. If only they would risk the little self-regard, they might see the vast self-love they could generate if they would just invest the effort. We all deserve to travel through life with an abundance of self-love, rich with positive experiences and caring friends and family. Defensive people cut themselves off from what they deserve. They will discover that only when they are willing to see themselves accurately and get on with the process of growing up (character building) can they experience the mountain climb at its best.

While reading *The People Code*, you have experienced a new identity, and your journey to self-actualization has begun. With your commitment to developing your new identity you will experience many opportunities to appreciate yourself and others. Life's greatest moments are never more clearly experienced than in our genuine connection to ourselves and others. Our success comes with these rare yet magical moments. These moments occur throughout our lives as we honestly assess ourselves and lovingly value others.

Unconditional love is experienced when we accept and encourage others as *they* wish to be accepted and encouraged. Loving requires trust and risk. Loving allows for the limitations of those we love. It prevents our expectations from exceeding their abilities. We must believe in others' abilities to make healthy decisions. We accept and encourage their choices, regardless, at times, of how healthy or unhealthy their choices may be.

There are occasions when criticism is appropriate and helpful, but it must always stem from a pure motive in order to affect the individual for whom the criticism is intended. We must care and truly value the individual before we are in a position to offer criticism.

Enjoy your climb up the mountain. I have enjoyed the part of the trip that we have made together. As a Yellow, it has been challenging to commit myself so completely to something other than play. As with anything worthwhile, the slopes are high, but the sunsets—yes, the sunsets—have been even more rewarding than I could have dreamed.

I value intimacy, learning, and creating new insights. Unfortunately, distributing my thoughts in a book is less personal than I would like. However, I invite your feedback so that I can share in your life's journey as you have shared in mine. Happy mountain climbing. I hope that we will continue to cross each other's paths on our ascents to the top.

INDEX

being good vs. looking good in,
215–16
blame in, 224–25
complementary opposites in,
226–27
conflict and confrontation in,
223–24
control vs. freedom in, 219
distant vs. inviting in, 224
emotionality in, 217
forgiveness in, 223
giving in, 225
impatient vs. good natured in,
222–23
intimacy vs. playfulness in,
214–15
listening in, 225
love and commitment, 226
low vs. high profile in, 221
negative vs. positive in, 225
overview of, 212–13
perfectionism vs. scattered productivity in, 218–19
purposeful vs. playful in, 218
responsibility in, 219–20
security vs. adventure in, 216–17
sensitivity in, 222
sincere vs. insincere in, 220–21
suspicious vs. trusting in,
221–22
boldness, 44
Bombeck, Erma, 72
boredom:
Whites and, 87
in White-Yellow relationships,
235
business applications, 148, 259–67
assessing people reliably, 261
conflict resolution, 262
hiring employees, 296
leaders' self-awareness, 260–61
MASYC company testimonial,
265–67
motive-based training, 259,
261–63, 264–65, 266–67
testimonials, 263–64, 265–66

calculation, 47
calmness, 137
career people:

Blue limitations as, 77
Blue strengths as, 73
Red limitations as, 57
Red strengths as, 53
White limitations as, 96
White strengths as, 92
Yellow limitations as, 115–16
Yellow strengths as, 112
case histories:
Blue father, 71
Blue 13-year-old girl, 202
Blue woman, 71
Bob, 51
concerned hostess, 285
distressed mother, 110
free will, 278
Gayle and Paul Fesperman, 72
gifted White man, 91
Ginny, 51
Grace, 50
Herb Kelleher, 110
Jake, 27–28
Jeff, 90–91
Jenny, 70
Larry, 71
Linda, 151
Lynda Sherman, 109
Michael, 89–90
Monica, 35–36
older woman, 108
Red married couple, 155–56
Rob, 50
67-year-old woman, 70–71
strong, dominant widower, 283
Susan, 71–72
Taylor Hartman, 1–2, 121–22
university students, 91
White chief financial officer, 90
White couple, 90
White dentist, 202–3
White father and Red daughter,
177–78
White husband, 91
White woman, 177
Yellow attorney, 110
Yellow friend (a), 108
Yellow friend (b), 108–9
Yellow husband, 109
Yellow 16-year-old, 187
Yellow young man, 110–11

celebrities:
  Blue examples, 76
  Red examples, 55–56
  White examples, 95
  Yellow examples, 114
challenge:
  in Red-Blue relationships,
    161–62
  Reds and, 30
  in Red-White relationships, 172
  in Red-Yellow relationships, 185
change:
  in Red-White relationships, 173
  in White-Yellow relationships,
    235
character, 273–93
  advantages of building, 292–93
  behavior patterns and, 274–75
  defining, 275, 278
  development, 36–38, 124, 276,
    290
  education and, 271–72
  examples of, 291
  free will and, 278
  inhibiting behaviors and, 276–77
  life principles and, 279–92
  limitations, 274
  passion and, 291–92
  personality dimensions and,
    36–38
  positive influences and, 279
  strengths, 274
charisma, 104–5, 141
children:
  Blue limitations as, 77
  Blue strengths as, 74
  Red limitations as, 57
  Red strengths as, 53
  White limitations as, 97
  White strengths as, 93
  Yellow limitations as, 116
  Yellow strengths as, 112
clarity, 33, 136
Clinton, Bill, 8, 106, 113
Clinton, Hillary, 55, 106
Collins, Jim, 260
color-coding:
  birth order and, 296
  business applications of, 261,
    263–64, 296

character limitations, 274
character strengths, 274
dating success and, 297
parent-child relationship and,
  297–98
personality and, see Hartman
  Personality Profile
politics and, 297
questions about, 294, 295
students, teachers and, 268–72
team building and, 296
color connections, 147–48, 252–55
Color Your Future (Hartman), 36,
  38, 292
commitment:
  in Blue-Blue relationships,
    192–93
  Blues and, 62
  in Blue-White relationships,
    209–10
  and love in Blue-Yellow relation-
    ships, 226
  in Red-Blue relationships, 168
  Yellows and, 101–2, 142
  in Yellow-Yellow relationships,
    243
committed companions:
  Blue limitations as, 78
  Blue strengths as, 74
  Red limitations as, 58
  Red strengths as, 54
  White limitations as, 97
  White strengths as, 93
  Yellow limitations as, 117
  Yellow strengths as, 113
communication:
  in Blue-Blue relationships,
    193–94
  methods in relationships, 248
  in Red-Red relationships, 154–56
communicators:
  Blue limitations as, 76
  Blue strengths as, 73
  Red limitations as, 56
  Red strengths as, 52
  White limitations as, 96
  White strengths as, 92
  Yellow limitations as, 115
  Yellow strengths as, 111
compassion, 123

Hartman Communications is proud to offer a wide variety of products and services. For more information, go to our website www.thepeoplecode.com, call 801-531-1816, e-mail info@thepeoplecode.com, or write to Hartman Communications at PO Box 900550, Sandy, UT 84090.

OTHER PRODUCTS

Don't miss out on Dr. Hartman's successful follow-up books to *The People Code*; they are all available on our website. We also sell a wide variety of color code products, including quick reference cards and a seminar CD set narrated personally by Dr. Hartman.

IN-HOUSE TRAINING

Dr. Taylor Hartman provides in-house training programs. His principles of motive and personality are easily integrated into existing training programs, providing the "missing link" for better teams, improved customer service, quality management, and increased sales. He is skilled in resolving many of the cultural diversity issues within the workplace, by recognizing the value of individual contribution. He will customize curriculum to specifically address the needs of your organization.

KEYNOTE SPEECHES

Dr. Hartman may be retained as a keynote speaker. In addition, we provide other outstanding speakers who present his concepts of motive and personality in one-hour, two-hour, half-day, and full-day sessions.

PERSONAL RETREATS

Dr. Hartman personally supervises three-day sessions at his retreat center in Sundance, Utah. Intimate (only 12 guests per session) and extremely enlightening, these retreats are equal to 6 months' therapy. People come from all over the world and every walk of life for this rare experience. Both individuals and couples are welcome.